CW00557412

Metaphoric Worlds

SAMUEL R. LEVIN

Metaphoric Worlds

Conceptions of a Romantic Nature

YALE UNIVERSITY PRESS

NEW HAVEN AND LONDON

Designed by Jo Aerne and set in Bembo type by
Keystone Typesetting Co., Orwigsburg, Penna.
Printed in the United States of America by
BookCrafters, Inc., Chelsea, Mich.

Library of Congress Cataloging-in-Publication Data
Levin, Samuel R.
Metaphoric worlds : conceptions of a romantic
nature / Samuel R. Levin.
p.   cm.
Bibliography: p.
Includes index.
ISBN 0-300-04172-1
1. Metaphor. 2. Romanticism.
3. Literature—Philosophy.
I. Title.
PN228.M4L4 1988   87-28955
808'.001—dc19   CIP

The paper in this book meets the guidelines for
permanence and durability of the Committee on
Production Guidelines for Book Longevity of the
Council on Library Resources.

10 9 8 7 6 5 4 3 2 1

For Amy and John

Contents

Preface

This book is written around two major themes: one bears on the general problem of metaphor, as to which I propose a specific solution, the other on a certain conception of how the world is ordered, a conception which I attribute to William Wordsworth and which constitutes, moreover, a significant component of the Romantic outlook. What links the two themes together is the fact that the worldview which I attribute to Wordsworth can be properly appreciated only if his metaphors are construed according to the analysis that I propose.

Unlike many standard analyses of metaphor, in which the essential relationship is regarded as obtaining between what is said and what is meant (by what is said), in the analysis that I provide the essential relationship is held to subsist between what is thought and what is said. On the first approach the problem is seen primarily as one of semantics, on the second it becomes one of intentionality. In this change of perspective, the question at issue shifts from 'What meaning does the metaphor express?' to 'What conception does the metaphor imply?'

I am aware that to introduce conceptions into any theoretical discussion is to bargain for trouble. As I indicate below, one of the problems associated with the notion is that it may be understood in either an epistemological or a phenomenological sense. In each of these senses, moreover, it is susceptible of both a general and a particular interpretation. On a general interpretation conceptions can imply a comprehensive (conceptual) scheme of how the world and its contents are disposed: thus, one may have a conception of the world in which everything is created and watched over by a benevolent Deity, or one may have a conception according to which the world with all its contents is the accidental resultant of certain physical and chemical processes. Various other such conceptions are of course possible. To qualify as general they need only to schematize, according to some projection, the entire world or universe. On the other hand, a conception on this mode can be particular: it can conceive of success as attending hard work, say, or of good health as resulting from exercise. If, as here, one regards conceptions as projections upon reality, then in both their general and particular manifestations they enjoy the status of epistemological properties, very much like cognitions or beliefs.

If we shift our theoretical perspective, however, the general and particular aspects of conception can be made to appear not so much epistemological properties as functions of phenomenological behavior. We can think of conception generally, that is, as representing an intentional state, on a par with such general intentional states as volition or desire, and we can think of such states as being implemented in particular intentional acts, so that, just as we may wish for the sun to shine or desire a bar of chocolate, we may conceive of a pleasant day spent at the beach or a winning outcome in a game of chess.

The difference that I am adumbrating here between the two ways to understand conception may be subtle, but it is not without substance. In its epistemological sense a conception is a rationalization of how the world is organized; in this sense the notion has an objective cast. The phenomenological sense, on the other hand, has a subjective tone; in this sense the notion represents how we as individuals relate to—how we play our roles in—the organization that we make of the world. We may characterize the difference by saying that in its epistemological sense a conception implies a projection of reality, whereas in its phenomenological sense it implies a projection *of oneself* onto that reality.

In this study I employ the notion of conception both in the sense of general epistemological scheme and in that of particular intentional act. Thus the worldview that I attribute to Wordsworth is a conception in the sense of general schematization; as such, it constitutes a fundamental component of Wordsworth's epistemological outlook. On the other hand, in his employment of individual metaphors, notably in the respect that these metaphors describe unlikely factual conditions, Wordsworth expresses conceptions of a particular kind; these conceptions are local, constituting individual and specific intentional acts, acts in which Wordsworth responds in a characteristic way to features and events of his personal environment. It is by abstracting from the particular and characteristic conceptions that Wordsworth expresses in his metaphors that we arrive at his general conception of how the world is ordered.

Actually, it is only in its application to Wordsworth that the use I make of conceptions in this study attains to theoretical significance. Thus, in the preceding discussion, instead of conceptions, I might just as well have spoken of beliefs, imaginings, or other mental attitudes. But when a poet's observations about the world around him imply a cosmology of a preternatural or 'unreal' character, then the notion of conception, used to signalize such an outlook, may be held to define a *distinctive* epistemological outlook. And, as I argue in this study, the worldview projected in the work of Wordsworth, a view in which the objects of nature may be animated by affections and emotions which in normal or standard cosmologies are reserved to human beings, represents just such an outlook.

The preceding remarks have addressed two general topics: the theory of metaphor and the role played by conceptions in defining Wordsworth's relation to his universe. Chapter 1 of this book is devoted to a discussion of metaphor. In it I present my own views and compare them with those of several other theorists whose ideas on the subject resemble mine in certain critical respects. The essential condition of my analysis is that metaphors should be taken literally. This condition is not trivial, inasmuch as metaphors typically are expressed in language that is semantically deviant: an example would be a sentence like 'The trees were weeping'. The other general topic mentioned above, that of the role played by conceptions in relating Wordsworth to his universe, is dealt with in chapter 9, the last chapter of the book.

In the hope of helping the reader to understand the rationale that lies behind the book's organization, I should like to say a few words about the contents of the intervening chapters as well. The claim that semantically deviant expressions (occurring as metaphors) are to be taken literally gives rise to a wide but connected set of questions. Chapter 2 begins to deal with some of these questions. Among the questions raised is that of what type of intentional act it is that lies behind and prompts the utterance of a deviant expression. My proposal is that the intentional act in question is one of conception, or conceiving of. The discussion of this as well as related questions is carried out in the framework of Husserl's theory of phenomenology. Deviant expressions raise questions also of an ontological and linguistic nature. By way of dealing with these questions I invoke some other aspects of Husserl's work and also some ideas of Chomsky on the form of grammars.

If conceptions are the intentional acts that prompt semantically deviant expressions, the question arises as to what sort of mental representation is associated with the performing of such an act. Chapter 3 focuses on this question. In the discussion conceptions are contrasted with concepts in terms of the phenomenological, referential, and semantic properties that respectively characterize the two notions. A section of the chapter deals also with the difference between conception, as here envisaged, and imagination. The chapter concludes with a consideration of infinity; the purpose is to show that there are similarities between attempting to 'conceive of' infinity and the attempt to 'conceive of' what it might be that is expressed by a semantically deviant expression.

If conceptions are expressed in semantically deviant language, it follows that the states of affairs thereby conceived of will in some sense lie beyond conventional notions of how the world is constituted. In this respect metaphoric conceptions resemble conceptions that arise in the progress of science, where such conceptions also entail states of affairs (aspects of nature) hitherto unthought of. Chapter 4 contrasts these two types of metaphysical extension, corollaries of metaphors in poetry on the one hand and of new theories in science on the other. A further contrast is drawn in regard to the nature of the truth claims that poetic metaphors and scientific theories are presumed to make; finally, an argument is presented for the validity of what I call conceptual truth.

Chapter 5 deals with the work of Giambattista Vico. Vico's work is relevant in view of his claim that metaphoric language should be taken literally. Since this is also the claim that I am making in this study, some comparison of the two viewpoints is indicated. It turns out that there is only a surface similarity between them. Vico's strictures apply to the function of 'metaphor' at the origin of language. At that time, according to him, the view taken of the universe is entirely anthropomorphic. The reason that we should take literally a sentence like 'The trees were weeping' in early poetry is therefore that the first poets in their *general* conception of how the world was ordered thought that trees, like humans, actually wept. For us, however, to take literally such a sentence in a modern poem, it becomes necessary to form a *particular* conception, one that transgresses our standard view of reality.

Chapter 6 raises the question of the adequacy of language for the expression of certain affective experiences. It argues that such experiences may provoke conceptions of such complexity that the language is ill suited to their expression—that the best it can do is approximate to such expression by means of deviant sentences. The linguistic problem of how properly to discourse about God is brought up for consideration, and Aquinas' solution to this problem—his theory of analogy—is described and discussed. The suggestion is made that the problem for which Aquinas developed his theory of analogy is similar in its intellectual and spiritual complexity to the problem faced by poets who feel an affinity for the objects of nature and attempt to express that feeling in their poetry. I argue that such expression realizes itself in linguistically deviant metaphors and that it is only by taking those metaphors literally that we stand some chance of approaching to an understanding of the feelings that they are intended to express.

Chapters 7 and 8 describe the intellectual background—the

legacy of Newton and Locke—that prevailed in England during the eighteenth century, which Wordsworth and other Romantic poets had to react against and overcome in the formation of their own philosophical outlooks. Newton's account of the universe made of it an assembly of inert and reactive particles, governed from without by fixed and immutable laws. In consequence of this essentially mechanical picture, eighteenth-century poets saw nature as a static and orderly arrangement of physical objects, responsive to (not interactive with) the needs of the human observer. In the same way that Newton's cosmological scheme ascribed strict and limited properties and functions to the physical objects in the universe, so the attributes and capacities that Locke allotted to the human mind were meager and restrictive. In the development of his own Romantic outlook, Wordsworth had to react against the confining ideas of Newton and Locke—and he had to redefine for himself both the nature of the universe and the mental capacities of the human being. In terms of the points made earlier in this discussion, we could say that Wordsworth's *general* conception, his idea that human beings and the objects of nature stand to each other in a relation of mutual and interacting responsiveness, is a departure from Newton's cosmology and that his *particular* conceptions issue from mental capacities that lie outside the complement of such capacities as specified in Locke's theory of mind. Without an understanding of the intellectual background out of which his ideas grew—an account of which is given in chapters 7 and 8—we could not fully appreciate the turn taken by Wordsworth's mental development.

Chapter 9 presents a discussion of Kant's *Critique of Judgment*, focusing on his analysis of the sublime—its nature and its (mathematical and dynamical) variants. Against this background I discuss the character of Wordsworth's general conception and argue that, in the effort to make his intuitions conform to this conception, Wordsworth attains to a state of mind that bears a strong resemblance to the condition of mental tension that Kant defines as the characteristic mark of the sublime. But whereas for Kant the tension results from the effort to make intuitions conform to a principle of reason (that of totality), the principle that interacts with those intuitions for Wordsworth is his general conception. Because of the role played by this conception in Wordsworth's mental process, I call the type of sublimity characteristic of his thought the conceptual sublime. A final section then contrasts the conceptual sublime with the egotistical sublime, a disposition of mind sometimes attributed to Wordsworth.

Acknowledgments

It is a pleasure for me to acknowledge the assistance that I received from a number of people during the writing of this book. I wish first to record my gratitude to Arthur Collins, Alex Orenstein, and Mary Wiseman who, at various stages of the book's composition, each read a chapter of it and gave me the benefit of their comments. I am grateful also to George Ridenour for conversations which helped me to understand the complex nature of the Romantic period. I am grateful further to Robert Fiengo for vetting the section in Chapter 2 on the linguistic treatment of deviance. This is also an opportunity for me to voice my appreciation to Jane Tompkins for a timely expression of confidence in my work. From an early stage in my thinking on these matters I discussed them with Mary Pat Kelly. For the interest, the enthusiasm, and the insights that she brought to those discussions I remain indebted to her. I am also under a weighty obligation to my friend Thomas McFarland, who read several chapters of this book and gave me advice and encouragement which were of great value to me. Finally, the support provided by my wife can only be referred to; it is beyond valuation.

July 1987   New York City

I

Conceptual Metaphor: A New Approach

The discussion that follows grows out of a simple but fundamental shift in the approach that is customarily taken to the analysis of metaphor—where by 'metaphor' I intend expressions that evince a degree of linguistic deviance in their composition. It follows from this deviant character that the 'claim' made by such expressions is bizarre, absurd, ridiculous, false, outlandish, non- or contrasensical. In other words, between an expression of this kind and the world as we are accustomed to think about it there is a mismatch, a lack of fit or correspondence. Unlike ordinary expressions, therefore, whose meanings need merely to be grasped to be understood, metaphors require first to be construed before understanding can be achieved. Now when presented with an expression of this type, most theories of metaphor—however much they may differ in methodology—proceed to analyze its language. An expression like 'The trees were weeping', say, might be construed to mean that the trees were dripping moisture, shedding their leaves, exuding sap, or something similar. If we think about it, we see that behind any such approach to the interpretation of metaphor there lies a tacit assumption, namely, that in any incompatibility between what an expression says and our conception of the world, it is the expression that is 'at fault'. It is assumed that our conception of what the world is like is fixed—a given—and that whenever an expression contradicts or is inconsistent with that conception it is the expression that must be modified, into a form that consists with our conception of the world.

In the face of this incompatibility, however, it is logically possible to regard the expression as the fixed quantity, with the consequence that it is our conception of the world that has to be modified. We can try, that is, to conceive, or conceive *of*, that state of affairs that the expression, taken *literally*, purports to describe; we try to conceive of trees—those very things—as weeping. The latter approach to the problem of metaphor represents the 'shift' that I am speaking of; from being linguistic, construal becomes conceptual. Moreover, the world onto which this conception is projected is no longer the actual world, the world in which we live; it is a world which, in respect of the description comprised in the linguistic expression, departs from and transgresses the conditions that obtain in the actual world. Such a world then is a deviant world, one which, inasmuch as its reality becomes for us a matter for construal, we may call a metaphoric world. On this approach, in other words, what is metaphoric is not the language, but the world.

The notion of metaphoric world fills out and completes a chiastic pattern that is implicitly generated by semantically deviant expressions. This pattern is represented in figures 1 and 2 below.

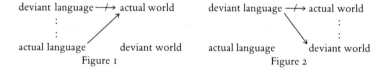

deviant language —/→ actual world   deviant language —/→ actual world

actual language   deviant world   actual language   deviant world

Figure 1   Figure 2

Figure 1 represents the interpretive route taken by standard approaches to metaphor. The language being deviant, its interpretation against (conditions in) the world is blocked. Interpretation against a deviant world not being taken seriously as a possibility, the move is made to reinterpret, to construe, the language of the (deviant) expression (a process represented by the dotted line). The construal, expressed in nondeviant (what I am here for purposes of symmetry calling 'actual') language, can then be plotted against conditions in the actual world (the diagonal). In figure 2 the first move is the same as for figure 1, and is similarly blocked. In the next move, however, it is not the language that is construed, but the world. Then the original (deviant) language is mapped onto that world. It is the positing of deviant worlds, introducing thereby a counterpart to the role and status of deviant language, that fills out and completes the chiastic pattern. Figure 1 then represents the interpretive strategy whereby a metaphoric meaning is construed for the actual world, figure 2 whereby a metaphoric world is construed for the literal meaning.

Granted the *logical* possibility of approaching the study of metaphor in the shifted fashion that I am proposing, the question still arises whether any practical benefit may derive from adopting this approach. I believe not merely that there may, but that there does. I believe that in the works of certain poets (I instance chiefly Wordsworth) an insight can thereby be gained into some of their deepest intellectual and spiritual strivings, an insight whose possibility is completely foreclosed if their metaphors are interpreted in the usual way. It is part of my argument that the language at our disposal, for all its utility and excellence, is for the expression of certain profound and out-of-the-ordinary experiences an inadequate vehicle and that it is only by taking his metaphors literally that we stand a chance of approaching to an understanding of the thoughts and emotions that the poet is striving to communicate. In doing so we implicitly acknowledge our awareness of the poet's struggle against limitations inherent in the capacities of human language. Wordsworth is alluding to both those limitations and those strivings in the following lines:

> 'tis a thing impossible to frame
> Conceptions equal to the soul's desires,
> And the most difficult task to keep
> Heights which the soul is competent to gain.
>
> [*Excursion*, IV, 136–39]

It is for conceptions of this profound and difficult nature that metaphoric language is enlisted, and it is my contention that only by taking those metaphors literally can one appreciate in some measure what the poet is attempting by their means to express. I would say that the essential characteristics of my view of metaphor—the respects in which, as it seems to me, it differs significantly from other theories of poetic metaphor—consist in its taking the metaphoric expression literally and in accepting the epistemological consequences that ensue from adopting this approach. I am aware of no modern theory of metaphor that deals with the problem in just this way. It would be time consuming and not to the purpose if, in attempting to validate my sense of the situation, I were to survey the field, providing detailed expositions of the major theories with accompanying commentary. It seems to me advisable instead to review just those recent publications I know of which bear some affinity to my own proposal and comment on the differences which comparison discloses. Among the significant theories that by this rationale will go unexamined are those of Richards (1936), Jakobson (1956), Beardsley (1962), Black (1962), Derrida (1974), Searle (1979), Gumpel (1984), and Mac Cormac (1985). Those that I shall deal with are the theories of Lakoff and Johnson (1980), Davidson (1978), and Ricoeur (1977).

Lakoff and Johnson

It is the argument of Lakoff and Johnson in *Metaphors We Live By* that in respects which are important but largely unnoticed metaphors influence the manner in which we view the world and determine the roles that we play in it. Their primary concern is not with poetic metaphors but with such as occur commonly in everyday language and which betoken the influence of a certain other class of metaphors, which they call 'conceptual'. The important fact for Lakoff and Johnson is not so much that we use metaphoric *expressions* in our everyday language (although as we shall see such expressions do play a significant role in their account); what matters essentially is that we bring to bear metaphoric *concepts* in the ordinary affairs of our lives. So that the interest in a metaphor like ARGUMENT IS WAR (one of their examples) is not that it displays the formal characteristics of metaphor (in fact, it is not even necessary that this, being a *conceptual* metaphor, even be expressed); what counts is that we conduct ourselves in argument as though we were in fact waging war. Evidence that we do indeed so conduct ourselves is deducible from satellite metaphors which *are* expressed, metaphors like 'Your claims are *indefensible*', 'He *attacked every weak point* in my argument', 'I *demolished* his argument, and so on (pp. 3ff.). A similar discussion is presented for the conceptual metaphor TIME IS MONEY. Among its satellites are 'You're *wasting* my time', 'How do you *spend* your time these days', and 'I've *invested* a lot of time in her'.

The class of conceptual metaphors comprises a number of subclasses. The two that I have mentioned above are referred to as structural (conceptual) metaphors. Thus the concept of war (comprehending its elements, aspects, and practices) structures the way we conduct arguments, and the concept of money structures the attitude that we take toward time. As the satellite metaphors indicate, we *contend to win* arguments and we *place a value* on time. Other types of conceptual metaphor are the orientational (for example, HAPPY IS UP) and the ontological (for example, INFLATION IS AN ENTITY) (pp. 14–32).

As we have seen, conceptual metaphors are not, as such, linguistically expressed. They are given implicit expression by the occurrence of their satellite, or linguistic, metaphors. The role of conceptual metaphors is to fashion, in ways that we are largely unconscious of, our view of reality, a view to which our linguistic behavior, in the form of the satellite metaphors, bears implicit testimony. The significance of Lakoff and Johnson's theory of metaphor thus does not bear on the problem of poetic discourse and the part played in it by metaphor; its significance lies rather in its character of metaphysical theory. A good part of *Metaphors We Live By* consists of arguments attempting to show that the question of truth—what the world is really like—depends on taking toward it an 'interactional' approach, an approach that sees reality as something that happens *to* people and that people participate in *making*, rather than as some objective state of affairs which one tries to account for by means of abstract, depersonalized theories (pp. 156ff.). These claims, of considerable interest in their own right, do not bear centrally on the question of poetic metaphor. However, since the idea of conceptual metaphor figures significantly in both the Lakoff-Johnson theory and my own, it will be useful to examine the role that it plays in each.

A series of fundamental differences between our respective theories derives from the fact that whereas the conceptual metaphors of Lakoff and Johnson express concepts, mine express conceptions. In chapter 3 I discuss the difference between these two notions, concluding that concepts in the relevant sense are clear and distinct representations, the products of conceiving, whereas conceptions are mental schemas, the product of conceiving of, and I argue that the interpretation of poetic metaphors devolves upon the latter type of representation. As between concepts and conceptions so defined, the mental representations embodied in Lakoff and Johnson's conceptual metaphors are closer to concepts, though differing from them in the following respects: as being of a propositional rather than an imagistic nature; as being metaphorical rather than literal; and as involving the generality of speakers of a natural language rather than only the limited group consisting of the poet and his readers. Even though the differences between concepts in my sense and the concepts of Lakoff and Johnson are thus considerable, it is with concepts rather than with conceptions that Lakoff and Johnson's conceptual metaphors are to be associated. Essentially, this is because concepts, of whatsoever description, have a character of definiteness, whereas conceptions, being schemas, lack this property.

As the discussion in chapters 2 and 3 will make clear, the reason that poetic metaphors have for us to be rationalized in terms of schemas—not imagistic or propositional representations—is that such metaphors are typically expressed in language that is semantically deviant. This fact prompts the question of just what linguistic status is enjoyed by the metaphors in Lakoff and Johnson's theory. The fact that their theory comprises two types of metaphor (the conceptual metaphors, those 'we live by', and those we employ in our 'living thereby', that is, in our actual speech) imparts to the question a certain complexity. It is clear of course that the 'language' of the conceptual metaphors is metaphorical. The question is not so clear as it applies to the expressions actually used in speech, the linguistic, or what I have been calling 'satellite', metaphors. Some arguments bearing on this question are contained in the following passage where Lakoff and Johnson, speaking of the conceptual metaphor ARGUMENT IS WAR, comment as follows (p. 5):

> *The essence of metaphor is understanding and experiencing one kind of thing in terms of another.* It is not that arguments are a subspecies of war. Arguments and wars are different kinds of things— verbal discourse and armed conflict—and the actions performed are different kinds of actions. But ARGUMENT is partially structured, understood, performed, and talked about in terms of WAR. The concept is metaphorically structured, the activity is metaphorically structured, and, consequently, the language is metaphorically structured.
>
> Moreover, this is the *ordinary* way of having an argument and talking about one. The normal way for us to talk about attacking a position is to use the words 'attack a position.' Our conventional ways of talking about arguments presuppose a metaphor we are hardly ever conscious of. The metaphor is not merely in the words we use—it is in our very concept of an argument. The language of the argument is not poetic, fanciful, or rhetorical; it is literal. We talk about arguments that way because we conceive of them that way—and we act according to the way we conceive of things.

At the end of the first paragraph in the above passage, the authors say: 'The language [of argument] is metaphorically structured'. In the second paragraph they say that the language of argument is literal. The only apparent way to achieve consistency between these two characterizations is to assume that by the first formulation they mean not that the language *used* in argument is metaphorical but that lying behind and 'structuring' that language is the metaphorical concept. This leaves us with the claim that the actual language in which argument is conducted is in fact literal.

An argument assuming metaphorical concepts to be expressed in literal language (even though the expressions need not be of the concept per se) calls for close examination. Some additional considerations bearing on this argument occur in a subsequent portion of Lakoff and Johnson's discussion (pp. 52–55). Claiming that typically the structuring achieved by conceptual metaphor is only partial, and using for illustration the conceptual metaphor THEORIES ARE BUILDINGS, they assert:

> The parts of the concept BUILDING that are used to structure the concept THEORY are the foundation and the outer shell. The roof, internal rooms, staircases, and hallways are parts of a building not used as part of the concept THEORY. Thus the metaphor THEORIES ARE BUILDINGS has a "used" part (foundation and outer shell) and an "unused" part (rooms, staircases, etc.). Expressions such as *construct* and *foundation* are instances of the used part of such a metaphorical concept and are part of our ordinary literal language about theories.

Lakoff and Johnson then contrast expressions employing the 'unused' part of the THEORIES ARE BUILDINGS metaphor with those that employ the 'used' part. Among the examples they provide for the former type of expression are 'His theory has thousands of little rooms and long, winding corridors' and 'He prefers massive Gothic theories covered with gargoyles'. They then comment, 'These sentences fall outside the domain of normal literal language and are part of what is usually called "figurative" or "imaginative" language. Thus, literal expressions ("He has constructed a theory") and imaginative expressions ("His theory is covered with gargoyles") can be instances of the same general metaphor (THEORIES ARE BUILDINGS)'. In these passages again examples that count for them as metaphors (that is, 'He has constructed a theory') are said to be expressed in literal language.[1]

---

1. Lest it be thought that the equivocation I am calling attention to is one that I am myself introducing, by transporting what is properly the metaphorical status of the conceptual metaphors onto the linguistic level, I adduce the following statements of Lakoff and Johnson which should make it perfectly clear that in their theory the linguistic expressions that testify to the existence of their concep-

As part of their discussion in this same chapter Lakoff and Johnson introduce another type of metaphorical expression, which they call 'idiosyncratic'. As examples they offer 'the *foot* of the mountain', 'a *head* of cabbage', and 'the *leg* of a table'. Because such metaphors are isolated, because they do not interact with other metaphors to form part of a system of interrelated metaphors, such metaphors are characterized by Lakoff and Johnson as 'dead'. Metaphors like 'wasting time' and 'attacking position', on the other hand, are 'alive'. Lakoff and Johnson conclude their discussion by asserting that expressions like the latter 'are metaphors we live by'. And they add, 'The fact that they are conventionally fixed within the lexicon of English makes them no less alive'.

It happens that those metaphorical expressions that Lakoff and Johnson call 'idiosyncratic' are classical instances of the type which in the standard rhetorical treatises is referred to as catachresis. By *catachresis*, Quintilian says, 'is meant the practice of adapting the nearest available term to describe something for which no actual term exists' (1953, III, 321). The function of catachreses is thus to fill lexical gaps; they are metaphors by default, we might say. Because of their background and function their 'metaphoricity' is of a compromised nature. The indeterminacy of their metaphorical status was highlighted by Fontanier (1977, 213ff.), who allowed to catachreses the status of tropes but denied that they were figures. His reasoning took the following form: he defined tropes (metaphor, metonymy, and so on) as expressions in which the meaning of a word (or larger form) was modified or altered, and he defined figures as expressions in

---

tual metaphors are in their own right metaphorical: 'Since metaphorical expressions in our language are tied to metaphorical concepts in a systematic way, we can use metaphorical linguistic expressions to study the nature of metaphorical concepts' (p. 7); on page 9 they say, 'Of the expressions listed under the TIME IS MONEY metaphor, some refer specifically to money (*spend, invest, budget, profitably, cost*), others to limited resources (*use, use up, have enough of, run out of*), and still others to valuable commodities (*have, give, lose, thank you for*). This is an example of the way in which metaphorical entailments can characterize a coherent system of metaphorical concepts and a corresponding coherent system of metaphorical expressions for those concepts'.

which a word was used where a different word was customarily or normally used. Catachreses, therefore, since they did not replace or substitute for another expression—there being none—could not be figures. In this respect, thus, they differed from metaphors, which did so substitute and which consequently displayed the characteristics of both trope and figure.

What Fontanier's analysis makes clear is that the metaphoricity of an expression does not derive from the additional sense it may develop when used in a new context (polysemous extension of this sort is a routine development in the semantic careers of many words); it derives rather from the tension and interplay that the word in its extended use enters into with the term normally used in that context. Lakoff and Johnson admit that metaphors like 'wasting time' (a paradigm case for them) are 'conventionally fixed within the lexicon of English'. This means that the language of such expressions is in no way deviant, consequently that there is no encroachment by any of their terms on the semantic domain of another, normal term. In other words, there is no tension or interplay between 'waste' and a nonmetaphorical term that would otherwise be used with 'time' to mean 'waste time'; as with 'foot' in 'foot of the mountain' we are dealing here with catachresis. Lakoff and Johnson claim, however, that 'wasting time' is a metaphor and that, moreover, unlike 'foot of the mountain', it is alive. But it is one thing to claim that there are metaphors we live by (the conceptual metaphors); it is another thing to modulate from this to the claim that certain literal (originally catachretic) expressions are living metaphors. This equivocation figures at the heart of Lakoff and Johnson's theory.

It thus appears that while we may agree that conceptual metaphors embody metaphorical concepts, we may at the same time reject the claim that so much of the language in which we express ourselves is metaphorical—according to Lakoff and Johnson, *vitally* metaphorical. Appealing as the notion may be that the bulk, if not the entirety, of our language is metaphorical, it appears that its application to the facts leads to theoretical inconsistency. When I say 'I spent three hours on this problem' or 'This theory is weak', I am not aware that these statements are conditioned in any way by concepts like TIME IS MONEY or THEORIES ARE BUILDINGS. My awareness of such conditioning is not much increased when I say 'My time is precious' or 'This theory is shaky'. Of course, I can be made aware of such dependencies, and making one so aware is part of Lakoff and Johnson's achievement. However, to claim *on this basis* metaphorical status for both terms of this dependency is to make a move of questionable validity. The linguistically expressed metaphors of Lakoff and Johnson involve originally catachretic uses that, by their own account, have become completely lexicalized. From this it follows that the concepts they express (not those they may imply) are unexceptionable. So that it is only of the conceptual metaphors in Lakoff and Johnson's treatment that one may speak nontrivially of metaphorical concepts. And I have already indicated above the respects in which those concepts differ from my 'conceptions'.

I said at the beginning of this chapter that the essential characteristics of my view of metaphor consist (1) in its taking of the metaphorical expression literally and (2) in accepting the epistemological consequences that ensue from adopting this approach.[2] If we now examine the theory of Lakoff and Johnson in respect of how it compares as regards these two requirements, the following picture emerges: their conceptual metaphors are not taken literally; the language in which they are formulated, according to Lakoff and Johnson, is 'figurative' (p. 53), so that metaphors like TIME IS MONEY and ARGUMENT IS WAR are not taken at face value; we may manage our time as though it were money and conduct ourselves in argument as though it were war, but we do not try to conceive of time as in fact being money or argument

---

2. A few words may be in order to dispel what may appear to be an air of paradox, if not of oxymoron, in the idea of taking metaphorical expressions literally. Normally, we take the language of a metaphorical expression to be metaphorical, that is, we assume that it does *not* mean what it says, that the language—the semantic product of the words in the expression—cannot be read sense into just as it stands, that a sense must be *construed of*, not simply read off, the expression. Further, it is normally ordinary expressions whose meanings we take at face value, interpret literally. What makes my requirement nontrivial is that it is imposed on the reading of expressions which normally receive metaphorical readings, that is, on expressions that are deviant.

as being war. The language of the satellite metaphors, on the other hand, *is* taken literally, but this, as I have tried to show, is no more than should be expected, inasmuch as the meanings of the words in these expressions have been semantically domesticated and have taken their place in the lexicon of English. So that taking literally an expression like 'I wasted my time' or 'I demolished his argument' does not, as does the taking of deviant expressions literally, result in the need to project novel conceptions, conceptions whose realization would entail the actualization of metaphoric worlds.

Davidson

The theory of Lakoff and Johnson required our examination because of the role played in it by conceptual metaphor. In the discussion I tried to show that the epistemological consequences that derived from their conceptual metaphors were very much different from those that derive from my idea that poetic metaphors express conceptions. The interest that Davidson's theory holds for us stems from its relation to the other characteristic of my view of metaphor, namely, the requirement that the language of metaphor is to be taken literally. Davidson lays it down that 'metaphors mean what the words, in their most literal interpretation mean, and nothing more' (p. 32). In particular, a metaphor incorporates no collateral cognitive content which it is the business of analysis to read into or out of it; it 'means' simply and strictly what it says. The process effecting it as a metaphor takes place exclusively in the reader, and the metaphoric interpretation consists in the set of relations, resemblances, and analogies that the sentence taken literally brings to the reader's notice and induces him to attend to (cf. p. 46). This process is activated by the fact that what the sentence asserts is patently false (or obviously true) (cf. pp. 41f.).

Davidson's theory, in its major bearings, might be characterized as a pragmatic theory of metaphor. Apart from the fact that the focus of his analysis is on the reader, and his denial of any specially semantic property to metaphors, the pragmatic nature of Davidson's treatment is explicitly suggested in the following statement: 'I depend on the distinction between what words mean and what they are used to do. I think metaphor belongs exclusively to the domain of use' (p. 33). There is nothing special about metaphor linguistically (that is, semantically); its special property is to be explained by the uses to which it is put, specifically as it serves to activate a series of conceptual maneuvers in the reader.[3]

Now metaphors typically are semantically deviant. For Davidson such 'absurd' sentences taken literally are patently false, and it is this fact alone (the possibility having been denied that anything special in their meanings could serve this purpose) that sets into motion the metaphorical construal in the hearer. But let us examine this argument. There are of course other types of sentence that are patently false. Consider 'The earth moves around the moon'. This sentence is patently false.[4] But it does not engender any metaphorical construal (notice that if it should, it would be by taking some of the words in a nonliteral sense). What then is the difference between such a sentence and a metaphor? Compare that sentence with 'The earth pirouettes around the sun'. According to Davidson, both would be false. One, however, instigates construal, the other does not. Patent falsity cannot, therefore, be a sufficient condition for metaphor. And since Davidson himself admits that obvious truths ('Business is business') may function as metaphors, it is not a necessary condition either. It thus seems that the prompting mechanism of metaphor cannot be reduced to

3. In a footnote (pp. 46f.) Davidson claims that in this respect metaphor is no different from any use of language, the process of conceptual elaboration (paraphrase in his terms) being endless in all cases. This reduction (or assimilation) follows from (or consists with) Davidson's denial of any special import to metaphor.

4. It might be objected that the falsity of this sentence is a factual matter and thus cannot be read off its face. We judge it false, however, not by conducting an empirical investigation but, immediately, on the basis of an astronomical law. If it should still be objected that precisely because it requires knowledge of that law its falsity is not patent, we have the right to ask in what *different* respect the falsity of an 'absurd' sentence is patent. And the answer, it seems to me, would devolve upon its semantic incompatibility or, as we might say in this context, the contravention of a grammatical rule.

patent falsity (with the corollary that its generative function resides solely in the reader). Davidson in fact does not make this strong a claim for the efficiency of patent falsity (hedging it by saying that it functions 'generally' as such a mechanism). My argument, however, is not intended so much to show that this claim is mistaken as to show that where Davidson is wrong is in denying to metaphor any special significance for its meaning. When we encounter a sentence like 'The earth pirouettes around the sun', we do not question whether it is true or false, we ask: 'What could it mean'? This is especially the case if it occurs in a poem.

It is in my opinion a mistake to conflate, as is so frequently done, absurd sentences and false sentences. False sentences are false in virtue of a disagreement between what they assert and facts in the world; 'absurd', or semantically deviant, sentences, if they are reckoned false, are so reckoned because there are held to be no facts in the world of which they may be properly asserted. In the latter case, therefore, the judgment is arrived at not by checking the world but by examining the expression. Such expressions are thus on an altogether different footing from bona fide false sentences. Their absurdity is a function of their semantics. If one wishes still to term them false, it must be with a recognition that prima facie their 'fault' lies in their meanings, not in their truth claims. In fact, unless some distinctive truth-conditional method is proposed for determining their truth value, 'patent falsity' is simply an inaccurate and misleading characterization of semantic deviance.

Consider again 'The earth moves around the moon'. If this sentence is negated (that is to say, 'The earth does not move around the moon'), the consequence is agreement with the facts, and the resulting sentence (or its assertion) is true. If the assertion made by an absurd sentence is negated, the resulting sentence is also true ('The earth does not pirouette around the sun'). But these results, although the same for the two types of false sentence, have only a superficial significance. For although in both cases the negated counterparts of the false sentences are true because what they deny is in fact not observed to occur—the earth neither moves around the moon nor pirouettes around the sun—where the bona fide false sentence (not its negation) is concerned, the falsity is demonstrable—by adverting to the fact with which it is in disagreement, namely, that the earth moves around the *sun*. The falsity in this case, we might say, is of a propositional nature. With what fact of the matter, however, can the absurd false sentence be shown to be in disagreement? In answer to this question there is no decisive factual evidence; we do not show the falsity of 'The earth pirouettes around the sun' by pointing to the fact that the earth *moves* around the sun (in fact, even the truth of its negation is in some sense trivial). All we accomplish by doing this is to show that 'pirouette' is not the appropriate word to use of the earth's actual behavior. But then there is here no propositional falsity; there is only a lexical misuse. The point is that it is improper to say of the earth either that it pirouettes around the sun or that it does not pirouette around the sun. Yet this is not because as a matter of fact it does not pirouette around the sun but because what the earth does is not properly described as pirouetting—around the sun or anywhere else.

It could still be maintained that since the earth does not pirouette, it follows that an assertion that it pirouettes around the sun is false. But this only drives home the point. In absurd sentences the conclusion that what they assert is false follows on the recognition that there is a semantic incompatibility in the sentence making the assertion; no one, in the face of such a sentence, would think of investigating the world to ascertain its truth value. Thus this falsity ('patent' falsity) is on a different footing from truth-conditional falsity. In fact, although I have been speaking above of the assertions made by deviant sentences, to speak so is really inappropriate. In response to Davidson's claim that metaphors mean what they say, we might ask whether they also say what they mean, that is, whether they assert anything. It seems to me that if asserting is taken to mean making a factual claim, the answer has to be no.[5]

5. Compare Davies (1982–83, 79): 'Davidson regards the sentence [the metaphorical statement] as preserving its literal meaning and as being used to perform a *saying*, but not an *assertion*'.

Another question raised by Davidson's thesis concerns the relation between what we might call the input and output conditions of metaphor. Davidson's analysis treats of the linguistic expression and the hearer's (reader's) response. The expression is to be taken literally, and in the response to that expression there is engendered a proliferation of relations, resemblances, and analogies, in the entertainment of which the metaphor is held to consist. Now it is fair to assume that some counterpart to this proliferation has occurred in the mind of the poet and that the linguistic expression is intended to serve as its conveyance. If we thus make symmetrical the two terms of the process, the claim that the linguistic expression means just what it says—that the metaphoric interpretation is a function solely of the reader— emerges in a still more dubious light. For on Davidson's analysis it seems we must conclude either that the complexity of senses active in the poet's mind has been neutralized in the expression or that the poet entertained no such complexity. In this case it is hard to see why or how the expression suggests to the reader the need for metaphoric construal. On the other hand, if the poet's complexity of senses is held to have been represented in the expression, the difficulty is in seeing how it can mean no more than what it literally says. The claim that the expression's patent falsity suffices to activate the construal process seems hardly to the point in the broadened perspective. Why should the poet entrust his metaphoric intention to the elaboration of a patent falsity? Why should not his choice of language reflect the complexity of thought which he trusts his reader will attempt to reproduce?

In the foregoing paragraphs I have raised some general objections to Davidson's theory of metaphor. At this point, however, let us recall the respect in which Davidson's theory was selected for comparison with mine, that is, its stipulation that the language of metaphor is to be taken literally. Although Davidson says that 'metaphors mean what the words, in their most literal interpretation mean, and nothing more', this stipulation is contravened by the effects of his pragmatic approach, for it results from that approach that though the words of a metaphor mean what they say and nothing more, what they are *taken* to mean is something else again. It is in this *taking* of the meaning, this processing of the linguistic expression, that the metaphoric work consists—in the relations, resemblances, and analogies that the reader, in the course of processing the metaphor, imposes upon or draws out of the expression's literal meaning. The interpretation of the metaphor can thus be said to grow out of the literal meaning of the expression, but it is not, as it is on my approach, an interpretation *of* that meaning.

The upshot of all this is that there is less in Davidson's stipulation than meets the eye. Its innovatory significance is more of a technical than of a substantive nature. The interpretation of a metaphor is still something quite other than what the expression in fact says; it is only that the difference is attributed not to any semantically special property inhering in the expression but to the work of processing that the reader has performed in the construing of that expression. Coupled with my requirement that the language of metaphor be taken literally is the further requirement that we accept the epistemological consequences that ensue from adopting this course, where this means that we try to conceive of the state of affairs actually described by the language of the metaphoric expression. This further requirement is not observed in Davidson's theory.

Thus in the course of his argument Davidson discusses the metaphor in 'The Spirit of God moved upon the face of the waters' and says that if in this expression 'face' is used correctly with 'waters', then waters by inference, really have faces and 'all sense of metaphor evaporates' (p. 34). Davidson is right if we understand him to mean that all sense of *linguistic* metaphor would then evaporate (in the circumstances described by Davidson 'face of the waters' would represent a natural extension of 'face' into a new linguistic environment whose sense in this environment would have been lexicalized). If the metaphor is construed conceptually, however, then the taking of the expression literally has epistemological consequences that are not trivial. We are then not in the artificially manufactured situation in which waters in fact have faces, a situation that would indeed normalize the expression but would imply the *actuality* of a world that is ontologically fantastic; nor are we in a construal mode in which we might interpret the phrase to mean roughly 'surface of the waters'; rather, in the face of all evidence to the contrary, but impelled by a conviction that the poet is striving to express a highly personalized view of reality, we must try to conceive of the possibility that a state of affairs which exceeds anything that our experience has acquainted us with and which in fact transcends what we know the world to be like might yet somehow obtain.

Ricoeur

Ricoeur's discussion of metaphor, perhaps the richest and most comprehensive of those published in recent years, offers a well-thought-out and well-worked-out theory of metaphor. Its essential character is represented by the claim that metaphors, both in their semantics and their reference, display a characteristic ambivalence, promoting interpretive impulses that alternate between sense and non-sense and between reference and nullity. The aim of interpretation is to effect a stasis out of these opposed impulses. Ricoeur's theory impinges on mine in the respect that one term of the ambivalence that he describes results from the taking of metaphor literally and incorporating the epistemological consequences into its interpretation.

Figuring as a kind of theoretical springboard for the elaboration of Ricoeur's views is a pregnant notion of Jakobson's. In his 1960 essay, 'Closing Statement: Linguistics and Poetics', Jakobson writes of the poetic function that among its powers or faculties was that of making reference ambiguous. By way of supporting this notion of 'split reference' he alludes to the preambles of various fairy tales and 'the usual exordium of the Majorca story-tellers: "Aixo era y no era" ("It was and it was not")' (p. 371). This notion of split reference becomes the principle around which Ricoeur develops his theory of metaphor. Before reaching in his discussion the question of reference, however, Ricoeur provides a thorough analysis of metaphorical expressions in terms of their meaning (cf. pp. 65–133). So that when he comes to the discussion of reference, that discussion is carried out in close conjunction with analogous issues raised by the problem of meaning. The following statement provides a clear exposition of how Ricoeur understands meaning and reference to interact in metaphoric expressions (p. 230):

> It is within the very analysis of the metaphorical statement that a referential conception of poetic language must be established, a conception that takes account of the elimination of the reference of ordinary language and patterns itself on the concept of split reference.
>
> Initial support comes from the very notion of metaphorical meaning; the way in which metaphorical meaning is constituted provides the key to the splitting of reference. We can start with the point that the meaning of a metaphorical statement rises up from the blockage of any literal interpretation of the statement. In a literal interpretation, the meaning abolishes itself. Next, because of this self-destruction of the meaning, the primary reference founders. The entire strategy of poetic discourse plays on this point: it seeks the abolition of the reference by means of self-destruction of the meaning of metaphorical statements, the self-destruction being made manifest by an impossible literal interpretation.
>
> But this is only the first phase, or rather the negative counterpart, of a positive strategy. Within the perspective of semantic impertinence [deviance], the self-destruction of meaning is merely the other side of an innovation in meaning at the level of the entire statement, an innovation obtained through the 'twist' of the literal meaning of the words. It is this innovation in meaning that constitutes living metaphor. But are we not in the same motion given the key to metaphorical reference? Can one not say that, by drawing a new semantic pertinence out of the ruins of the literal meaning, the metaphoric interpretation *also* sustains a new referential design, through those same means of abolition of the reference corresponding to the literal interpretation of the statement? A proportional argument, therefore: the other reference, the object of our search, would

be to the new semantic pertinence what the abolished reference is to the literal meaning destroyed by the semantic impertinence. A metaphorical reference would correspond to the metaphoric meaning, just as an impossible literal reference corresponds to the impossible literal meaning.

We see on inspection of Ricoeur's statement that one term of the split reference is in fact no reference at all (it is, rather, null reference) and that the other, the positive term, functions to sustain 'a new referential design'. These results (for reference) run in tandem with the conclusion that Ricoeur arrives at for the meaning of metaphorical statements: taken literally, they have no meaning, their meaning 'self-destructs'; construed, they become, by a semantic 'twist', metaphor. It thus turns out that although on its face the notion of split reference suggests a kind of referential duality, both aspects of which would have a positive value, the case in fact is otherwise. This does not mean, however, that the two-termed character of reference as interpreted by Ricoeur does not play a significant role in his theory. The sense in which split reference plays such a role may be deduced from a proper evaluation of the conjunction represented in the 'It was and it was not' of the Majorca storytellers. To appreciate its significance in the present context, we have to understand by it not that a metaphoric statement makes the claim that a certain state of affairs *alternately* is and is not the case; rather, we are to understand the state of affairs as *simultaneously* being and not being the case. Although the existence of the latter condition is an obvious impossibility, the interpretation of a metaphor, according to Ricoeur, grows out of the effort to comprehend just such an actuality. The interpretive stasis that I referred to in the first paragraph of this section, were it attained to, would represent the achievement of this comprehension.

From the phenomenological standpoint any such comprehension represents an interpretive limit which though it can be approached cannot be reached. Ricoeur says, 'Interpretation is . . . a mode of discourse that functions at the intersection of two domains, metaphorical and speculative. It is a composite discourse, therefore, and as such cannot but feel the opposite pull of two rival demands' (p. 303). To support this notion of a 'pull' in the interpretive process Ricoeur adverts to the *Critique of Judgement* and Kant's discussion there of aesthetic ideas. Concerning the latter Kant writes, 'By an aesthetic idea I mean that representation of the imagination which induces much thought, yet without the possibility of any definite thought whatever, i.e. *concept*, being adequate to it, and which language, consequently, can never get quite on level terms with or render completely intelligible' (1952, 175f.). Now an aesthetic idea is, like an idea of reason, a noumenon; as such, it cannot find its realization in experience. No concept of the understanding, therefore, can comprehend it. Commenting on this phenomenological impasse, Ricoeur says, 'But where the understanding fails, imagination still has the power of presenting" the Idea. It is this "presentation" of the Idea by the imagination that forces conceptual thought to *think more*' (p. 303). In the respect that the effort at comprehension imposes on conceptual thought a demand to 'think more' Ricoeur's theory resembles mine, since the same necessary failure to achieve completion or fulfillment that disables comprehension attaches also to any attempt at the 'conceiving of' states of affairs—in my sense of that notion. For the states of affairs of which it is here a question are those that are projected by expressions that are semantically deviant and as such embody empirical discordancies.

Thus when I say that in interpreting metaphor we must try to conceive of things like trees (literally) weeping, it is clear that in any such effort no definite understanding of that state of affairs can be produced. At the same time, however, the interpretive imperative impels or urges the process on to completion (the 'thinking more' aspect). In chapters 2 and 3 I shall present in greater detail just what I regard the process of *conception*, or *conceiving of*, to consist in. Now, however, it is sufficient to indicate that as a phenomenological activity the process of conception, in its incapacity to issue in a clear-cut representation, resembles the activity of 'comprehension' that I have described above as characteristic of Ricoeur's interpretation. It is therefore necessary to ascertain the respects in which the two forms of interpretation differ. The interpretation of metaphor is a conceptual exercise induced by a challenging (because deviant) linguistic form. On the basis of what I have said about it thus far, I would say that the theory of Ricoeur, in virtue of the pains it takes to elucidate the complexities of the semantics and reference comprised in metaphor, is oriented in large part toward the challenge posed by the linguistic form, whereas my theory, committed as it is to dealing with the epistemological consequences of that form, is oriented essentially to the conceptual exercise. Raised for Ricoeur on his orientation are questions of ontology and metaphysics: he must consider the extent to which the conflicting claims made by metaphorical statements can be made to conform to conditions of the real world.[6] Raised for me, on the other hand, is a phenomenological problem—I must consider the extent to which the conceptions that I claim to be the essential product of the construal process are in fact 'conceivable'. Consideration of this question will be taken up in the next chapter. Yet we must not leave Ricoeur without examining a pendant to his book on metaphor, the article entitled 'The Metaphorical Process as Cognition, Imagination, and Feeling', which appeared in 1978.

In this article Ricoeur fleshes out and supplements his earlier, 1977 treatment of the phenomenological problems associated with the interpretation of metaphor. (Examination of this paper may thus suggest a mitigation or extenuation of the contrast that I drew above between the 'epistemological' and the 'ontological' implications of our respective views on metaphor.) In the course of his discussion Ricoeur develops an analysis whose structure is similar in certain respects to that which underlies my rationalization of 'conception'; the difference is that in his case it is not the

6. Ricoeur's final chapter, 'Metaphor and Philosophical Discourse', contrasts the role played by analogy in Aristotle's theory of metaphor with the role it plays in his theory of the Categories, discusses the efforts made by Aquinas to assess properly the language in which being should be attributed to God and to man, examines the contention of Derrida that all language contains traces of metaphor, and considers the view of Heidegger according to which metaphysics is ineluctably metaphoric—all these profound and weighty matters by way of attempting to 'place' metaphor in the world.

nature of conception but the function of the imagination that the analysis attempts to account for. In this effort Ricoeur again avails himself of Kant, utilizing this time, however, not the Third Critique but the First; in particular, it is Kant's notion of the schema and the role it plays in the operations of the imagination that Ricoeur presses into service. Where, however, for Kant the function of schematization is to provide a means of transition from experience to understanding—to bring intuitions under concepts—for Ricoeur schematization is employed to assimilate to each other, on the basis of a likeness discerned by imagination, the disparate elements comprised by a metaphoric predication. Here are Ricoeur's words on the subject (1978, 148f.):

> . . . I want to underscore a trait of predicative assimilation which may support my contention that the rapprochement characteristic of the metaphorical process offers a typical kinship to Kant's *schematism*. I mean the *paradoxical* character of the predicative assimilation which has been compared by some authors to Ryle's concept of 'category mistake,' which consists in presenting the facts pertaining to one category in the terms appropriate to another. All new rapprochement runs against a previous categorization which resists, or rather which yields while resisting, as Nelson Goodman says. This is what the idea of a semantic impertinence or incongruence preserves. In order that a metaphor obtain, one must continue to identify the previous incompatibility *through* the new compatibility. The predicative assimilation involves, in that way, a specific kind of tension which is not so much between a subject and a predicate as between semantic incongruence and congruence. The insight into likeness is the perception of the conflict between the previous incompatibility and the new compatibility. 'Remoteness' is preserved within 'proximity.' To see *the like* is to see the same in spite of, and through, the different. This tension between sameness and difference characterizes the logical structure of likeness. Imagination, accordingly, is this *ability* to produce new kinds by assimilation and to produce them not *above* the differences, as in the concept, but in spite of and through the differences. Imagination is this stage in the produc-

tion of genres where generic kinship has not reached the level of conceptual peace and rest but remains caught in the war between distance and proximity, between remoteness and nearness.

When earlier in this section I compared Ricoeur's and my views on metaphor, the focus of attention was on his notion of split reference. The contrast that I drew between my 'epistemological' and his 'ontological' concerns derived from that focus. In the passage cited above we see Ricoeur attempt to reconstruct the activity of the imagination in its struggle to realize a meaning out of the incongruent *semantic* elements of a metaphoric predication. We thus have Ricoeur here on epistemological ('cognitive') terrain, and it becomes possible to compare our views on relatively the same grounds. In respect to one aspect of the construal enterprise, Ricoeur and I are in agreement: the effort to achieve interpretive consummation is doomed, ultimately, to failure. Where we differ is in what we take the effort to consist in. For Ricoeur the effort is one of adjudicating incompatible meanings; for me it is to rationalize a constrasensical state of affairs. For me, in fact, the effort consists in trying to form a conception, from what is for Ricoeur the metaphor's negative sense (that of the expression taken literally), of a state of affairs described by that sense. That term of Ricoeur's split reference which functions in his analysis as the null term is for me, therefore, not vacuous; I hold that the state of affairs described by the expression taken literally is conceivable of under a schematization. On Ricoeur's account schematization is employed by the imagination to assimilate incongruent meanings, on my account it is employed to schematize a conception of an unreal or irreal state of affairs.

A Note on Conceptions

It is all well and good to say that we are to take deviant sentences literally and try to conceive of the states of affairs that, so taken, they define or project. The question is whether the projections prompted by such sentences have any phenomenological substance or delineation. If my view of metaphor is to have any usefulness or feasibility, it must be shown that between a deviant sentence and a metaphoric world there in fact does mediate some sort of mental state or process. In large measure one of the burdens of this study is to develop a proper understanding of this mental condition and a just appreciation of the role it plays in causing to transpire certain experiences of a heightened and exceptional nature. It is in fact this mental condition that is associated with the experience we call 'the sublime'. In the concluding chapter of this book I shall try to bring the notion of conception and the idea of the sublime together by way of analyzing a state of mind that I shall characterize as the 'conceptual sublime', and I shall attribute such a state of mind to Wordsworth, whose poetry I shall then adduce as a testing ground for the validity and utility of my theory of metaphor.

In fact Wordsworth himself, whose poetic mind habitually ranged on the brink of sublimity, makes occasional attempts to describe this mental state, a state which in his case is usually induced by ministrations made to his spirit by the forces of nature. In one such description he writes of how he would 'walk alone / In storm and tempest' and feel 'whate'er there is of power in sound / To breathe an elevated mood', how he 'would stand / Beneath some rock, listening to sounds that are / The ghostly language of the ancient earth'. Commenting then on the significance that such experiences had for him, he writes,

> I deem not profitless those fleeting moods
> Of shadowy exultation; not for this,
> That they are kindred to our purer mind
> And intellectual life, but that the soul—
> Remembering how she felt, but what she felt
> Remembering not—retains an obscure sense
> Of possible sublimity, to which
> With growing faculties she doth aspire,
> With faculties still growing, feeling still
> That whatsoever point they gain they still
> Have something to pursue.
>
> [*Prelude* II, 331–41][7]

7. Except where the 1850 edition is indicated, *Prelude* references are to the 1805 edition.

In these lines the soul is remembering a former mental state, a state of which it retains but an 'obscure sense'; this state is one of a 'possible sublimity', whose fundamental character—that of the mind straining toward an unattainable closure—Wordsworth effectively captures in the concluding lines. As I shall argue particularly in the following two chapters, the upshot of this mental straining, this cognitive tension, precisely is a conception.

2

Conceptual Metaphor in the Context of Husserl's Phenomenology

It should be clear by now that the approach I am taking to metaphor in this study raises a difficult set of problems—problems of ontology, of linguistics, and epistemology. In more compact terms, it raises the question of the extent to which language mirrors thought and thought reality. In the general case, to be sure, the relations obtaining between these three constants of the human condition pose few if any problems. We are generally able to express our thoughts and to know the states of affairs that we intend by them. There are occasions, of course, when we feel that an expression is imprecise, a thought unclear, the knowledge of our surroundings inadequate. But we tend to regard such occasions as transient, attributing any inefficiency or uncertainty to momentary or contingent lapses on our part. When we are not completely indifferent to the problem, we act in a placid confidence that there exists between language, thought, and reality a happy compatibility, each member of the triad essentially reflecting and being reflected by the other(s). It is at the same time obvious, however, that we can think of and express things for which reality, taken strictly, provides no backing. We can think of nonexistent objects and 'impossible' states of affairs. And when we give utterance to these thoughts we may produce expressions that have a peculiar character. A subset of these expressions, those termed 'deviant', have a particular interest. They disturb our accustomed indifference or complacency and cause us to consider carefully their linguistic form, the thought that prompted them, and the kind of 'reality' that might be intended by them; they cause us, in other words, to focus our attention on precisely the question raised at the head of this paragraph. The fact that such expressions are common in poetry—almost a trademark—imparts to them a special significance. And the fact that many such expressions are responded to as metaphors throws them into higher relief. In any discussion of metaphor, therefore, an investigation of the status and nature of deviant expressions is unavoidable. Before this investigation is undertaken, however, I shall make some general observations on the background against which such expressions stand out.

Conceptual Space

The words of a language stake out positions in the field of meaning. Thinking, conducted as it is in language, is a passage between and through those positions. Where the thought is ordinary the passage is along preestablished pathways connecting those positions. By contrast, a novel thought projects a previously unrealized trajectory across this field; it is a pioneering foray into space not yet traversed by the mind of man. Noteworthy as such projections may be, however, they are not all of equal significance. Thus the statement 'The telephone was dissolving' expresses a novel thought, in the sense that it has presumably never before occurred to anyone to make that particular statement. In making it, a new trajectory has been thrown across fixed semantic positions; standing words have been combined in an unprecedented way. But the facts underlying the statement—the knowledge that it expresses—have always been available. Novel thoughts that are expressed on this mode are thus relatively trivial. They are thoughts that are 'possible' given the disposition of the field but which for purely accidental reasons have not previously been induced (presumptively, no one has ever dropped a telephone into a vat of acid). Some novel thoughts are not trivial, however; their novelty consists not merely in the relatively insignificant fact that they may never previously have been occasioned but in the fact, critical for our purposes, that they conceive of the world in an unprecedented way. Such thoughts therefore represent new conceptions, and their expression embodies those conceptions. We might say that where in expressing thoughts of the first type we throw light on preexisting facts, in expressing those of the second we present such facts in a new light.

We said above that certain novel expressions conveyed knowledge that was previously available, accordingly that the novelty of such expressions was trivial, and we contrasted those expressions with such as embodied new conceptions, expressions whose novelty was thereby nontrivial. Seen in the framework of our spatial model, novel expressions of the former type connect elements situated in the semantic space between which there previously existed no trajectory. The absence of such a trajectory, however, we said was accidental, being barred by no systematic principle. Novel expressions of the latter type we said embodied new conceptions. In the discussion to follow, the claim of embodying new conceptions will be made for certain metaphoric expressions, for example, 'The sea was laughing' (Wordsworth's *Prelude*, IV, 326). In such cases also new trajections are involved. We need therefore to draw a distinction between the new trajections accomplished here and those involved in the thought expressed by a statement like 'The telephone was dissolving'. The appropriate distinction can be drawn if we assume that the conceptual space is not general and undifferentiated but rather is divided into subspaces, each such subspace being defined by an a priori conceptual coherence. Of 'The sea was laughing', then, we can say that its production implies the crossing of subspatial boundaries.

To specify exhaustively and in detail the determinants of conceptual coherence is obviously impracticable and at best can be done only in part. At this stage I shall merely give some guidelines of a grammatical nature. In the first place, to be set outside our concerns are regimentations like agreement of verb and sub-ject, quantifier and noun, sequence of tenses, gender agreement, and the like. Constraints of this sort are narrowly grammatical in nature. They govern a superficial dimension of syntactic struc-ture and apply equally to all the subspaces. In any case their transgression has no bearing on conceptual coherence. Where the conceptual aspect proper is concerned, we may find clues to the delimitation of these subspaces in certain analytic decisions made in the course of constructing a grammar. To a large extent these decisions reflect the conceptual subspaces. Thus the division among nouns into concrete, abstract, animate, and human, and the corresponding marking of predicates as compatible with one or another of these subclasses, is motivated by and reflects the fact that the conceptual space is divided into subspaces.

A more detailed account of the bearing that linguistic analysis has on the problem of deviant sentences will be presented later in this chapter. Now we shall simply state the conclusions that we arrive at when we plot our two types of novel sentence against the background of conceptual space. In connection with the sen-tence 'The telephone was dissolving' we said that although its expression presupposed a new conceptual trajection, the facts underlying the statement have always been known, that it ex-presses no new knowledge. In light of how the conceptual space is divided, we may suggest that such expressions are accom-plished without the crossing of subspatial boundaries. The new trajectory, although previously unrealized, is projected across points that all lie in the one conceptual subspace. This conclusion correlates both with the fact that the novelty of the thought is unremarkable (occurrence of the fact may be remarkable) and that grammatically the sentence is routine.

We have now contrasted two sentences: 'The sea was laughing' and 'The telephone was dissolving'. The thought expressed by the one, we said, crossed the boundary of a conceptual subspace, whereas that of the other did not. Correlated with this difference is the fact that the first sentence is linguistically deviant, whereas the other is not. Since the first sentence is the one whose novelty is nontrivial, and since it seems to be a characteristic of such novelty that the sentences projecting it are in some sense deviant, it will be worthwhile to examine some approaches to the problem of deviance and the questions it raises.

Among the questions raised by deviant sentences is whether they can be said to describe anything or, to put it another way, whether any state of affairs corresponds to what they 'assert'. If we take as our frame of reference conditions as we know them in the actual world, the answer to this question would seem to be straightforward: to a sentence like 'The sea was laughing' nothing in the world corresponds; or, as we might put it more directly, the sea does not laugh. A second question raised by such sentences, more problematic and more interesting, is whether we can entertain any such notion or idea as that of the sea laughing. To this question the answer is not so obvious; however, that such mental exercises are possible cannot be ruled out a priori.

Apart then from its purely grammatical aspect, our question thus appears in both an ontological and a phenomenological guise. For discussion of the phenomenological aspect it is natural to think of Husserl, particularly his work in *Ideas* and the *Logical Investigations*. As it happens, the *Logical Investigations* is also one of the few places to treat of the question in its ontological aspect. I have therefore thought it useful to examine these two question in the context of Husserl's discussion. This examination, I may say in advance, will not serve to validate my view of metaphor. But it will prove useful in providing a comprehensive theoretical background against which to consider the two questions that interest us and also in sharpening our awareness of just how severe are the problems raised by the consideration of those questions.

The Inadequacy of an Ontological Approach

In the *Logical Investigations* we find that the Fourth Investigation, entitled 'The Distinction Between Independent and Non-Independent Meanings and the Idea of Pure Grammar', is devoted to the general question of linguistic form. In the course of his analysis Husserl distinguishes two types of deviance: nonsense (*Unsinn*) and absurdity (*Widersinn*) (1970, 493). The norm defining nonsensicality is constituted by the general syntactic patterns of a natural language; thus for a language like English (or German) by patterns like Nom V Nom, Nom *be* Adj, and the like. Husserl treats these patterns as defining conditions on well-formedness. Any departure from these patterns violates these conditions and as such yields nonsense. Thus strings like 'If the or is green' and 'A tree is and' are nonsensical (1970, 512). Strings like 'Furiously sleep ideas green colorless' and similar jumbles would count a fortiori as nonsense for Husserl; the examples he adduces, however, are selected to show *specific* transgressions in a syntactic pattern; thus 'or' occurs where a nominal is required, 'and' where an adjectival is required, and so on.[1]

Conversely, any expression that conforms to the general syntactic patterns of the language makes sense, has meaning. Husserl introduces as a formalization of the syntactic pattern realized by the sentence 'This tree is green' the formula 'This *S* is *P*'. As other realizations of this formula Husserl then offers 'This gold . . . ', 'This algebraic number . . . ', 'This blue raven etc. is green'. Concerning this procedure he says (1970, 511f.), 'any nominal material—in the wide sense of "nominal material"—can here [that is, for the "*S*"] be inserted, and so plainly can any adjectival material replace the "*P*". In each case we have once more a meaning unified in sense, i.e. an independent proposition of the prescribed form, but if we depart from the categories of our meaning-material, the unitary sense vanishes'. Subsequently he says, 'In such free exchange of materials within each category, false, foolish, ridiculous (*falsche, dumme, lächerliche*) meanings—complete propositions or elements of propositions—may result, but such results will necessarily be unified meanings, or grammatical expressions whose sense can be unitarily realized. When we transgress the bounds of categories, this is no longer true. We can string together words like "This careless is green", "More intense is round", "This house is just like"; we may substitute

---

1. For Husserl elements like Nominal, Adjectival, and so on are semantic categories, or 'categories of meaning-material', rather than syntactic categories. Similarly, instead of general syntactic patterns he speaks of basic propositional forms. It makes for ease of presentation, however, to set the facts out as above.

"horse" for "resemble" in a relational statement of the form "*a* resembles *b*", but we achieve only a word-series, in which each word is as such significant, or points to a complete, significant context, but we do not, in principle, achieve a closed unity of sense'. The preceding exposition contains the gist of Husserl's analysis. So long as the rules determining syntactic well-formedness are observed, any lexical realization will be meaningful (departure of course yielding nonsense). Among these realizations, however, some will be '. . . ridiculous'. At this point one would welcome a criterion for distinguishing those meaningful expressions that are '. . . ridiculous' from those that are not. No such criterion is offered, however.

After distinguishing sense from nonsense, with 'ridiculous' expressions partaking of the former, Husserl turns to the explication of another opposition—this time between absurd and consistent expressions (1970, 516ff.). As examples of absurdity Husserl instances 'a round square' and 'wooden iron'. Of these expressions Husserl again says that they yield unified meanings.[2] But at the same time (speaking of 'a round square') he says, '*It is apodictically evident* that no existent object can correspond to such an existent meaning'. A sentence like 'All squares have five angles' is treated similarly: it is meaningful, but there is no state of affairs that corresponds to its meaning. The criterion for distinguishing between consistent and absurd expressions is thus the possibility for objects or states of affairs to exist that correspond to the meanings conveyed by those expressions. As we see, however, the ontological criterion is provided for expressions that comprise *analytic* contradictions, thus either such as designate 'impossible' objects ('a round square'), or in the case of sentences ('All squares have five angles') such as are analytically false—thus designate 'impossible' states of affairs.

Earlier we saw Husserl offering as sentences that were sensical (though perhaps false, foolish, or ridiculous) 'This gold is green', 'This algebraic number is green', and 'This blue raven is green'.

2. Thus in the context of the sense/nonsense division, consistent, absurd, and 'ridiculous' expressions all belong to the former class, the last type being indeed a variety of the consistent as well.

The first and third of these sentences would seem to be just as analytically contradictory as 'All squares have five angles'. In the third example the contradiction appears on its face, in the first it derives from the definition of gold as yellow. Inasmuch, therefore, as the meanings of these sentences would by Husserl's ontological criterion be unsatisfiable, it is hard to see on what basis he withholds from them the status of absurdity. We may pass over this point, however, since our interest devolves upon the type of sentence represented by Husserl's second example, 'This algebraic number is green'. This sentence is not absurd, since it comprises no *analytic* contradiction. Unlike what is true of Husserl's other examples, there is nothing in the definition of '(algebraic) number' that explicitly precludes greenness. As it happens, 'This algebraic number is green' is the only example of Husserl's that represents our crucial type. This fact is of little consequence, however, since according to Husserl's own principle of free interchangeability within syntactic categories, we are sanctioned in generating from 'This *S* is *P*' all manner of other sentences representing the same type, for example, 'This wish (fear, sigh) is green' (as well of course as 'This tree is (sincere, angry) ambitious'). Here, as with 'This algebraic number is green', we have to do not so much with analytic contradictions as with semantic anomalies, and in such cases the impossibility of ontological correspondence, Husserl's blanket criterion for absurdity, is not 'apodictically evident'. Failing that criterion, moreover, there is nothing in Husserl's analysis to tell us that such sentences have a special property (we are told only that their meanings are 'ridiculous'). Since they are not absurd, however, it is left open on Husserl's analysis that some possible state of affairs corresponds to their meaning. Husserl might very well deny this possibility, but he offers no grounds in his analysis for doing so.

Some Remarks on 'Possible Worlds'

Let us at this stage consider the question of ontology and the use which Husserl makes of it in his analysis. Ontology is the study of being, its nature and its manifestations. Now of the various positions that one can take in respect to this study, the one adopted by Husserl is severely and unnecessarily limited. For him existent objects are such as exist in the actual world, nonexistent objects (and impossible states of affairs)—thus the objects and states 'meant' by absurd expressions—such as exist in no possible world. Yet between these two extremes there lies the possibility of existence in *some* 'world' not necessarily actual. And this possibility, which is the crucial one for our purposes and which really requires consideration even for his own analysis, is left unexamined by Husserl. What I am suggesting is that besides ontology *tout court*, we entertain the possibility of personal nonce ontologies.

The notion of possible worlds is associated primarily with systems of modal logic, in which interpretations provide for the truth or falsity of sentences incorporating the modal notions of necessity and possibility (or in some systems also for sentences containing verbs expressing propositional attitudes, for example, 'believe' and 'know'). The possible worlds in these systems are not to be thought of as extraterrestrial planets, places which could be visited by spaceship and on which one might find life; they are to be regarded, rather, say with Kripke (1972, 267), as descriptions of constitutive conditions or, with Hughes and Cresswell (1972, 75), as 'conceivable or envisageable states of affairs'. With these suggestions in mind, let us consider an interpretation (first) of a language that contains no modal operators and whose domain is the class of New York Yankees baseball players. Such a restricted interpretation makes claims that obtain in the actual world; thus for it the sentence 'All New York Yankees are over five feet tall' would be true. The same sentence, however, prefixed by the operator 'Necessarily', could be false, since it is possible to conceive of a 'world' in which Don Mattingly, say, is a midget. In other words, if it is not necessary that all New York Yankees are over five feet tall, it is possible that some are under that height. Notice that we said of the 'Necessarily'-prefixed sentence that it *could* be false. It could, however, be true; that is, it is not *necessarily* false. Since the height of a New York Yankee is a contingent matter, since there is nothing in the definition of

'New York Yankee' that stipulates an exact height or range of heights, we can just as well conceive of a set of possible worlds in which all the New York Yankees are over five feet tall as a set comprising one in which some are not. From the preceding we can see that whereas nonmodal interpretations are directed at those states of affairs that happen to obtain in the actual world, those of modal logic comprehend also states that we may entertain, additionally, as obtaining in alternative 'possible worlds' and that, depending on the scope of the possible worlds that we entertain, the same 'Necessarily'-prefixed sentence can vary in truth value.

In the context of the a priori available 'possible worlds', Husserl's discussion of absurdity is conducted exclusively through sentences which in a modal logic would be *necessarily* false, that is, false in a strictly logical sense. Unlike the example above about the New York Yankees, where the *Necessity*-operator was prefixed to a sentence whose truth value could be true or false contingently, the examples offered by Husserl consist of sentences which are analytically false. Thus there is no conceivable set of circumstances in which a sentence like 'This square has five angles' (Husserl's example) could possibly be true. So that the latter sentence if prefixed by 'Necessarily' would be false and if by 'Possibly' would still be false. (Husserl deals largely with names rather than sentences, thus is more apt to say that nothing exists that corresponds to the meaning of 'a round square', but the respective conclusions have the same implications.) Now there is no reason to question the conclusions that Husserl arrives at for phrases and sentences that comprise analytic contradictions. These conclusions, however, are not self-evident for sentences like 'This algebraic number is green' or 'The sea was laughing'. Such sentences occupy a level lying somewhere between sentences like 'All New York Yankees are over five feet tall', whose truth value is contingent, and sentences like 'A square has five angles', whose truth value is analytic. In Husserl's analysis, however, limited as it is to just the two extreme cases, the ontological implications of a sentence like 'The sea was laughing' (or 'This groan is green', etc.) remain unspecified. In particular, he has not shown that such sentences are *necessarily* false; thus the possibility is not ruled out that they might be true.[3] Although its primary object is natural language, Husserl's analysis is directed ultimately toward the establishment of a priori laws governing the form and combination of his meaning-categories. Toward this end he draws a distinction (1970, 523f.) between what he calls material (synthetic) absurdity and formal, analytic absurdity. The former is realized in actual realizations of syntactic patterns, that is to say, 'A square is round'. The latter is governed by laws such as those of Contradiction, Double Negation, and Modus Ponens. The latter laws 'show us what holds for objects in general in virtue of their pure "thought-forms", i.e. what can be said regarding the objective validity of meanings on a basis purely of the meaningful forms in which we think them, and in advance of all objective matters signified. These laws may not be violated if falsehood is not to result, even before objects in their factual particularity have been taken into account'. Here again Husserl confines himself to sentences that are necessarily false. A sentence like 'A square is round' is materially absurd. Its material absurdity follows from the Law of Contradiction, one of the formal laws the violation of which entails falsehood. As before, the status of sentences like 'The sea was laughing' or 'This wish is green' is left unaddressed. None of Husserl's formal, analytic laws would predict absurdity for sentences of this type. Moreover, as we have seen, neither does his criterion of ontological correspondence have obvious application for such sentences. They thus escape his analysis from both above and below.

A Linguistic Approach

It was mentioned earlier (and illustrated in passing) that light can be thrown from one direction on the structure and configuration of the conceptual subspaces by examining the constraints placed by a linguistic description on the co-occurrability

3. For the applicability of possible worlds in the analysis of fiction, see Pavel, 1986, and Doležel, 1988.

of grammatical classes. Recast in conformity with the present focus of discussion, this becomes the problem of deviance and the mechanisms developed by a grammatical analysis for identifying it and characterizing its varieties. In perhaps the most comprehensive and relevant scheme devised for dealing with this problem, that in Chomsky (1965), two such contraints are introduced.[4] First, nouns are subcategorized according to their grammatical properties: *boy* would be analyzed as comprising the features [+N, +Count, +Common, +Human, . . .], *sand* as [+N, −Count, +Common, −Animate, . . .], *pathos* as [+N, −Count, +Abstract, . . .], and so on. The rules that make these assignments are context free, applying to nouns on the basis of their *inherent* properties. The constraints, which are context sensitive, then take two forms: strict subcategorization rules, which limit the grammatical *categories* with which a verb (or other predicate) may co-occur, and selection rules, which impose a further limitation, one which restricts verbs to co-occurrence with *subclasses* of these categories. Rules of the first type ensure, for example, that the grammar will not generate strings in which intransitive verbs occur with direct objects, rules of the second type apply to ensure that, given the satisfaction of strict subcategorization, the grammar does not go on to generate strings that transgress a narrower restriction of co-occurrability.

The procedure implies that verbs will incorporate in their lexical representations features relating to both their strict subcategorizational and selectional valencies. Thus the first part of a verb's representation will be sensitive to the *categorial* marking of a noun's feature composition (the element 'N'), the second part to its *syntactic* markers (the features 'Count', 'Human', etc.).

To illustrate briefly how the procedure works, the phrase-

---

4. Grammatical theory since 1965 has not, so far as I can see, made any significant progress in the treatment of linguistic deviance. The extensive syntactic machinery developed in the *Aspects* model for defining well-formedness conditions has played less and less of a role in the subsequent development of grammatical theory. A major innovation has been to reduce drastically the role played in the grammar by transformational rules and the enrichment of the lexicon by way of compensation. But this has had little if any significance for the treatment of deviance.

structure rules of the grammar will generate a phrase-marker as shown in figure 3.

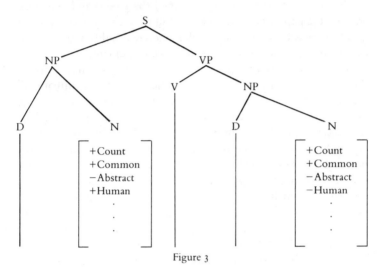

Figure 3

Into this phrase marker the lexical entry for *boy* may be inserted in the first noun position and that for *paper* in the second. Let us assume *the* for both Determiner positions. A verb appropriate for insertion in the V position will have to be compatible both with the categorial configuration of the phrase marker (thus at least be transitive) and with the syntactic features assigned to the two N positions. This sensitivity obtains not in respect to the actual nouns that we have suggested as inserts. Since those nouns conform to the syntactic specifications of the Ns, they merely reflect the selection problem; they have been introduced simply in the interest of perspicuity. Turning now to the lexicon in the search for possible candidates among the verbs for this phrase marker, we find representations like the following: *arrive* [+V, - —NP, . . .]; *amuse*, [+V, + —NP, +[+Human], . . .]; *tear*, [+V, + — NP, +[−Human], . . .]. Thus *arrive* is barred from insertion because it may not take a following NP (a strict subcategorization requirement), *amuse* is barred because its following NP must be [+Human] (a selection requirement), and *tear* may be inserted as satisfying both types of restriction.[5]

The two sentences 'The boy arrived the paper' and 'The boy amused the paper' are both deviant, but they appear to be deviant in different ways. One way to characterize the difference would be to say that the former is syntactically deviant, whereas the deviance of the latter is conceptual. Since nothing can be arrived, the conceptual dimension of the (object) nouns is immaterial; whatever differences they may exhibit on this dimension are neutralized in the syntactic category, which alone is relevant for the description. Since, however, there are things that can be amused, it is necessary to consider the things named by the nouns. For Chomsky of course both types of deviance are strictly syntactic in nature (thus talk of things, as in the above, is a departure from his approach). The strict subcategorization restrictions relate to syntactic categories, the selection restrictions to syntactic feature complexes ('complex symbols'). Restrictions of the former sort can therefore be accounted for by stipulating that a noun phrase (any one) may not follow a verb like *arrive*, and restrictions of the latter sort by specifying the syntactic feature composition of nouns and stipulating that the selection restrictions in the lexical representation of verbs be consistent with those feature complexes. Chomsky's treatment of the problem thus does not of itself warrant us in claiming that a sentence like 'The boy amused the paper' is conceptually deviant. Because the approach is linguistic, certain aspects of the problem are either presupposed or left out of account. But Chomsky's analysis does represent an advance over that of Husserl, for whom 'The boy arrived . . . ' and 'The boy amused the paper', as both satisfying the syntactic requirements, are meaningful. For Chomsky, neither is.[6] However, where under Husserl's analysis they are *equally* meaningful, Chomsky's model implicitly enables us to measure the respective *degrees* of their unmeaningfulness.

---

5. As we see, the categorial symbol that the verb is sensitive to is 'NP', not 'N' as stated earlier. Explaining the difference at the early stage, however, would have complicated the exposition needlessly.

6. For Husserl well-formedness guarantees meaningfulness; for Chomsky it does not.

If we turn now to the linguistic analysis of the sentences 'The telephone was dissolving' and 'The sea was laughing', we find that the results are consistent with the conclusions that we arrived at in our earlier discussion of those sentences. We said then that although both sentences might be held to express novel thoughts, the novelty of the *telephone* sentence was trivial, of little or no theoretical interest, whereas the novelty of the *sea* sentence we said was nontrivial and might be theoretically significant. We reasoned further that in the production of the *telephone* sentence no subspatial conceptual boundaries were transgressed, whereas the production of the *sea* sentence entailed precisely such a transgression. Let us now look at the treatment that the two sentences would receive in the grammatical framework sketched above. The phrase-structure rules would generate for both sentences a phrase marker, as shown in figure 4.

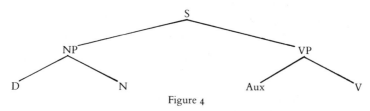

Figure 4

Since *dissolve* is an amphibious and *laugh* an intransitive verb, the insertion of either into this phrase marker would be in conformity with the strict subcategorization requirements. Whatever difference there might be between the two sentences should then emerge in connection with how they relate to the selection rules. We proceed then to consider the sentences in terms of the co-occurrability of their nouns and verbs. The 'complex symbol' that would be generated under the N for one derivation would comprise the features [+Common, +Count, −Abstract, −Human, . . .]. Inserted for the N in this phrase marker could then be the lexical item *telephone*, since its feature specification agrees with that in the complex symbol. Following this the verb *dissolve* may be inserted for the V, inasmuch as its feature complex specifies that it may co-occur with a subject noun marked [. . . , −Abstract (i.e., Concrete), −Human, . . .]. In the derivation of our other sentence, the complex symbol generated under the N would comprise the features [. . . , −Count, −Abstract, −Human, . . .]. This feature specification would permit the insertion of *sea*. The verb *laugh* is specified in its lexical representation as requiring a subject noun that is, among other things, [+Human] (or at least [+Animate]). If, therefore, *laugh* should be inserted in the phrase marker there would result a conflict between the minus and plus values on the feature [Human]; this conflict defines the violation of a selection restriction. So far as the grammar is concerned, then, its 'comment' on a sentence like 'The sea was laughing' is simply that it departs in a certain respect from strict well-formedness. It is not concerned, that is, with the possible significance that such a sentence may have in poetry—as a metaphor—or, generally, as a means for expressing new conceptions. However, the fact that the selection rules involve considerations of Humanness, Animateness, Abstractness, and the like, implies that they are sensitive to linguistic properties and relations that lie close to the semantic surface. It stands to reason, therefore, that operations at this level would figure in 'extensions' of thought and conception.

In the preceding exposition of Chomsky's treatment of deviant sentences, no mention was made of meaning as such. It is understood, however, that the lexical entries of words will comprise, in addition to the features which determine their privileges of occurrence, representations of their meaning. This is obviously necessary if the grammar is to provide an interpretation for those strings which are not filtered out by the selectional rules. To provide such an interpretation a grammar of the sort described above needs to be supplemented by a semantic component. For present purposes we need not go into a description of the semantic component of such a grammar and the rules it contains which effect these interpretations (for such a description see Katz, 1972). It is sufficient for us to know that the definitions of lexical items are cast in the form of semantic markers and that a projection rule progressively amalgamates on the basis of these markers sets of words in the string until finally the entire sentence receives its semantic interpretation. For our purposes the important fact is that the entire process may be carried out without reference to concepts or conceptions. The elements figuring in the syntactic and semantic rules are all linguistic units or such units analyzed into primitive elements. The entire procedure operates on the single plane of language.[7]

Obviously, considerations of reference and concept will have been entertained in the construction of the grammar. But once the grammar has been constructed, abstraction is made of those considerations and the grammar operates autonomously. Thus when we said above that common to all Husserl's absurd sentences is the fact that their falsity is analytic, following from the Law of Contradiction, it is this fact, distilled into semantic features, which serves in a linguistic description to characterize a sentence like 'All squares have five angles'. Following from the marking of *square* as +[+Having four angles] and the assertion made by the predicate, the semantic component will mark the sentence 'Contradictory'. On Husserl's analysis, on the other hand, the sentence is absurd in having no ontological grounding—that is, no state of affairs corresponds to the statement made by the sentence. A similar treatment would be accorded to sentences like 'This algebraic number is green', 'The boy amused the paper', and 'The sea was laughing'. On the basis that the selection requirements for their predicates are not satisfied by the subject nouns, they would be labeled 'Anomalous' by the semantic component and receive no interpretation. Thus, as compared with judgments like Husserl's 'false, foolish, or ridiculous', judgments which represent reactions to the ontological claims made by certain well-formed sentences, a judgment like 'Anomalous' is

---

7. Katz (1972) does in fact discuss concepts. On p. 38 he writes, 'Concepts and propositions are senses of expressions and sentences'. This is thus, as we mentioned above, to regard the meaning of a word as the concept expressed by it (and similarly for a sentence and a proposition). Katz's actual analysis, however, is carried out strictly in terms of linguistic units and theoretical constructs related to such units, the concepts in all this being essentially presupposed. And this is quite consistent with his project, which is to develop a *semantic* component for a general *linguistic* theory. As we shall see, later, however, Katz is well aware of the problem posed by concepts—how a different approach to the language phenomenon may elevate the notion of concept to a more prominent position.

based entirely on the incompatibility of semantic features assigned to lexical items.

Toward a Phenomenological Approach

Quite apart from the question of what if any sort of truth claims are made by deviant sentences, and the question of how they are treated in a generative grammar, deviant sentences raise the further question of what one might be thinking of—what mental processes one might be experiencing—when one produces or interprets such a sentence. To examine this question we return to Husserl, focusing this time on his discussion of intentional acts and their varieties.

Since Husserl claims that deviant sentences make sense, have unitary meanings, we might expect that when he turns to his analysis of intentional acts the question of deviant sentences would again arise, this time in terms of their phenomenological properties, and that in this discussion he would assess for us what we might call their semantic cash value, that is, describe what if any image, notion, concept, or conception we entertain when we 'grasp' the meaning of a sentence like 'The sea was laughing'. This expectation is encouraged by the fact that intentions make up a class of entities for which one can claim an existence quite regardless of whether extramental conditions obtain that are correspondent to them; in other words, the existence of intentions does not depend necessarily on matching facts or states of affairs in the actual world. This is obvious in the case of volitional or affective intentions—of wishing, desiring, hoping, expecting, dreading, and the like—whose very nature is such that their corresponding actualizations are precluded from occurring in concert with the intentions. Other types of intention, like those of memory, regret, and imagining, similarly do not require that the original perception or experience on which the intention is based be present in actuality, this again by definition. The same point can be made in regard to other varieties of intention. In all such cases the fact follows from the nature of the intentional act in question and is relatively trivial, since actualization in these cases stands in a relation of temporal disjunction to the act in question: with memory or regret it has occurred, with wish and expectation it is to occur. Nonactualization becomes nontrivial, however, and highly important, when the intentional acts are such that the possibility of phenomenal actualization is out of the question. When in such cases we have only the intentions, without the corresponding phenomena, we need not take the situation to be partial or impoverished; the domain of intentions remains as a field of operations. The significance of the phenomenological approach is thus that it accords prominence to our conscious experiences; it lends substance to certain types of mental phenomena that otherwise are seen as obscure, indistinct forms with little or no significant content. Phenomenology provides us with intentions. In its context these have a reality as mental or psychical entities subsisting in their own right.

In point of fact Husserl does not explicitly take up the aspect of the problem which here concerns us. He does not, that is, consider the phenomenological implications of sentences like 'This algebraic number is green' or 'The sea was laughing', that is, the kind of intentional experience that should be associated with sentences which according to him have 'ridiculous' meanings. As we shall see, however, his very failure to do so may be used to throw light on the problematic nature of such experiences.

Presentations

To bring us in the way of ascertaining Husserl's position, it will be necessary as a preliminary to examine certain notions that figure prominently in his subsequent discussion. We consider first the notion of presentation and its variants. Presentations are primitive intentional acts, correlatives of either verbal or intuitive functions, in which the matter of experience is promoted to consciousness. They thus represent the aspect in which the intentional 'objects' are viewed phenomenologically. In this process the object or state of affairs may be presented in either of two modes, one in which they carry an implicit claim of existence, the other in which they appear 'merely' in presentation.

The verbal or intuitive acts inducing the presentations are then referred to as *positing* or *nonpositing*, depending on which mode the presentation assumes. Thus in the naming function—where 'name' is meant to include definite descriptions as well as proper names—the objects that the names refer to may be understood as really existent, in which case the name is positing, or the name may be used nonpositingly. In the latter case the 'mere presentation' of the object is promoted in consciousness, no implicit claim being made for its existence. Husserl gives as an example of the latter possibility the case of a discussion in which the question of existence is itself at issue, so that the existential commitment of the names used in that discussion remains suspended (1970, 626).

Judgments as well as names can occur either as positing or nonpositing. Referring to the shifting of a term from the one to the other status as a 'modification', Husserl says (1970, 638): 'We find exactly the same modification in the case of judgments. Each judgment has its modified form, an act which merely presents what the judgment takes to be true, which has an object without a decision as to truth and falsity'. As an example of such a modification where judgments are concerned, Husserl offers '2 x 2 = 5', uttered to express mere understanding, hence not asserted (1970, 641). In the field of intuitive acts the distinction likewise obtains. Acts of perception, recollection, anticipation normally posit the existence of their presented 'objects'. These same acts, however, carried out in the frame of an illusion or an exercise of fancy would be nonpositing; hence they promote merely the presentation of their 'objects' with no implicit commitment to their existence.

Given the theoretical significance for Husserl of the distinction that he draws between positing and nonpositing acts, we might expect that the question of acts involving contrasensical thoughts or their expression would come up in his discussion. But it does not; he offers us instead a couple of uninteresting examples— where names are concerned, the special case of a discussion which is itself about existence, and for propositions, the obviously false '2 x 2 = 5'. We might then assume that Husserl neglects to raise the question because the answer is obvious: intentional acts, if they involve contrasensical thoughts or expressions, are necessarily nonpositing. As we shall see later, however, this assumption would be unwarranted.

Fulfillment

We turn now to consider another pertinent consequence deriving from Husserl's investigations. This one follows from his analysis of intentions and their fulfillments. Husserl begins his discussion with an examination of expressive acts, primarily that of naming (1970, 687ff.). To each such act there is related a meaning-intention. The meaning-intention is fulfilled when there occurs in connection with it the corresponding act of intuition, which for Husserl is an act of perception or imagination. The required association may appear simultaneously with the expressive act, in which case the fulfillment of the meaning-intention is *static*, or it may appear subsequently, in which case the fulfillment is *dynamic*. As an instance of static fulfillment Husserl cites the case where he says 'I see my inkpot' and the inkpot is before him in a perception. If, on the other hand, one should say 'I am looking for my inkpot' and then find it somewhere the meaning-intention of the expression would be fulfilled dynamically, in that a temporal lapse would have intervened between its enunciation and the intuitive act connected with it.

Acts of perception and imagination may of course take place without the accompaniment of verbal expression. In this mode the intentional acts are also fulfilled statically, the percept and the image being integral parts of the act. This coincidence of act-phase and object-phase is characteristic of *intuitive* intentional acts. If we shift our attention now to types of intentional act other than the perceptual or imaginative, the picture changes. For it is clear that where volitional or affective intentions—wishes, fears, doubts, expectations—are concerned, fulfillment, if it supervenes at all, can only be dynamic. Unlike what is true for (veridical) acts of perception and imagination, where (static) fulfillment is guaranteed by the intuitive nature of the act, intentional acts of volition or affection depend on an empirical sequel for their fulfillment. Thus although such acts may succeed in fulfilling their intentions, their fulfillment is necessarily deferred. We mention this point in passing. What interests us primarily is the situation in which intentional acts, whether expressive or otherwise, succeed in their intention even though fulfillment, in the form of empirical realization, is foreclosed on a priori grounds. Obviously, what is wished for in a wish may remain unrealized, what is judged to be the case may in fact be otherwise, what is feared may turn out to be harmless. If so, the intentions in question fail of fulfillment. On the other hand, the intentions in such acts may in fact achieve fulfillment: the wish may be realized, the fear borne out, and so forth (all this dynamically of course). These alternatives are characteristic of the standard, or normal, situation. As we said above, however, the interesting cases for us are those in which the intentions do not simply fail of fulfillment but whose character is such that their fulfillment is impossible—such that they must always, in the nature of the case, remain mere intentions.

To illustrate: we could wish to grow a third eye, we could judge Goldbach's conjecture to be correct, we could fear being swallowed by a coffee bean. In all such cases the intention as such exists. Yet (on the assumption that the various acts were performed seriously) there would pertain to the intentions in the examples given what might be called a 'vain' or 'pathological' character, in that they would require for their fulfillment the *actualization* of a sequel that is a priori impossible. For without the actualization of this sequel there would be no experience to provide grounds for the fulfillment of the intentions.

We wish now to contrast such 'vain' intentional acts, in which the intention fails of fulfillment because actualization of consequences is presupposed that is impossible of realization, with another class of acts, in which, even though the actualization of corresponding consequences is likewise impossible, the result is not one of self-stultification—the intentions are nevertheless realized. I refer here to acts of conceiving. If I conceive (of) the sea as laughing, I realize an intention in my conception of that 'state of affairs'. For intentions like this there is also no possibility of actualization. Thus it might appear that they likewise fail of fulfillment. But there is a difference between those intentional acts that are 'vain' and acts of conceiving like the one just described. In the former the impossibility of actualization stultifies the act. There is no point in wishing for something that cannot occur, judging something that in undecidable, or fearing what cannot harm. It is not pointless, though, to conceive (of) absurd states of affairs. The difference has to do with the nature of the intentions which are associated with the two types of act. Wishing, judging, fearing, and so forth are acts that are *dependent* on their actualizing sequels in a way in which conceiving is not. If the empirical correspondents of these 'dependent' acts are unactualizable, then the entire intentional act is rendered moot, inasmuch as the intention by definition cannot be fulfilled. On the other hand, an act of conceiving and its intention—the conception—stand to each other in a relation of *static* fulfillment. We may, if we take the notion of fulfillment to be unexceptionably dependent on intuitive support, speak where conceptual intentions are concerned of satisfaction rather than fulfillment. The thing to stress, however, is that acts of conceiving are autotelic; they carry within themselves the grounds of their satisfaction: although their intentions cannot be realized, neither can they be defeated. Where conceptions are concerned one brackets both the possibility of intuitional fulfillment and the need for it.

Conception and Imagination

It is necessary to make clear that the term *conceiving (of)*, as I am using it, is to be distinguished from *imagining*. The latter term refers to intentions directed toward states of affairs (and objects) that are not present, the former toward such as do not exist. In bringing the respective states to consciousness, I imagine the sea as being calm, but I conceive (of) it as laughing. Some such distinction as the one I am drawing seems to be indicated. If we say simply that we 'think of' both the sea as calm and as laughing, or that we have the 'idea' of both, then the difference in the ontological statuses of those two states of affairs is neutralized in the common description. If, on the other hand, we use the term *imagine* for experiences of both types, it would imply that intuitional fullness is achieved as much for our presentation of a laughing sea as of a calm—also a contraindicated result. It appears, therefore, that introduction of the term *conceiving* is well motivated.

On the question of what the phenomenological difference is between acts of imagination and acts of conception (in my sense), Husserl is essentially unhelpful. We might expect that the difference would be noted in his discussion of positing and nonpositing acts, namely, that acts of the former type would be positing, and would thus imply the existence of their intended objects and states of affairs, whereas those of the latter would be nonpositing, that is, would promote the 'mere presentation' of their objects and states, with no implication of their existence. This does not happen, however. Husserl conducts his discussion throughout by means of nonvacuous names and descriptions of possible states of affairs, his purpose in this section being to show that such names and descriptions are susceptible of *both* statuses, the difference depending on whether the names and descriptions are (as we might say) asserted or merely mooted.[8] Ultimately, at all

8. The *Logical Investigations* does offer one discussion bearing on vacuous names; it appears, however, in the section on presentation, not in that treating of positing acts. Speaking of the intentional experience, Husserl writes (p. 558):

> If this experience is present, then, *eo ipso* and through its own essence (we must insist) the intentional 'relation' to an object is achieved, and an object is 'intentionally present'; these two phrases mean precisely the same. And of course such an experience may be present in consciousness together with its intention, although the object does not exist at all, and is perhaps incapable of existence. The object is 'meant', i.e. to 'mean' it is an experience, but it is then merely entertained in thought, and is nothing in reality.

Continuing, he says,

> If I have the idea of the god Jupiter, this means that I have a certain presentative experience, the presentation-of-the-god-Jupiter is realized in my consciousness. This intentional experience may be dismembered as one chooses in descriptive analysis, but the god Jupiter will naturally not be found in it. The 'immanent', 'mental object' is not therefore part of the descriptive or real make-up of the experience, it is in truth not really immanent or mental. But it also does not exist extra-mentally, it does not exist at all. This does not prevent our-idea-of-the-god-Jupiter from being actual, a particular sort of

events, any expectation that vacuous names and, more important, absurd descriptions might be specially considered in this
section is dashed by the following statement (1970, 626): '*To each
positing act there corresponds a possible non-positing act having the same
matter, and vice versa*'. The converse in this postulation would
appear effectively to rule out under the positing/nonpositing
dichotomy the comprehension of expressive acts comprising either vacuous names or absurd descriptions. For in order that such
acts should indeed be comprehended they would have to be
capable of employ in a positing function, a function which,
according to Husserl, attributes to the object or state of affairs
named 'the status of an existent' (1970, 626), and this would seem
to be a presupposition that is ruled out for these expressive acts.

I take it that Husserl does not mean by his principle that the
same proposition can be uttered positingly or nonpositingly depending on the syntactic environment in which it occurs, so that,
for example, the proposition that 2 x 2 = 5 would be positing if it
occurs after 'since' or 'I know', but nonpositing after 'if' or 'I
doubt'. The fact that the existential claim made by propositions
can be modified by such means is so obvious that one cannot see
Husserl putting such great theoretical store by his principle (it is
repeated several times in the *Logical Investigations*). Besides, the
form of the postulation seems to be making a stronger claim,
namely, that the *very same* expressive act can be uttered either

---

experience or particular mode of mindedness, such that he who experiences it
may rightly say that the mythical king of the gods is present to him. . . . If,
however, the intended object exists, nothing becomes phenomenologically
different. It makes no essential difference to an object presented and given to
consciousness whether it exists, or is fictitious, or is perhaps completely
absurd. I think of Jupiter as I think of Bismarck, of the tower of Babel as I
think of Cologne Cathedral, of a regular thousand-sided polygon as of a
regular thousand-faced solid.

In this passage Husserl does not say whether the presentations promoted by
vacuous names are positing or nonpositing. And as mentioned above, the answer
that appears obvious—that presentations of this sort are (necessarily) nonpositing—turns out to be unwarranted. What this passage does argue is that one can
intend nonexistent objects. But this aspect of Husserl's phenomenology is well
attested and not at issue (cf. Smith and McIntyre, 1984, 12, 90). Not addressed by
the passage, however, is whether the use of vacuous or nonreferring names posits
or does not posit the existence of the objects denoted by those names.

positingly or nonpositingly. Suppose then that we assume that Husserl means us to take his principle at its fact value. This would indeed give us a warrant to conclude that intentional acts involving vacuous names or descriptions of absurd states of affairs may be positing and thus presuppose the existence of the 'objects' named by their constituent elements. It is hard to know, however, just how seriously we should take this possibility. Since the objects of vacuous names are not referents and the states of affairs 'described' by deviant sentences are not actual, what in fact would it mean to say that intentional acts comprising such elements were positing? The only possibility left open, it seems to me, is that Husserl intends such positings to be made by agents who are in some way divorced from reality, people like mystics, seers, shamans, assorted lunatics, and perhaps also poets. This would not be an unwelcome inference for me to draw, but there is little in Husserl's discussion of this problem to suggest that this is what he means.

It appears that, following Husserl, all we are entitled to say about what I am calling conceptual acts is that they promote to consciousness a presentation of the state of affairs intended in the act. Yet this presentation is supposed to be far less substantive and potent than the analogous presentation promoted by an act of the imagination. This difference between these two types of intentional act, which prima facie appears to be so radical, can be attenuated, however. To see this, let us compare with an act of conception the type of imaginative act that we may call 'far-fetched'. It would be supposed, in terms of such a comparison, that one should be able to imagine, say, a volcano erupting pineapples but not the sea laughing. Now in these two cases the possibility of factual validation is just as remote for the act of imagination as it is for the conceptual act involved in regarding the sea as laughing. This implies that in neither act is the state of affairs posited, that is, presupposed as actually existent. So that in both acts, from the phenomenological standpoint, the intentional experiences promote to consciousness 'mere' presentations (this despite the fact that imaginative intentions are supposed to constitute a variety of intuitive act). Thus if imaginative acts of the kind here in question are to have any status as full-blown intentional acts it would have to be on the basis of the same kind of phenomenological self-sufficiency that, as I have argued, obtains in the case of conceptual acts. As between the two types of self-sufficiency there is, it must be granted, the following difference: even for 'farfetched' imaginative acts the presentation can take the form of a clear image, whereas in acts of conception (in my terms) this does not occur. Entertained instead is a progressively lapsing impression which the conceiver, bent on its realization in consciousness, impels and urges to attainment. Although attainment is not reached, that is, no definite presentation is achieved, there stands behind and activates the process what may be regarded as a schema of the presentation.

The phenomenological process I have just sketched consists very closely with the sentiments expressed by Wordsworth in the lines from *The Excursion* cited in chapter 1:

> 'tis a thing impossible to frame
> Conceptions equal to the soul's desires,
> And the most difficult task to keep
> Heights which the soul is competent to gain.

My 'schema' corresponds to the 'heights which the soul is competent to gain', and the attempt to *keep* those heights (a 'most difficult task') spells out as 'a progressively lapsing impression which the conceiver . . . impels and urges to attainment'. I would argue that for a person who for some reason is intent on bringing such an impression to attainment, acts of conception will constitute intentions of a more significant order than acts of 'farfetched' imagination, even though the latter promote to consciousness the phenomenologically weightier 'presentations'.

Of Some Acts That for Husserl Are Phenomenologically Substantial

Husserl's failure to take a clear position with regard to what I am calling conceptions stands out when we consider his readiness to commit himself otherwise on the question of phenomenological substantiality. Consider, for example, the claims he makes for intentional acts of the kind he calls categorial. On pages 784ff. of the *Logical Investigations*, as part of his discussion of complex intentional experiences, Husserl introduces a distinction between sensuous and categorial acts: sensuous are those acts (or parts of acts) whose intuitional fulfillment is produced by empirical matter or 'stuff', categorial by relations between those 'stuffs'. Thus the intentions correlated with a perception or imagining of a tree or a house would be sensuous, that correlating with the notions of, say, conjunction, existence, or definiteness would be categorial. So if someone should say 'That tree and house are green', the acts correlated with the (perception of the) tree, the house, and greenness would be sensuous, those correlated with the other—the formal—parts of the experience would be categorial; and the act correlated with the entire experience (the perception of the state of affairs) would be a categorial act *founded* on the sensuous intentions.

Husserl says of these categorial acts that they have objects, that they are perceived, and that they are fulfilled intuitionally. The object ultimately perceived by them is typically a state of affairs, and this object, being a 'percept', is presented with intuitional fullness. If we see that a certain tree and house are green then are not only the percepts of the tree, the house, and the greenness presented intuitionally but also the logical categories of definiteness, conjunction, and predication; finally, the act founded on these intuitions—the perception of the entire state of affairs—is also presented with intuitional fullness. The same analysis applies if we give expression to our perceptions. Moreover, as Husserl makes clear, whatever holds in regard to categorial forms when they appear in acts of perception applies with equal force to acts of imagination. Of such experiences generally, Husserl says (1970, 785): 'The object with these categorial forms is not merely referred to, as in the case where meanings function purely symbolically, but it is set before our very eyes in just these forms. In other words: it is not merely thought of, but intuited or perceived'. As we see, when it serves his theoretical purposes Husserl finds it quite feasible to attribute intuitional fullness to intentional experiences of a rather attenuated, highly abstract nature.

Another example of the latitude with which Husserl employs the notion of intuition in his analyses occurs on page 686 (1970), where he discusses the indicative functions of the deictic 'this'. After distinguishing this function as it applies to the speaker or the hearer, Husserl says that for the former (unlike the latter) there is no indefiniteness as to what object the 'this' may be indicating: the object is presented along with the 'this'; more precisely, for the speaker the object is intuited *before* it is indicated by the pronoun. Husserl then goes on to say,

> If the thing meant cannot be intuitively picked out, as in a reference to a theorem in a mathematical proof, the conceptual thought in question plays the part of an intuition: the indicative intuition could derive fulfillment from an actual re-living of this past thought. . . . If the previous conceptual thought is not now being performed, an intention which corresponds to it survives in memory; this attaches itself to the act-character of the indication, thereby lending it definiteness of direction.

Here Husserl is saying that a conceptual thought can play the part of an intuition, and that when that thought is indicatively re-trieved from memory and 're-lived', the intentional act of which it is a part can achieve intuitional fullness. The thought in ques-tion here, involving a mathematical theorem, would no doubt incorporate categorial forms in its formation, thus constituting a categorial act; it would therefore be to a certain extent abstract. This type of categorial act, however, is even more abstract than the type treated of in the preceding paragraph, in that its founda-tional elements consist not of sensuous acts but acts that are themselves constituted of conceptual (not sensuous) matter.

It is plain that for Husserl intuitive support can be enlisted for experiences that extend beyond those that involve concrete ob-jects, that it can be enlisted also for experiences involving highly abstract phenomena, phenomena thus that are conceptually grasped rather than sensuously apprehended. It is therefore un-fortunate that he does not discuss the possibility that such support might be available for intentional experiences of the sort that I am calling conceptions.

The possibility of intuitive backing for expressive acts that constitute conceptions is part of a larger question, namely, just how far does the correlability between intuitive and expressive acts extend? We have seen that Husserl, despite his failure to treat of acts constituting conceptions, is otherwise quite prepared to enlarge the domain of acts for which such correlation holds. But in the long run, even if it should be possible to add other types to the domain of such acts, the correlation is not complete. As Husserl says (1970, 824), '*The realm of meaning is . . . much wider than that of intuition*, i.e. than the total realm of possible fulfillment. For, on the meaning-side, an endless host of *complex meanings* arises, which lack "reality" or "possibility". They are patterns of meanings assembled together into *unitary meanings*, to which, however, *no possible unitary correlate of fulfillment* can correspond'. It is at this point in Husserl's exposition that we might expect our question regarding the status of a sentence like 'This algebraic number is green' to come up for discussion, and the question raised of whether the intention promoted by this sentence can be fulfilled intuitionally. We know from Husserl's earlier discussion of meaning-intentions that sentences involving sort crossings have unitary meanings and make sense. So this is the place for Husserl to tell us whether with such meanings a correlate of intuitional fullness is or is not possible. Here again, however, Husserl fails to confront the issue that interests us. As before, he moves directly to the case of analytic contradictions. He tells us that to expressions like 'an *A* which is not an *A*' or 'All *A*'s are *B*'s and some *A*'s are not *B*'s there is not a corresponding type of categorial objectivity, that is, a state of affairs which would provide intuitional fullness for the expression. He continues,

> Only in connection with primitive types can and must such parallelism [that is, between meaning and intuition] obtain, since all primitive meanings "originate" in the fullness of correlated intuition, or, to put the matter more plainly, since talk of compatibility and incompatibility applies only in the sphere of what can be put together, or is to be put together, simple meanings, as expressions of what is simple, can never be "imaginary". This applies to every simple *form* of meaning.

While "Something that is at once A and not-A" is impossible, "an A and a B" is possible, since the *and*-form, being simple, has a "real" sense.

This elaboration gets us no further. With a string like 'an A and a B', Husserl says, intuitional fullness can be correlated. Now if we take the A and B as propositional variables, we can substitute—as having unitary meanings and hence permitted—sentences like 'This algebraic number is green' and 'The sea was laughing'. Instead of discussing this possibility, however, and considering the implications that such substitution would have for the question of intuitional correlation, Husserl comments on the *and*-form, repeating a point he has already made. What interests us about this passage is the question it suggests concerning the relation that deviant sentences bear to what Husserl calls 'primitive meanings', those meanings that he says can never be 'imaginary'. But Husserl does not address this question.

The same opportunity to discuss the question of deviance as it pertains to intentions and the possibility of their fulfillment is presented in *Ideas* (1967). After showing that various types of intentional act may comprise the same noematic nucleus, Husserl directs our attention to the different 'characters' that may co-occur with that nucleus and on the basis of which it is variously *presented* (1967, 290ff.). The experiencing of a particular tree, for example, may be constituted of the identical noematic nucleus in acts of perception, memory, and imagination, but that nucleus will appear in those acts in the respective characters of a percept, a reproduction, and an image. After thus introducing the notion of character, Husserl extends its scope to comprehend the type of *being* associated with noemata in intentional acts. He tells us that in straightforward acts of perception or recollection the noematic nucleus is presented in the character of 'real' or 'actual' being. The correlate of being on the noetic side is belief; acts that are noematically 'real' being characterized noetically as 'certain'. These two types, actual (real) being and certain belief, are fundamental characters of intentional acts; upon them various 'modifications' may be registered. Thus the being characteristic of a noematic nucleus may be registered in the intentional acts as *possible*, *probable*, *questionable*, or *doubtful*. The noetic (belief) counterparts of these ontic statuses would then be *suggestion, presumption, question*, and *doubt* (1967, 297). Further, beliefs held in the mode of certitude are *primary* beliefs, or protodoxa, and, as the 'unmarked' member in the series, represent the reference point of the other belief-modalities. Protodoxa, as having correlated with them on the noematic side the presumption of ontic actuality, make the most implicit of claims regarding the content of their intentional representations; by definition, those representations have complete intuitional support.

Here again Husserl has laid out a background against which he might consider whether such thoughts as that algebraic numbers are green or that the sea was laughing have any *conceptual* currency. It is here, that is, that one might look for Husserl to consider the question of deviance in its epistemological aspect and to comment on the doxastic attitude by which such thoughts are 'characterized'. Instead of acknowledging and addressing this problem, however, Husserl focuses on the formal elaborations which introduction of his doxastic characters makes possible. The thought that S is P, it is shown, may now take the form 'S is certainly (possibly, doubtfully, etc.) P'. That which interests us, on the other hand, is the question of what *specific* belief-modality should be assigned to that thought when the combining of a particular 'S' with 'P' produces conceptual 'deviance'. But this question does not arise in Husserl's discussion.

Husserl's Notion of 'Horizon' in Relation to 'Possible Worlds'

On the taking of deviant sentences literally, two questions arise: whether they are meaningful and, if so, what sort of meaning they can be said to have. Husserl answers the first question in the affirmative but to the second question he provides no clear answer. My own answer to the second question is that if we have a principled reason for taking deviant sentences literally, say as part of a critical theory of how to read the metaphors in certain poems, then in the face of such a sentence we try to conceive of the state of affairs that it literally describes. The linguistic description engenders a mental schema, which I try to fill with intuitional content. Given the nature of the case this attempt to fill out the schema will fail. In the process of trying to conceptualize the state of affairs, however, I bring myself to consider its possibility credible, and the crediting of possibility to the state of affairs then represents the meaning of the sentence.

We might now ask whether there is any way to accommodate the notion of a credible possibility within a Husserlian framework. I don't think there is, and this despite the fact that Husserl's phenomenology holds out the promise of a possible-worlds analysis. In *Ideas* § 47 he even talks of possible worlds. His notion of possible worlds is very heavily constrained, however. Since for him the world is not the world transcendent of us, not the actual physical world, that is, but only our experience of it, what is possible for Husserl means what is experienceable. And experienceability, he says, '*never betokens any empty logical possibility*, but one that has its *motive* in the system of experience'. To explain what he means by 'motive' here we have to introduce his notion of 'horizon'. According to that notion, each intentional act experiences its transcendent object only partially and incompletely. But the aspects of the object that are theoretically left out are implicity *motivated* in the experience, and they constitute the object's horizon. Correlatively, the intentional act has its horizon. When I see a tree, for example, I see it from a particular angle; the tree itself, moreover, is in a contingent state. The other a priori possible angles of approach and the tree's other possible states are in the object's and my act's horizons. The tree approached from those other angles and appearing in those other states could then be regarded as the tree in different possible worlds, and statements about the tree, that say, its leaves were falling or that a bird was singing in one of its branches, might then be true or false depending on their correspondence with the situation of the tree in those worlds, all of those worlds, to reiterate, being functions of the act's horizon. For a statement like 'The sea was laughing' to have a truth value relative to a possible world, it would therefore have to be the case that that condition of the sea should be in the horizon of the sea (and of my act) when I experience it in one of its actual empirical aspects. But for that to be possible, a perception of the sea as laughing must fall within the bounds of experienceability—which it does not. So that since no possible experience correlates with deviant sentences, casting Husserl's analysis in the framework of possible worlds throws no light on the phenomenological properties associated with such sentences.[9]

Nor do I see that the problem is alleviated if we move from an experientially oriented possible worlds approach to one that is more formal. We could try, for example, to frame our problem in the type of semantics that Hintikka (1969, 87–111) has developed for propositional attitudes. Suppose, that is, that we consider 'conceive (of)' an intensional verb. The problem, as I see it, would be how to get the semantics off the ground. The truth of a proposition in the actual world being given, Hintikka's semantics makes it clear, in extensional terms, why substitutivity of identicals and existential generalization should fail in intensional contexts. Our problem, however, is not with what happens to the truth value of the embedded proposition when co-referring or individuating noun phrases are substituted for any of its singular terms; our problem is with the original proposition. In line with Hintikka's formula for belief contexts, $B_a p$, we could form $C_a p$, for conceptions. As an instance of this formula we could then have 'John conceives of the sea as laughing'. What John conceives of would then be true in all the possible worlds compatible with what he conceives of in the actual world. But as the proposition that he conceives of—that the sea was laughing—has no definite truth value in the actual world, we are back where we started from.

---

9. For an extensive discussion of the adaptability of Husserl's horizon concept to a possible worlds framework see Smith and McIntyre (1984, 310ff.).

3

Meaning and Representability

In accord with our interest in the relations that obtain between language, thought, and reality, we considered in chapter 2 the question of deviant sentences from the standpoint of their ontological, linguistic, and phenomenological implications. During our discussion of the phenomenological implications the problem of conceptualization was raised, in particular the question of its feasibility as it pertains to concepts and conceptions. As regards this question we found Husserl's exposition to be essentially uninformative. In this chapter, therefore, we shall return to that problem and try to make clear the sort of mental experience that is to be understood by our use of those terms.

In any examination of such notions as concept and conception, it soon becomes apparent that it is hardly possible to proceed without incorporating in the discussion elements from the fields of meaning and reference;[1] the attitude taken, in fact, is one of general orientation, not exclusive focus. And although the refer-

1. The problem of keeping clear in discussion the way in which these notions relate to each other is not a new problem; cf. the introduction to the commentary of Averroes on Aristotle's *Categories*, in which Davidson (1969, xvi f.) writes, 'Aristotle introduced his familiar list of the ten categories, writing: "everything that is stated without composition designates either substance, quantity, quality, ... " The sentence is reformulated by Averroes as follows: "Simple concepts which are designated by simple expressions necessarily designate one of ten things: substance, quantity, quality. . . . " Averroes' version is a little fuller and clearer, but, what is more important, it suggests the commentator's view concerning the true nature of the categories; they are "concepts" in the mind, designated by "expressions," and, in turn, designating "things" '.

ential dimension may be tacitly assumed in all discussion, an initial clarification of the conceptual approach is best achieved by contrasting it with the approach from meaning.

Concept, Meaning, Reference

The notions *meaning* and *concept* are frequently used interchangeably in discussions with no real harm done. Thus it is possible to regard the meaning of a word as the concept expressed by it; for example, the meaning of the word *horse* is the concept horse. In this sense 'meaning' and 'concept' are interchangeable. It is also possible, however, to regard the meaning of 'horse' as that expressed in the definition 'a large, solid-hoofed herbivorous mammal of the special *Equus cabbalus*'. Meaning as concept is thus something that is entertained in the mind, and meaning as meaning is something expressed in language. One moves in the one case from language to thought, in the other from language to language. Of course, concepts entertained in the mind will, if expressed, be expressed in language, and meaning expressed in language (as a definition) will imply concepts in the mind. This correlation lies behind their easy convertibility. But just as we can discriminate two species deriving from the notion *meaning*, so it is possible to discriminate two species of the notion *concept*. We have already indicated that we can speak of concepts as the implications of a definition. Thus the definition of 'horse' implies the concepts underlying 'large', 'herbivorous', 'mammal', and so forth. These are semantic concepts. Besides concepts of this nature, however, we can, if we unpack what is contained for many people in their conception of a horse, find constituent concepts like 'beast of burden', 'animal used in round-ups', 'quondam mail carrier', and so on. These notions are not part of the meaning of 'horse', but they are part of people's beliefs about horses. We might distinguish between the *concept* 'horse' and people's *conception* of a horse. The former is expressed by a dictionary entry, the latter by a set of general beliefs.[2]

2. Katz (1972, 450f.) draws a distinction between 'the narrow notion of a concept' and 'the broad notion of a concept'. The narrow notion is expressed by a

Granted the close and complex relationship existing between meaning and concept, we need now to consider a relationship equally close and complex: that between concepts and facts in the world. We speak here of facts in the world rather than simply reference so as to leave open the equivocation that inheres in the notion of concept(ion)—as it does in that of the 'world' in which the facts are taken to exist. If the notion is taken semantically, that is, strictly as concept, then what is designated is a reference. A concept on this view stands for, is related directly to, objects or facts in the world. But the notion may also be taken in an intentional sense. On this view it designates 'facts in the world' as an individual may conceive them to be or, more precisely, as they appear in an individual's mind. The crucial question here is whether the 'facts' as they appear in an individual's conception are limited to and may not exceed the facts as they obtain in the world. It is clear that there is no such limitation.

Earlier we drew a distinction between ontology *tout court* and one's personal ontology. By ontology in the former sense we mean what there is in the natural world (we leave open the status of universals, whether they exist in reality or merely conceptually, but we reject any form of nominalism). This ontology provides the raw materials for individual ontologies. From these raw materials an individual may constitute all manner of personal ontologies. By the exercise of his conceptual and imaginative faculties an individual may combine, alter, modify, and in various ways rearrange and transmute the materials of the natural world. In this process the individual is limited only as to the raw materials; as to their combination and rearrangement he enjoys wide latitude.[3] By the raw materials of the natural world we

---

dictionary definition (e.g., 'Martian' = 'an inhabitant of Mars'); the broad notion by the average person's conception of a Martian. His distinction is thus the same as the one we have drawn above. His point is that any account of meaning is inadequate unless it takes the concept of meaning in the broad sense of the notion.

3. Compare Hume (1966, 16f.): 'To form monsters, and join incongruous shapes and appearances, costs the imagination no more trouble than to conceive the most natural and familiar objects'. Hume goes on to say that these conceptions amount to 'no more than the faculty of compounding, transposing, augmenting, or diminishing the materials afforded us by the senses of experience'.

understand, of course, not only substances but also the various attributes—states, activities, processes, properties, relations, and so forth—that affect or are affected by those substances. Thus if universals are taken to exist only conceptually, the phrase 'raw materials of the natural world' is being used equivocally. Since, however, I think that setting the problem out as I have done serves a useful purpose, and since I do not believe that the equivocation is pernicious, I shall proceed with this line of exposition. In essence, then, one can conceive all sorts of objects and states of affairs that exceed what is given by the raw materials of the natural world. Thus we can conceive, in the sense of 'bring to mental awareness', a Santa Claus, a Pegasus, centaurs, griffins, unicorns, mermaids, werewolves, wyverns, and various other 'objects' that do not exist in the world of natural facts. Moreover, one can conceive dogs with antlers, trees with hearts, men with tails, and one can conceive such dogs as melting, such trees as flying, and such men as petrifying (the same activities obviously being conceivable for uncompounded dogs, trees, and men).

We next consider the question of whether, granted the wide latitude enjoyed by individuals in their conceptual capacities, there are constraints that limit those capacities. Can just any combination of characteristics be entertained as a concept? It appears that to a considerable extent the possibilities are conditioned by relations between inherent characteristics found in natural phenomena, relations that provide the basis for various taxonomic schemes. Thus we can easily cross one member of a species with marks from another member of that species; we can conceive a Napoleon with red hair, a Black Beauty with a white mane, and the like. Further, we can conceive an object produced by the crossing of marks between two species of the same genus and thus form concepts like those already given of dogs with antlers, men with tails, and so on. In these and the other examples mentioned above we are dealing with physical phenomena, and the concepts are correspondingly feasible. The problem becomes attenuated and the feasibility less obvious when we include in our exercise attributions of an affective or emotional nature. Can we conceive a tree as sad or the sea as laughing?

Conceiving and Conceiving Of

At this stage I would like to introduce a distinction between *conceiving* and *conceiving of*. I take conceiving to be, substantively, the stronger notion; thus, we might be unable to conceive something and yet be able to conceive *of* it. The evidence from language bearing on this distinction is not clinching, but it is suggestive. Consider the following sentences:

(1) John conceived a solution to the problem.
(2) John conceived of a solution to the problem.

In response to (1) we are entitled to conclude that John has a solution and, if asked, he should be prepared to produce it. We may ask the same thing of John in response to (2), but it would not be inconsistent for him to answer that he conceived only of the possibility that there was a solution, not that he had thought of one. This sense of (2) would be more explicitly expressed as 'John conceived of there being a solution to the problem'.

A similar difference is manifest in the following pair of sentences:

(3) I conceive a woman performing miracles.
(4) I conceive of a woman performing miracles.[4]

The speaker in (3), it seems to me, is obliged, if asked, to describe the miracles that the woman in his conceptual act performed or was performing; the speaker in (4), on the other hand, is under no such obligation. In saying 'I conceive of a woman performing miracles', he has committed himself only to the possibility that a woman might perform miracles, not that in his conception any such miracles actually took place.

The difference in semantic force that I am postulating in respect of these examples is interestingly similar to a difference described

4. I would say that (4) but not (3) is paraphrasable as 'I conceive of a woman's performing miracles' or 'I conceive that a woman might perform miracles'. It might be remarked here that the difference between our two verbs is somewhat similar to that between 'know' and 'know of', where to know something or somebody is to have had direct experience of that object, whereas to know of it is to be in possession of some facts or reports about it.

by Lakoff and Johnson (1980, 128ff.). Their claim is that closeness in the syntactic order of the words in a sentence correlates directly with strength of (semantic) effect. Among the examples they adduce in support of this claim are the sentences 'I found that the chair was comfortable' and 'I found the chair comfortable'. Concerning these examples they comment: 'The second sentence indicates that I found that the chair was comfortable by direct experience—by sitting on it. The first sentence leaves open the possibility that I found it out *indirectly*—say, by asking people or by taking a survey'. This subtle difference in semantic implication they attribute to the fact that the 'I' is (syntactically) closer to 'chair' and 'comfortable' in the second sentence than it is in the first. In similar fashion there is in the four examples I have analyzed above a greater closeness (between the subject and complement) in the sentences containing 'conceive' than in those containing 'conceive of'; thus, consistent with the claim of Lakoff and Johnson, the experiences described in the odd-numbered sentences are semantically 'stronger' than are those of the even-numbered sentences.[5]

Consider now

> (5) John conceived a golden mountain.
> (6) John conceived of a golden mountain.

Of these two sentences, (5) implies that John has brought the concept of a golden mountain to mind, whereas (6) does not have that implication but suggests, rather, that John has carried out a *projection*, such that not the concept of a golden mountain but only a schema of that concept has been brought to mind. We might note, as variants of (5) and (6), the sentences

> (7) John has the concept of a golden mountain.
> (8) John has a conception of a golden mountain.

What is noteworthy here is the respective selection of articles, definite in (7), indefinite in (8). This lack of definiteness consists with the schematic character of conceptions as I am developing

---

5. Compare the remarks about 'know' and 'know of' made in footnote 4 above.

the notion in this study. We might say that a conception is the schema of a possible concept.[6] The respective semantic (or presuppositional) properties of the two verbs are rendered more pronounced if we augment the syntax (along indicated lines), namely:

(9) John conceived there to be a golden mountain.

(10) John conceived of there being a golden mountain.

Although referentially the contexts in both sentences are opaque, (9) would appear to have more epistemological substance than (10), where this is to be referred to the formation of a concept in (9) and its mere schema in (10). The different semantic valences ('valences', to comprehend possible presuppositions) of the two verbs can be brought out in other ways as well. If we compare

(11) I conceived a mountain

and

(12) I conceived of a mountain

we feel, I think, that there is something semantically tense or muscle-bound about (11) and something semantically slack about (12). Unlike the concept of a golden mountain, which is not common property and has as it were to be fabricated for the nonce, that of a mountain is general and antecedently available. Therefore, to say that one conceives a mountain is to semantically overcharge the sentence (beyond, say, 'I thought of a mountain'). In the same way, to say that one conceives *of* it is to underutilize the semantic force of the verb. In general, when the concept is

6. The notion of a schema is of course associated with Kant and the function he ascribes to it in *The Critique of Pure Reason* (1965, 180ff.). For Kant a schema is a rule of the imagination which mediates between an appearance and a pure concept of the understanding, in this way bringing intuitions under concepts. The appearance must be sensible and the concept one of the a priori categories. As I am using the notion of schema, the 'appearance' would be a concept and the 'category' a conception. Moreover, where for Kant the schema, in subsuming intuitions under concepts, leads to a cognition of an object or state of affairs, on my use it leads to entertaining it as a possibility that such an object or state of affairs may obtain.

readily available, it is inappropriate to invoke conceptions. On the other hand, in a sentence like

(13) John conceived of a mountain covered with mermaids

where the object of the verb does not represent a generally available concept, the semantic force of the verb, in being exploited, is properly utilized. Again, because of the ad hoc nature of the concept involved, in the sentence

(14) I conceived a mountain covered with mermaids

we once more feel a sense of slackness, this time, however, for reasons converse to those in (12). In (12) the verb was 'undersaturated' by its object, in (14) the object is 'oversaturated' by the verb. These latter characterizations are perhaps more impressionistic than intuitive, but I believe they are not without some substance.[7]

Concepts and Conceptions

In the preceding discussion concepts have been seen as the consequences of conceiving, conceptions of conceiving of, and concepts have been accorded the greater epistemological weight. Where concepts particularly are concerned, this is not an obvious conclusion. Katz (1972), for example, sees in concepts elements that figure in a semantic framework. He writes (p. 39), 'Speakers . . . communicate without confusion of reference about particular abstractions and use them to investigate the characteristics of concrete objects. What enables them to perform such individuation is that *concepts* and propositions are *senses* of

---

7. The different evaluations of 'conceive'—(by inference) acceptable in (5), questionable in (14)—derive from the differing focus in the contrasts being drawn in the two cases. In the contrast between (5) and (6) the focus was on the verbs and the degree of definiteness associated with their respective mental representations; in the contrast between (12) and (14) the focus was on the relation between the object ('mountain covered with mermaids') and the verbs, from which point of view, considering the fanciful nature of what was to be conceptualized, 'conceive' could be thought too strong. As I say, however, the latter evaluations may be somewhat tenuous.

expressions and sentences' (my italics). Katz thus represents the position, mentioned above in our discussion, which aligns concepts with meanings. Earlier (p. 38) he writes,

> . . . a semantic marker is part of the sense of morphemes and other constituents of natural languages. By a concept in this connection we do not mean images or mental ideas or particular thoughts. These, which we will refer to collectively as *cognitions*, form part of the experience of some individual person, in the same way as do sensations, feelings, memories, and hallucinations. Cognitions are individuated in part by the persons who have them. . . . Concepts, on the other hand, are abstract entities. They do not belong to the conscious experience of anyone, though they may be thought about, as in our thinking about the concept of a circle. They are not individuated by persons: you and I may think about the same concept. They are not, as Frege ['The Thought'] urges, elements in the subjective process of thinking, but rather the objective content of thought processes, which is "capable of being the common property of several thinkers".

Now in our account, concepts (and conceptions) precisely *are* mental phenomena, and they *are* individuated by persons. We view them as the products, the intentions, of individual mental acts.

Thus, to continue with our own line of investigation and try to draw more sharply the *phenomenological* difference between concepts and conceptions, we shall say that to conceive something, say *x*, is to have a clear and distinct image or idea of that *x*, whereas to conceive of *x* is as it were to prepare a mental space into which that *x* might be placed. If *x* is a flying horse then to conceive it means to have before one a clear and distinct image of a flying horse; to conceive of it means to allow for the possibility that such an image might be produced. In the same way, to conceive a golden mountain means to have before one a clear and distinct image of a golden mountain; to conceive of a golden mountain means to allow for the possibility that such an image might be produced. In both our examples, where *x* is either a flying horse or a golden mountain, the mental space prepared by the conception can in fact be filled—that is, both objects can be conceived. A flying horse and a golden mountain can be conceived because, even though neither exists, the elements out of which they are composed are physical characteristics, and those elements can be combined, both in a conception and as the components of a concept.

In the two examples thus far considered, the distinction between conceiving and conceiving of (and the correlative one between a concept and a conception) has had no operative role to play; the objects in both of our examples (and the types that they represent) can both be conceived of and conceived. The utility of the distinction emerges, however, when we consider examples in whose composition there figures an attribute of affection or emotion. Earlier we asked whether we can conceive a tree as sad or the sea as laughing. I would now say that we can conceive *of* such 'objects' but we cannot conceive them. In terms of our distinction we can focus on an area in our minds such that it delimits the space into which the concept of a sad tree would fit, but we are unable to fill that space with a concept. In the process of focusing on that area, however, we project a schema, an abstract model or framework which, given the purpose of our exercise, we take to be an implicit or potential representation of that 'object'. This schema or model conveys the sense in which I am using the notion of conception.

It should be clear by now that we have explained concepts and conceptions in two different ways. Earlier we spoke of concepts as the constituent senses of a dictionary entry (in this concurring with Katz) and conceptions as the set of general beliefs held by individuals in respect to an object. Now we have used 'concept' to designate the mental image produced by a linguistic expression and 'conception' to designate a mental function performed preparatory to the formation of such an image. Such seeming inconsistency is hardly avoidable, however, in any discussion that tries to canvass the various relations that subsist between language, meaning, thought, and reality. The terms *concept* and *conception* (like the terms *meaning*, *sense*, *reality*, and so forth) figure at several theoretical intersections and, depending on the standpoint taken, will bear one or another radical signification. The two senses assigned to 'concept' and to 'conception' derive from the notions having been developed out of different theoretical starting points. Even though this general rationalization may be given, it will be useful to consider at greater length the theoretical contexts in which the notions of concept and conception may properly be said to have the respective senses that we have assigned to them.

Our initial distinction between a concept and a conception was drawn against a background that was primarily linguistic. Against this background it is customary and useful to distinguish a semantic and a pragmatic dimension of language. Correspondingly, a linguistic description will contain a semantic and a pragmatic component. The function of the semantic component is, among other things, to render the meanings of lexical items, that of the pragmatic component to account for people's common knowledge concerning the 'objects' that those meanings (or the speakers using those lexical items) refer to. In such a context one may reasonably employ 'concept' as a primitive term to be explained by the semantics and 'conception' as one to be explicated by the pragmatics. Thus, as we indicated earlier, the item 'horse' is explained *semantically* on the basis of the concepts underlying 'large', 'herbivorous', 'mammal', and so on; the same item is explained *pragmatically* by analyzing the conception—the sum of commonly held beliefs—that people have about horses.

Empirically, it is not clear how to separate the kind of information that is reducible to semantic concepts from such as is comprised by conceptions. It is not even clear that there is anything to be separated. People know the concepts that underlie the meaning of a word, and they also know the facts that constitute their conception of that word, facts that they associate with the referent of that word's meaning. The allocation of the one sort of information to semantics and the other to pragmatics is thus usually made on theoretical grounds, depending on what goals the investigator has in view. If the goal of a semantic theory is taken to be the explication of certain properties and relations like analyticity, antonymy, contradiction, and the like, then a line may be drawn so as to exclude information of a 'pragmatic' nature (this is the approach taken in Katz, 1972). If, on the other hand, the goal is to account not merely for the way in which certain semantic features interact with each other in sentences, but also with the way in which 'semantic' features are understood and processed by speakers in their *use* of the language, then pragmatic information is requisite. The first approach would suffice to mark a sentence like 'A horse is an animal' as analytic, 'A pony is an old horse' as contradictory; the second approach is necessary to understand the implications registered by a speaker on hearing a sentence like 'This horse is headed for the glue factory' or 'This horse is Kentucky bred'. To understand the former sentences one needs to know only the meaning of 'horse' (allowance being made for the remainder), to understand the latter one has to know certain facts about a horse—concept and conception.

The issue over whether there is a dividing line between semantic 'information' and pragmatic 'knowledge' is a vexed one, on which it is not necessary for us to dwell. Here it is necessary only for us to see that both semantics and pragmatics are aspects primarily of language, of its meaning and its use. Thus although it is true that concepts and conceptions, as treated above, are presumed to be mental entities, they amount in the context of a linguistic orientation to unanalyzed units—primitives in the analysis, as observed above—mere placeholders that stand in temporarily for the elements which analyze and explain them (we thus have, it is true, definitions of individual concepts; the notion, however, of concept is undefined, as is that of conception). This status is thus to be contrasted with their treatment as approached phenomenologically, where concepts and conceptions are considered not as static counters in some theoretical framework but as aspects of dynamic and individuated mental functions. We shall have more to say about the phenomenological status of concepts and conceptions later in this chapter. Before proceeding to that discussion, however, we must introduce and discuss another mental activity, one which bears closely and significantly on concepts and conceptions when the latter are in fact viewed in the context of mental process; I refer here to imagination. Indeed, it may have appeared that a good deal of what has been claimed above for the operation of concept(ion) should properly have been assigned to the imagination.

Imagination

We must here recall that the purpose of this study is to develop a theory for the interpretation of metaphor—thus, of certain *linguistic* expressions. Our analysis therefore centers on mental operations that are *reactive* to immediate verbal stimuli. The stimuli for an act of imagining, on the other hand, are of a quite different order. If they can in fact be tracked down, they will usually be found to consist in the memory and recollection of events and experiences that occurred at times variously re-moved—at a distance—from the actual act. Moreover, in those cases at the limit, where an act of imagining follows hard on a perceptual experience, the perception in no way constrains the form or direction that the imaging may take. Thus, though in such cases we may speak of an immediate stimulus, the situation is unlike what obtains with metaphor, where the language not merely stimulates the interpretation but also constrains the form that it will take. But the freedom from constraint enjoyed by imagining may be seen even when it operates at a distance, that is, in the absence of an immediate perceptual experience. In *Imagining* (1976), Casey describes two modes of imagining: the sponta-neous and the controlled. All acts occur of course in a context. Where imagining is concerned, however, that fact is essentially trivial. When the act is spontaneous, what is imagined appears '*of and by itself,* as quite independent of the imaginer's immediate practical situation' (p. 68). By the same token, when an act of imagination is controlled, it can take whatever form the imaginer chooses. Acts of imagination, therefore, are not constrained by any circumstances, attendant or otherwise.[8] Imagining is thus

8. They are to be sure *limited*, but only in the general sense in which the laws of logic and the dictates of ontology apply to any type of mental act. Thus Casey points out that one cannot imagine what comprises contradictory concepts (like a square circle), nor can one by an act of the imagination *effect* existence or nonexis-tence (pp. 77ff.).

seen to be independent and initiatory, in a way in which one's response to a metaphoric expression cannot be.

Although we have in the discussion to this point rather consistently treated of both concepts and conceptions, it should be clear that for us the significant notion is the latter. It is the mental act of conception that correlates with the type of linguistic expression that we deem characteristic of metaphor, such, that is, which involves a sort crossing, in particular of the type where a 'human' predicate is applied to a nonhuman object or aspect of nature. In comparison then with conception, imagination displays another, and highly significant, difference. Acts of imagination are supported by intuitions, either immediate or recollected. This fact separates them further from acts of conception wherein, as will be brought out more clearly in the next section, intuition is precisely the phenomenological component that is lacking in the mental act.

Hitherto our discussion in this section has considered the role that imagination might be presumed to play in the interpretation of metaphoric expressions. We should now consider its role in the theory and practice of the Romantic poets. By way of throwing the discussion into proper relief it will be useful to refer again to Casey's work on imagining.

Casey's analysis deals primarily with the phenomenological aspects of imagination, that is, with the mental processes concerned when a particular act of imagining takes place. His primary concern, moreover, is with ordinary, or run-of-the-mill, acts of imagination, acts such as the average person might perform a dozen times a day.[9] Of interest to us now, on the other hand, is imagination in its so-called creative aspect; it is this aspect of the imagination that is usually invoked when one reflects on the poetic mind and practice, particularly in connection with the Romantic poets. There is a sense, of course, in which all acts of the imagination are creative. In this sense the claim is trivial, following from the definition of imagination. The sense in which

9. Casey (1976, ix): 'The investigation will . . . take the form of a descriptive account of imagination in its ordinary, even banal, modes of activity'.

creativity is claimed for the poetic imagination is far from trivial, however. According to Casey (1976, 183f.), ' "Imagination" [for figures like Blake, Coleridge, and Shelley] became a watchword denoting the source of all human creativity. In its world-creating and visionary role, such creativity mirrors that of God; more modestly conceived, it enlivens nature and converts the merely mechanical into the profound and purposeful'. Between a faculty for which claims of this power and magnitude are made and the essentially utilitarian role and function of the imagination Casey sees no fundamental correspondence. After examining the grounds of their relationship he concludes that 'there is no inherent or necessary connection between imagining and being creative; they are only contingently connected' (p. 188). It appears that in default of the ability to specify what faculty of mind (or spirit) is responsible for human endeavors of a most profound and significant order, that faculty has been equated with the imagination. In the words of Wordsworth, 'Imagination' is a 'Power so called / Through sad incompetence of human speech' (Prelude, 1850, vi, 592–93).

What then might be the mental or spiritual faculty or faculties implicitly (and perhaps illicitly) incorporated in the extended conception of the imagination? In Originality and Imagination (1985, 150), his comprehensive study of the imagination and the role it played in the outlook of the Romantic poets, McFarland suggests as a possible candidate for this theoretical contraband the notion of soul. As part of the support for this suggestion he cites Coleridge's Biographia Literaria (chap. 14): the poet 'described in ideal perfection,' Coleridge writes, 'brings the whole soul of man into activity', but he does so specifically 'by that synthetic and magical power, to which we have exclusively appropriated the name of imagination'. Expressions indicating a comparable belief in this interdependence may be found in the writings of others, including Wordsworth, so that it is possible to conclude with McFarland that 'Romantic imagination . . . not only moves in the sphere of the soul, but it reciprocates and draws to itself the very meaning of soul'. In the course of developing his argument McFarland shows that introduction of the soul adds to the idea of the imagination a component that consists with and explains the human need to envisage a purposeful and divinely ordered universe.

Although there is no doubt that for the Romantic temperament the imagination was indeed involved in projections of such a universal nature, I believe it is a mistake to explain such projections by moving directly from imagination to soul, from a common ingredient of cognition to a refined instrument of faith. In passing so directly from one to the other of these terms, it seems to me that an important mental function is bypassed. In book XIV of the *Prelude*, after an admonition that earthly love must be sustained by love of the Almighty, Wordsworth says,

> This spiritual Love acts not nor can exist
> Without Imagination, which, in truth,
> Is but another name for absolute power
> And clearest insight, amplitude of mind,
> And Reason in her most exalted mood.
>
> [*Prelude*, XIV, 188–92]

In this passage the imagination is explicitly allied with spiritual Love, a function of the soul. On the basis of this alliance Wordsworth at the end of the stanza proclaims his

> Faith in life endless, the sustaining thought
> Of human Being, Eternity, and God.
>
> [*Prelude*, XIV, 204–05]

This selection provides ample evidence (consistent with McFarland's argument) for the numinous function performed by the imagination when it is allied with soul. But we should not overlook the affiliation that Wordsworth effects earlier in the stanza between imagination and reason. It is this rational element that I believe must be added to our idea of the imagination when it is credited with being creative. Of course, creativity comprises for me the specific sense of conception. A Wordsworth, say, conceives of a state of affairs in which humans and natural objects are all beings that share in the grace and watchfulness of God. This conception, in the character of its metaphysical bearings, is obviously 'creative'. Properly to express this conception, however, the language suffers deviance, that is, it is used 'improperly'. The reader, to approach in his own mind the conception lying behind and determining the poet's expression, must take the language literally. Only in this way may he approach to the 'world' created—conceived of—by the poet.

Infinity and Other 'Conceptions'

Among the questions raised by deviant sentences is the question of what form their mental 'representations' may be said to take. As an answer to this question I have proposed a special sense of 'conception', a conception on this view being a schema whose form is defined by the linguistic expression and which the mind exerts itself to fit somehow with an image or representation. Although in the nature of the case the effort of the mind to provide the schema with intuitive content is bound to fail, it is this effort that makes of a conception more than a mere rational form. A conception can therefore be said to lie, in terms of phenomenological substance, somewhere between a Kantian category, which is purely abstract, and a cognition, where something intuitive falls under and satisfies a category. When seen in this way, it turns out that conceptions as the representations of deviant sentences have congeners in other areas of mental endeavor where the question of comprehensibility is likewise rendered problematic. One of these areas is that involving the notion of the infinite (and the continuous); another involves extremely complex geometrical figures. Other areas could be imagined, but consideration of these two will suffice for our purposes.

A very apposite exposition of the problem posed by conceptions is provided by Coleridge in the *Biographia Literaria* (1983, I, 288–89). At this point in his discussion Coleridge is attempting to justify the use of technical terms in his examination of certain metaphysical doctrines. Anticipating criticism for this practice on the grounds of unintelligibility, he writes: 'According to the creed of our modern philosophers, nothing is deemed a clear conception but what is representable by a distinct image. Thus

the conceivable is reduced within the bounds of the picturable'.
By way of support for his own practice he then appends a passage
from Kant's *De mundi sensibilis atque intelligibilis forma et principiis*,
which, in the translation that he provides, reads:

> Hence it is clear from what cause many reject the notion of the
> continuous and the infinite. They take, namely, the words
> irrepresentable and impossible in one and the same meaning;
> and, according to the forms of sensuous evidence, the notion of
> the continuous and the infinite is doubtless impossible. . . .
> But it is of the highest importance to admonish the reader, that
> those, who adopt so perverted a mode of reasoning, are under a
> grievous error. Whatever opposes the formal principles of the
> understanding and the reason is confessedly impossible; but
> not therefore that which is therefore not amenable to the forms
> of *sensuous* evidence, because it is exclusively an object of pure
> intellect. For this non-coincidence of the sensuous and the
> intellectual . . . proves nothing more but that the mind cannot
> always adequately represent in the concrete and transform into
> distinct images abstract notions derived from the pure intellect.

Where in the above citation the mind is judged unable '*adequately*
[to] represent' abstract notions 'in the concrete and transform
[them] into *distinct* images' (my italics), I speak of an effort made
by the mind to provide phenomenological substance for those
notions. It is in the making of this effort, unattainable as its goal
may be, that for me there lies the significance of conceptions.

Using slightly different terminology, a similar point about the
problem attendant on the comprehension of infinity is made by
Newton (Hall and Hall, 1962, 134):

> If anyone now objects that we cannot imagine that there is
> infinite extension, I agree. But at the same time I contend that
> we can understand it. We can imagine a greater extension, and
> then a greater one, but we understand that there exists a greater
> extension than any we can imagine. And here, incidentally, the
> faculty of understanding is clearly distinguished from imagina-
> tion.

The same point is made by Descartes, in his case concerning the representability of mere objects, when at the beginning of the *Sixth Meditation* (Haldane and Ross, 1931, I, 185f.) he writes:

> I remark the difference that exists between the imagination and pure intellection (or conception) ['intellectionem' in the Latin version, 'conception' in the French]. For example, when I imagine a triangle, I do not conceive it only as a figure comprehended by three lines, but I also apprehend these three lines as present by the power and inward vision of my mind, and this is what I call imagining. But if I desire to think of a chiliagon, I certainly conceive truly that it is a figure composed of a thousand sides, just as easily as I conceive of a triangle that it is a figure of three sides only; but I cannot in any way imagine the thousand sides of a chiliagon [as I do the three sides of a triangle], nor do I, so to speak, regard them as present [with the eyes of my mind]. And although in accordance with the habit I have formed of always employing the aid of my imagination when I think of corporeal things, it may happen that in imagining a chiliagon I confusedly represent to myself some figure, yet it is very evident that this figure is not a chiliagon, since it in no way differs from that which I represent to myself when I think of a myriagon or any other many-sided figure; nor does it serve my purpose in discovering the properties which go to form the distinction between a chiliagon and other polygons. But if the question turns on a pentagon, it is quite true that I can conceive its figure as well as that of a chiliagon without the help of my imagination; but I can also imagine it by applying the attention of my mind to each of its five sides, and at the same time to the space which they enclose. And thus I clearly recognize that I have need of a particular effort of mind in order to effect the act of imagination, such as I do not require in order to understand, and this particular effort of mind clearly manifests the difference which exists between imagination and pure intellection.

The faculty that is represented respectively in the three foregoing citations as intellect, understanding, and intellect is what I am characterizing as conceiving of or conception (in its productive aspect). The element that is lacking in the mental acts performed by (the various versions of) this faculty, and whose absence precludes them from constituting acts of cognition—acts, that is, in which something is *known*—is intuition. In the cases considered in this section this deficiency can neither be made good nor its effect compensated for through the agency of some other human faculty. Contemplation of notions like infinity, the continuum, and that of a thousand-sided figure arises in a context, usually of a mathematical nature, in which there is little or no incentive to close the epistemological gap. One understands and accepts the fact that intuition cannot be brought to bear so as to 'know' infinity (and kindred notions). I believe, however, that the situation is different where deviant sentences are concerned— that is, where such sentences are regarded as metaphors whose language is to be taken at face value. And it is to that extent that the notion of conception as used in this study differs from intellect and understanding as portrayed in the citations from Kant, Newton, and Descartes.

At the beginning of chapter 1 I said that requisite in approaching certain poems, poems which express strivings of a profound intellectual or spiritual nature, was a certain mental attitude on the part of the reader, and that a corollary of that attitude was the taking of metaphors at their face value. I would now argue that such a reader has a strong motivation to see in a deviant sentence more than just a syntactically allowable sequence of words, a sequence whose possible meaning can be entertained only by the understanding or intellect. The reader approaching the poem in this spirit has a stake in *validating* those sequences, that is, in *conceiving of* the states of affairs that, taken literally, they describe. Actual intuitive filling for these sequences not being possible, the reader will recruit elements of feeling and affect from his emotional store and form, out of a combination of those elements and the 'meaning' of the sequence, a conception. This process does not of course yield factual knowledge; it does, however, yield credibility. When Coleridge in chapter 14 of the *Biographia Literaria* described the plan that he and Wordsworth projected for the

Lyrical Ballads, he said that his own endeavors were to be directed 'to persons and characters supernatural, or at least romantic; yet so as to transfer from our inward nature a human interest and a semblance of truth sufficient to procure for these shadows of imagination that willing suspension of disbelief for the moment, which constitutes poetic faith'. Where Coleridge's purpose was to procure a measure of credibility for 'persons and characters supernatural', ours is to procure such a measure for the literal reading of deviant expressions. Both purposes require of the reader a show of poetic faith. The transfers 'from our inward nature' are earnests of that faith, and I am suggesting that what one transfers are elements of feeling and affect.

4

Scientific and
Poetic Truth

At the beginning of chapter 2 we described thoughts and their expression against the background of conceptual space and spoke of trajections across that space. Our primary interest was in those thoughts (and their expression) in which new conceptual ground was broken. Such thoughts we labeled '(nontrivially) novel', and by way of characterizing them we said that they involved the crossing of boundaries marking off conceptual subspaces. We contrasted such novel thoughts with such as were trivial, trivial in that, although they might never have occurred to anyone before, they resulted from the connecting of concepts which were all (antecedently) located in the same conceptual subspace. Thoughts of this type we said represented knowledge that was previously available (even if unregistered), and thus their novelty was 'accidental'. The novelty of such thoughts, we could say, resides entirely in their expression; the concepts expressed by them, on the other hand, are commonplace. Such thoughts, therefore, although they may bring knowledge to expression, bring none to light. As examples of the respective types we offered 'The sea was laughing' and 'The telephone was dissolving'. Let us now compare these two varieties of novel thought with those from another domain in which novel thoughts are also achieved—that of science—and see how those scientific novel thoughts differ from or resemble the two varieties previously described.

Among the novel thoughts occurring in science we may distinguish two subtypes. One subtype occurs when a new word, defining a new concept, is introduced into the semantic field. The other subtype occurs when the meaning of a preexisting word (or words) is shifted or extended so as to represent a new concept. Examples of both processes are common in science; we shall consider examples taken from the field of thermodynamics.

Some Terms from Thermodynamics

In 1854 Rudolf Clausius employed the term *entropy*— which he had derived from the Greek τϱοπή, 'a transformation'—by way of throwing a new light on the Second Law of Thermodynamics, a law which is based on the observation that certain physical processes tend to be unidirectional: heat flows from a hot to a cold body, solutes move from a more concentrated to a more dilute solution, magnets tend to become demagnetized, and so on. The reverse processes are not observed to occur spontaneously, that is, without the influence of some outside agency. To supply some additional background: when a physical body (liquid, solid, gas) is isolated from its environment, it reaches a state at which no (further) change in its physical constitution is perceptible—the density, pressure, and temperature remaining constant throughout the body. The body is then said to be in *equilibrium*. The same thing occurs when two bodies are placed in thermal contact. Any difference in original states between the two bodies will tend toward, then reach, an overall equilibrium. Entropy refers to the propensity and capacity of bodies (and systems) to undergo these changes. In the limiting case where the thermodynamic process is reversible, the system by definition is in equilibrium, and no (significant) change in entropy occurs; otherwise (in irreversible processes) it always increases—until the system reaches equilibrium. When a physical or chemical system is in equilibrium the entropy is thus at its maximum. Now since work is produced by the expenditure of energy, thus entailing a change in the energy state of the system, and since entropy conduces a system toward a state of equilibrium, that is, one in which further spontaneous change does not occur, it becomes possible to view the Second Law of Thermodynamics as positing an inverse correlation between the entropy of a system and the energy which it has available to do physical work. Consider now the Law of Entropy. It states: 'The entropy of an isolated system never decreases'. Here the expression of a novel thought is enabled by the meaning which has been secured for the word *entropy* in what was before a free place in the conceptual field. In the process a new trajection has been accomplished. This, then, is an example of the first subtype.[1]

The second and for our purposes more important subtype of new trajectory in science occurs when the trajectory results not from the introduction of a new word but from the use of preexisting words, one or more of which have had their meanings extended or shifted so as to represent a new concept. Here again we may serve ourselves with an example from thermodynamics. The First Law of Thermodynamics expresses the experimental finding that energy is conserved in chemical and physical processes. We shall consider this law to be reflected in the (simplified) form 'conservation of energy'. Now both 'conservation' and 'energy' had prior well-established uses before the enunciation of the principle (although the concept of energy had already under-

1. A process seemingly comparable to that undergone by 'entropy' occurs when a neologism is introduced in a poetic text. In *Paradise Lost* Milton writes (I, 756), 'A solemn Councel forthwith to be held / At *Pandemonium*, the High Capital / Of Satan and his Peers'. The term *pandemonium* is a coinage of Milton's, and although its meaning can be inferred from its etymology, Milton provides a gloss in the lines cited. 'Pandemonium' is therefore simply a new name given to a place that was previously known and hence that could be otherwise characterized. We might, it is true, claim that the poem performs the same defining function for 'pandemonium' that the theory of thermodynamics performs for 'entropy' and that therefore 'pandemonium' represents a novel thought in that it can be understood only against the machinery of the entire poem in which it is placed. But the analogy is not strict. Whereas the concept of entropy is simply inconceivable without the theory in which it is defined, 'pandemonium' could have been introduced and have assumed its meaning in a prosaic situation without the need of a poem as context. What this suggests is that neologisms introduced into poetic texts are compact synonyms for expressions that were previously available to represent the given phenomenon and that the thoughts they represent are therefore not novel. Such neologisms therefore differ in a fundamental way from those introduced in a scientific theory.

gone various extensions and modifications in its development). Underlying the development of the law, however, were a long series of experiments and the formation of a comprehensive theory governing chemical and physical processes. The terms *conservation* and *energy* were given new and precise meanings in the context of these developments. Correlated with these new meanings was the establishment of new positions in what were previously free spaces in the conceptual field. The expression 'conservation of energy', mapping as it did onto those new positions, thus represented a new trajection in the field of thought.[2]

It is important to understand that in the process of extension undergone by 'conservation' and 'energy' new conceptual space was occupied. In the usual case the extension of a word's meaning moves it into a position in the semantic field that is already occupied. Thus the corresponding concept is already in place, signaled by another word or phrase. Consider the word *attrition*. In earlier uses it referred to the wearing away of a material substance as the result of the abrasion caused by friction. In a phrase like 'attrition of personnel' it now means also the reduction of a work force as a consequence of death, retirement, or resignation. The latter meaning, as we see, represents a nonnovel concept, one that was previously available and expressible. Thus the extension of 'attrition' into that meaning does not involve the breaking of new conceptual ground. In the case of 'conservation of energy', however, the concept represented by that expression was not previously available in any form; it materialized only in consequence of the experiments, observations, and hypotheses that led to and were incorporated in the theory. It is this type of trajection—one in which a new concept takes its place in the conceptual field and figures as a term in the trajectory—that concerns us here. For by definition such trajections represent new knowledge.

2. The discussion of thermodynamics is based chiefly on Pippard (1966) and Denbigh (1968). The application is my own, as are also any technical errors that may appear in the exposition. For another example instancing a new trajection see Toulmin (1960, 17ff.), where he discusses the modification undergone by 'light' and 'travel' in the discovery that light travels in straight lines.

It should be evident that in speaking of a concept's previous availability we are not speaking of a priori availability. In that sense just about any concept is previously available. The question for us is, rather, whether the concept was available in the sense of being already *known*. In this sense the concept expressed by the extension of 'attrition' was previously available, while that expressed by 'conservation of energy' was not.

Notice also that 'conservation of energy', once the new meaning and corresponding concept had been gained for it by the development of the theory, could undergo a further, secondary extension of its meaning somewhat comparable to that experienced by 'attrition'. Apart from its original application to chemical and physical processes (with possibly already some nonnovel extensions in those areas), it may be applied with its newly acquired meaning in describing human, social, or political relations. We may analyze such extensions in one of two ways: either the meaning of 'conservation of energy' in these contexts is the same meaning as has been gained for the expression on its original extension or that meaning is modified in consequence of the new application. In the latter case, however, the meaning of 'conservation of energy' can be expressed using terms that signify antecedently available concepts. In whichever way we choose to analyze such secondary extensions, therefore, no new conceptual ground is broken.

Novel Thoughts in Science and Poetry

In the contrast that we drew in chapter 2 between trivial and nontrivial novel thoughts (and their expression) we said that the latter embodied new conceptions, whereas in the former nothing conceptually new was represented. At the same time, however, an *expression* like 'The telephone was dissolving' has a claim to novelty; it consists in the fact that just that sequence of words has presumably never before been articulated. We modeled the latter fact by a new trajectory in the conceptual space. This trajectory, however, is between points which were all antecedently present and fixed in that space. Thus between new trajectories of this type and those that occur in science there is the difference that in the latter the new trajectories involve *newly established* positions in that space. Where a notion like that of entropy is concerned, this is obvious. And it is no less true where those of conservation and energy (in the relevant sense) are concerned, since the notions have been split off from their former locations and extended to take up new and previously unoccupied positions. The different character of the new trajectories understood for novel scientific thoughts has as a corollary the fact that such thoughts are not epistemologically trivial; on the contrary, they embody new knowledge. Actually, this fact is truistic. What is interesting is that with it there can be correlated a distinctive kind of trajection in the conceptual space. Unlike the 'new' thought involved in an expression like 'The telephone was dissolving' which, as we have said, was always available, merely waiting, as it were, for someone to stumble on it, the thoughts involved in scientific discoveries need for their constitution the introduction of new concepts. These are represented by the theoretical definitions provided for coinages like *entropy* and the technical senses of words like *conservation* and *energy*.

Let us now compare the novel thoughts of science with those of poetry. It turns out that the novel thoughts occurring in science—of both subtypes—display a common property and that that property suffices to distinguish them from what is characteristic of the thought expressed by a poetic formation like 'The sea was laughing'. We claimed for the latter that in its production the boundaries of conceptual subspaces were transgressed. Examining the trajectories involved in our two examples from science we see that no such transgression has taken place. A neologism like 'entropy' is introduced into the semantic field in such a manner that other preexisting elements of the field are compatible with it. This means that the elements with which it comes to co-occur all belong (with it) to the same conceptual subspace. This follows almost by definition. The same result, although not so obvious, may be maintained for 'conservation of energy'. First, it seems implausible to suppose that the modification of meaning effected upon the words in this phrase should be such that either one or both of them should have been moved outside the original subspace. On the other hand, if this consequence should have ensued for either one of the words in its new meaning, we could argue that the meaning of the other word would have followed suit—with the same result as before. But a more substantive argument follows from the fact that the words in question derive and assume their modified, technical meanings in the context of a theory, and certainly a theory must define a consistent and unified conceptual space. Thus whether we take the position that the terms *conservation* and *energy* now occupy (shifted) positions in their original subspaces or positions in a new subspace, the trajectory that they define crosses no subspatial boundaries. The modeling of these thoughts therefore differs in a fundamental way from that of those representing poetic thoughts, thoughts which we are locating in metaphors.

We have now reached the conclusion that novel thoughts in science represent new knowledge. Consistent with this claim is the well-known fact that scientific statements make truth claims. This holds of course as well for those scientific statements that express novel thoughts. What now of the novel thoughts expressed in poetry? We have said that they embody new conceptions. Is there any sense in which those conceptions can be said to make similar claims about truth? More important, is there any sense in which those conceptions can be said to represent knowledge? By way of preparing ourselves to answer this question, let us recur to the conclusions arrived at in chapter 2 concerning conceptions. We said there that conceptions were the intentions of acts of conceiving of and that those intentions were fulfilled statically, thus that their fulfillments came into existence in the very acts that promoted them. We need now to reflect on this conclusion as it pertains to the present context.

Suppose I say 'I conceive of there being life on Mars'. It might appear that this statement makes a truth claim, that exploration might disclose facts that would confirm or disconfirm the claim that life existed on Mars. However, the only claim being made in the statement is that I have a conception; no direct claim is made about life on Mars or anything else. The verb *conceive of*, like

wish, *believe*, *suppose*, *imagine*, and so on, constitutes a referentially opaque context; any construction that occurs in such a
context makes no truth claims (see Quine, 1963, 142). Thus
whatever might be discovered about Mars—that life does or does
not exist on it—has no bearing on the truth of the statement.
What is significant, rather, is the fact that in making the statement
I do promote the corresponding intention—a conception. Suppose now I say 'I wish that there were life on Mars'. Here again
the discovered presence or absence of life on Mars would have no
bearing on the truth of the statement; the question of truth simply
does not arise (except in the trivial sense that I have made a
statement). What is significant in this case is that a wish has been
expressed and the corresponding intention promoted. But
whereas for the latter sentence fulfillment of the intention would
require that life be found to exist on Mars (thus fulfillment if it
occurred at all would be dynamic), no such consequence is required for the former sentence. Here again we see how the fulfillment characteristic of acts expressed in *wish* sentences differs
from that in *conceiving of* sentences. As pointed out in chapter 2,
the former acts require for their fulfillment an empirical sequel,
the latter do not. And the latter require no such sequel precisely
because they are fulfilled statically.

In the respect of being statically fulfilled, the intentional act of
conception is like those of perception and imagination. Of the
latter we may say that they are self-sufficient, satisfying themselves in their very exercise, meaning thereby that the act of
'recognition', which is the unifying function of the intentional
act—that which effects an identity between the act of perception
and the percept or the act of imagination and the image—is part
and parcel of the intentional act (see Husserl, 1970, 688). Thus
just as in every act of perception *some thing* is perceived and in
every act of imagination *some thing* is imagined, so in acts of
conception *some thing* is conceived of; conceptions, in other
words, partake, like perceptions and imaginings, of coinstan-
taneousness; they differ from the latter only in that they comprise
no intuitive counterpart of the percept or image, offering in their
stead merely a schema. In contrast to this self-certification char-

acteristic of statically fulfilled intentional acts, we find where volitional, purposive, and other types of intentional act are concerned the implication of a sequel, in that such acts 'look forward' to empirical realization. In a wish there is to be sure something wished, the correlate in consciousness of the act (namely, its noema), but such acts, inasmuch as their fulfillment is deferred, are in a sense unsaturated; they lack 'completeness'. Conceptions, we might therefore say, are 'inferior' to acts of perception and imagination in that their intentions have less phenomenological substance but 'superior' to acts that require dynamic fulfillment in being more self-contained than such acts. Where acts of the latter type must look beyond themselves for completion, conceptions are 'completed' by the exertions of the mind in its attempt to realize the schema. Conceptions are thus acts solely of a phenomenological nature, resembling in this respect acts of perception and imagination.

Metaphor and Knowledge

It will be argued here that certain conceptions, those that set in play such mental functions as are directed toward the apprehension of relations not previously thought of, represent new knowledge. Ordinarily, knowledge is defined as that which we are warranted in believing to be the case. The warrant is customarily grounded in the existence of a state of affairs corresponding to the belief, that state of affairs needing to be objective. These conditions are sometimes expressed by saying that knowledge is justified true belief. Now it was asserted above that conceptions—as intentions of acts of conceiving of—have content, the 'some thing' conceived of. Let us, therefore, in light of the above position regarding what constitutes knowledge, examine more carefully what that 'content' consists of. I have said that the representation of a conception is a schema, thus not anything that consists of an actual configuration of images. What kind of knowledge can the entertainment of such a representation be said to represent, what state of affairs can it be said to figure? A schema, in my terms, is a delimitation of mental space that is implicitly disposed to receive a configuration of a specific kind, namely, that configuration which would instantiate the conception. Since no such instantiation is actually represented in the conception, I suggest that what the schema represents is the *possibility* of instantiation, and that it is the recognition of this possibility that counts for us as an accession of knowledge. The claim that the recognition of possibilities is a species of knowledge may seem arbitrary and unjustified. I am making it, however, purely for conceptions activated by certain metaphoric expressions encountered in poetry, expressions which I regard as occurring in a special context. I described the sense in which I regard the context of poems to be special in Levin, 1977, where I proposed as implicitly defining that context the presupposed 'higher' sentence 'I imagine (myself in) and invite you to conceive a world in which . . . ' (for 'conceive' in the above sentence I would now put 'conceive of'). The implicit context that I assume for a certain type of 'expressive' poetry is, I think, of the sort that, as readers or hearers, we may also assume for the utterance of seers, prophets, mystics, and other visionaries—to which types may be added schizophrenics, the shamans of various tribes, and persons suffering from hallucinations or under the influence of drugs. Common to all these types is the conceiving of preternatural (and supernatural) schemes and an implicit belief in their reality.

The inclusion of poets with the types listed above, as agents who profess their deviant expressions to depict a reality, may seem to be an act of supererogation. Unless one views them in this way, however, perennial claims to the effect that the poet is a 'creator' and the poem a 'world' (claims which *are* intuitively congenial) amount to little more than rhetorical flourishes.

We have now reached the conclusion that in both scientific and metaphoric statements new knowledge is produced. And we have claimed that both types are to be modeled by new trajections across the conceptual space. The trajections differed, however, in that those for science were projected across newly established points in the one subspace, whereas those for metaphor were projected across old, preexisting points located in different conceptual subspaces—thus crossing subspatial boundaries. This difference in modeling derives from and reflects the difference between the structure of nature and the capacities of the human mind. Nature is consistent; it does not exceed itself. It was a scientific discovery that energy is conserved in physical processes, but it was always a fact of nature. When the fact was discovered, it represented new knowledge. But the knowledge was of properties *inherent* to the phenomena. Physical bodies and systems always conserved energy—it is in their nature to do so. There was just an 'accidental' gap in our knowledge. The trajectory was always implicitly there in the conceptual space. Thus the reason it is appropriate to model scientific new knowledge by trajectories across the one subspace is that the knowledge is of properties and relations that necessarily inhere in the phenomena. It would be counterintuitive to map such properties and relations onto a subspace different from the one in which are located the phenomena in which those properties and relations inhere. Thus when we predicate 'conservation of energy' of a physical system, we are predicating a property that belongs to that system in the nature of the case. This is why new knowledge in science is susceptible of truth-tests.

The picture is different for the new knowledge represented by metaphor. I said above that nature does not exceed itself. The mind, however, is not thus limited; it can exceed nature. It can combine elements and properties between which there exists no inherent relation, and between which there is not categorial compatibility. If we take literally an expression like 'The sea was laughing', we are projecting a relation which exceeds anything in nature, which exceeds, moreover, anything that future discoveries may disclose about nature. We are projecting a state of affairs that transcends anything that our experience has taught us or prepared us for. Of such projections it can truly be said that they yoke by violence two heterogeneous ideas together. The result of this process in the present instance is not a mere conceit, however, a farfetched and perhaps forced manner of expressing what could be expressed in simpler and more obvious terms. The result is a conception, one in which we entertain the possibility

that the sea might laugh. Because of the radical nature of the
yoking involved in such a conception, because the elements
yoked are so disparate, related neither inherently nor categoric-
ally, we are justified in modeling the trajectories of poetic metaphors as transgressing subspatial boundaries.

Aspects of Construal

Let us now take a look at the processes of construal that
may be prompted by a semantically deviant expression, the type
of expression, that is, which is pradigmatic of poetic metaphor.
For our present purposes we shall consider again our homely
expression 'The trees are weeping'. As we said in chapter 1, a
standard approach to the problem will see in this sentence a
figurative way of saying something like 'The trees are dripping
moisture' or ' . . . exuding sap' or ' . . . shedding their leaves', or
something similar. Behind all such interpretations, we said, there
lies a tacit assumption, namely, that when there exists an incompatibility between what an expression says and our notions of
how the world is constituted, it is the expression that must be
modified. So that, since trees do not weep in the world as we
know it, a sentence that says they do is in need of construal. Now
in the face of an incompatibility between a linguistic expression
and our notions of how the world is constituted, we pointed out
that there is logically another way to achieve conformity. Instead
of regarding our conception of the world as a constant, so that it
is the sentence that must be modified in any lack of fit between
that conception and what a sentence says, we can regard the
sentence as constant, so that what needs to be modified is our
conception of the world. In other words, we can try, on the basis
of some modality of thought, to validate what the sentence literally says—in the present instance, that the trees are weeping.

For reasons that are fundamental, this validation will have to be
achieved conceptually; that is, it cannot be achieved linguistically. The build of our language is strongly deterministic in this
regard; it reflects the fact that language was created by humans,
not by trees or horses. The consequence is that while we have in

English predicates that describe physical and dispositional states and activities for both humans and inanimate objects (one can say of a man that he is tall, fat, or sick, and of a tree that it is thick-boled, leafy, or flowering), when it comes to predicates describing mental, affective, emotional, or volitional states, almost all the predicates that the language makes available are those defined in the first instance for humans. Suppose now that trees have an emotional life. Our language offers us no predicates with which specifically to describe that life. We are asking how we would describe the activity of weeping, say, or the state of anger in a tree (let us leave aside for the moment the question of why we would think that that activity or state is to be described). We could of course simply say that the tree is weeping or is angry. As the language is now constituted, however, such descriptions would not serve our purpose, inasmuch as they activate interpretations that are adverse to the possibility of a tree's having an emotional life. This suggests that what are needed are not these predicates, which are defined for human activities and states, but predicates that are species-specific for trees.

But we have no such predicates. Suppose then that we introduce some into our lexicon; we coin the word *fliss*, say, and give as its definition 'to weep, *sp.* of trees'. We might now recast our original sentence as 'The trees are flissing'. This sentence would be understood literally, as meaning 'The trees are experiencing the arboreal equivalent of human weeping'. Even if we introduced 'fliss', however, it would be necessary, for a consistent program, to introduce hundreds of other terms if we wished to have species-specific predicates to counterpart all those describing human emotions, affections, volitions, and so forth. Suppose then that we forwent this remedy and decided instead to add species-specific *meanings* to the existing predicates, that is, we added the sense assigned above to 'fliss' to the meaning of 'weep', so that in reading 'The trees are weeping' we would understand 'weep' to mean what weeping is for trees. Now the sentence is again taken literally; there is no need to construe it (unlike the case for the same sentence before we introduced a species-specific sense for its predicate). However, although we now have, so to speak, domesticated the language to our purpose, we are faced with the problem of pairing with our arbitrary linguistic stipulation the corresponding understanding of what it means for a tree to weep. Where before ('The trees are dripping moisture') the language was construed to make sense of the world as we know it, we now have to construe our conception of the world to make sense of the sentence as it stands.

By way of assisting us to see that predicates can indeed be construed as described above, let us turn to a consideration of the metaphoric mode known as personification. Before doing so, we need to look somewhat more carefully at the two construal processes that have already been sketched for 'The trees are weeping'. In both construals the focus was on the predicate. In the first, 'weeping' was modified to yield 'dripping moisture' and so on; in the second, it was modified to mean 'to weep, *sp*. of trees'. Both these construals are 'forced' by the co-occurrence of 'weeping' with a noun that is semantically incompatible. Technically, construal proceeds by transferring certain values of the noun *tree* into the reading of the predicate—thus the direction of transfer is N → V—whereupon they serve to modify its meaning. In the former case the modification is semantic in nature, in the latter conceptual.[3] Suppose we now shift the construal focus to the noun, that is, we modify its meaning under the influence of the co-occurring verb—the direction of transfer thus being N ← V. In this process the syntactic requirement of 'weep' that it take a [+Human] subject, plus its semantic characteristics, impinge on the meaning of 'tree' with the result (under this particular construal process) that it is personified.[4] How do we understand the

3. I call modifications semantic when they are expressible as (ad hoc) definitions. When we say that 'weep' means 'to drip moisture', we are giving a definition of 'weep' (for a certain context). When, on the other hand, we say that 'weep' (in the same context) is to be read as meaning 'to weep, *sp*. of trees', we are obviously not providing a definition (since the same word appears in the definiens and definiendum). Thus our 'definition' is not cashable semantically. All it can serve to do is prompt us to an effort at conception.

4. This description is of course schematic, inasmuch as personification typically depends on a sustaining context. For a discussion of personification as it figures in allegory see Levin, 1981.

resulting 'object'? It seems that here we are able to conceive of an entity that is at once animate and inanimate: a tree which is, if not human, at least humanized. If our sentence occurred in an allegorical poem—a tree fable—it is in some such ontological guise that we would understand it. The fact that personification is a standard metaphoric convention suggests that it is possible for us to entertain conceptions whose content exceeds what our experience in the phenomenal world has prepared us for.

Although the point is not usually brought up for consideration, I think we are justified in claiming that in texts where inanimate objects are personified, the predicates undergo a corresponding modification, so that in allegories or beast fables the senses of the predicates are understood (perhaps subliminally) in such a way as to make them consistent with the amalgamated nature of the personified objects. Thus if in our example we take the tree as personified, we have as a concomitant the *dispersonification* of the predicate—resulting in a construal of 'weeping' that is congruent with an object that is both human and arboreal.[5]

In light of the above discussion, let us consider Blake's short poem 'Ah! Sunflower':

> Ah Sunflower weary of time,
> Who countest the steps of the sun:
> Seeking after that sweet golden clime
> Where the traveller's journey is done.
>
> Where the youth pined away with desire,
> And the pale virgin shrouded in snow,
> Arise from their graves and aspire
> Where my Sunflower wishes to go.

On the basis that the sunflower is said to be weary, that it counts, seeks, and wishes, I take it as personified.[6] Now if the predicates have been able to effect this result, how are they themselves then

---

5. For discussion of dispersonification as a construal process see Levin, 1977.

6. In the description that I give of this poem, it is to be understood that I discuss it in terms that are relevant to my thesis and that I exploit for purposes of that thesis.

to be regarded? They cannot be taken in their normal senses, since the subject is being understood as part plant. By the same token, whatever may be our notions of how a plant might experience these states and activities, these notions alone would not comport with a subject that is part human. We are forced, I believe, to conclude that the predicates in some sense neutralize attributes deriving from both types of entity. Pursuant to the personification of nouns, then, the predicates are dispersonified.[7]

Besides personification, there are other modes of construal possible on the N ← V direction of transfer. Thus, in a suitable context, 'tree' could be read as a metaphor for a man or woman (cf. 'The oak finally broke down and cried'). This construal would be the equivalent on the noun for the reading 'dripping moisture' on the verb, that is, semantic.[8] The conceptual counterpart on this direction of transfer would be the entertainment of a tree as capable of weeping. To be sure, when a tree's bark is scored and it then exudes sap the tree may then be said to be weeping—in other words, 'The tree is weeping' in fact then means 'The tree is exuding sap'. This fact in no way compromises the substance of what I have been saying about 'The trees were weeping'. We now simply have to add to our discussion the fact that when that expression is used to describe the exudation of sap, it is no longer metaphoric. Originally constituting a metaphoric extension of 'weep' in this context, the metaphor is now faded, if not dead, and 'weep' has had added to its semantic range the meaning 'to exude sap'. Thus, even though 'The trees were weeping' has an interpretation when taken literally, that interpretation is not the one associated with *conceptual* construal but is in fact semantic; in the conceptual construal the weeping of the

7. It is necessary to bear in mind that the holding in suspension of categorially mixed attributes obtains only in special poetic contexts. The critical words may subsequently develop new senses specific to the inanimate objects; as when we say that a tree is graceful or majestic, where little if any trace remains of what may originally have been a metaphoric predication. In the context of the poem, however, these subsequently emergent senses have not yet been linguistically ratified. The effort to rationalize their meanings is therefore purely conceptual.

8. For discussion of this and other modes of metaphoric construal that are a priori possible see Levin, 1977.

trees implies sorrow, grief, and the shedding of tears. If we conceive of a tree in this way, 'weeping' is understood as an activity actually experienceable by a tree. I refer to this way of construing as *radical dispersonification*.[9]

It is a critical contention that in poetry there is a fusion of form and content. In the customary application of this principle, form is seen largely as a matter of poetic conventions such as rhyme, meter, and the rest. The fact that the language is regimented by these conventions is held to constrict the language and effect a bonding with the content. We may grant that the conventions play such a role in poetry. But we are now able to rationalize this fusion of form and content at a significantly deeper level. In the stead of form and content, let us first substitute thoughts and their expression (we do this by way of abstracting from the conventions and constraining the problem to the terms of our argument). Bearing in mind that our focus is on deviant expressions, it is clear that if the language of such expressions is (semantically) construed, the thought (content) is rendered ordinary; only the expression of it is then to be regarded as novel. On the approach that I am taking, the thought is novel, and its novelty exacts a novelty of expression. On this approach the poet is not a mere wordsmith, decking out with unusual language a pedestrian view of the world; it is his vision of the world that is novel, and it is from this fact that there follows his uncharacteristic use of the language. On this view of the poetic enterprise there is no divergence of form (expression) from content—they are truly one. There is in fact no need to speak of fusion; the *unity* of form and content follow from the literal expression of a direct vision.

9. I introduce the notion of radical dispersonification in Levin, 1981. The difference between radical and ordinary dispersonification may be described as follows: in dispersonification, even though it leads to a conceptual construal, that conception still carries with it the preconceptions of anthropomorphism; since it accompanies personification, in which the inanimate object is understood as joined with human attributes, dispersonified predicates have a correspondingly mixed nature. Predicates are construed as radically dispersonified, on the other hand, when their subjects are understood simply in their own right—as inanimate or nonhuman objects. The predicates are then taken to mean what they say but predicable nevertheless of such objects.

Conceptual Knowledge

In the preceding discussion I have made a strong claim—namely, that conceptions of a certain sort represent new knowledge. As it stands this claim may appear counterintuitive; it certainly runs counter to accepted views of what constitutes knowledge. I grant that in making this claim I am pressing things and that its acceptance requires a reader's indulgence. But consider: in the course of our worldly experience we are continually made aware of new possibilities. Facts and events are disclosed to us of whose existence we were previously ignorant, and whose disclosure extended our notions of what is possible. As a result of these disclosures we acquire new concepts and gain new knowledge. In a conception, as I am using the notion, we conceive of a state of affairs that lies beyond our worldly experience and *we lend credence to its possibility*. The fact that the matter or substance of the conception is 'counterfactual' does not rule out for us the possibility of its realization. What we 'know' when we entertain such a conception is thus the matter of the conception and, additionally, that its realization is for us possible. We do not 'know for a fact' that the state of expressed affairs obtains, but we accord it credibility. It would perhaps be more appropriate to refer to this condition as one of belief rather than knowledge, but it is a new belief of which we were previously unaware. From my point of view it is reasonable to maintain that consciousness of this new belief is a form of knowledge, knowledge of our own capacities to be sure, but knowledge nonetheless.

Along the way of extending our discussion of the problems connected with the notion of conceptual knowledge, we may first point out that on the standard approach, which interprets 'The trees are weeping' as 'The trees are dripping moisture', an interpretation which we have characterized as semantic in nature, no new knowledge is produced: the interpretation describes an empirical condition which is conceptually routine; we already know that trees drip moisture (shed leaves and so forth). On the purely conceptual construal, by contrast, empirical grounding of this sort is missing. So that if knowledge should be produced on this type of construal it will have to be supported on grounds other than empirical.

We commonly speak of 'knowing our own minds'. In so expressing ourselves we trade on an equivocation in the meaning of 'know'.[10] The same equivocation is potential in the word 'knowledge'. In fact, in the concluding sentence two paragraphs back, the attribution of knowledge to conceptual construal was negotiated via just this equivocation; it was by its means that I modulated into a 'knowledge of our capacities'. We ought now, therefore, to examine that attribution more closely.

The doctrine that knowledge is justified true belief isolates a narrow and strict sense of what constitutes knowledge. The requirement that the true belief must be justified is designed to eliminate such 'knowledge' as may be arrived at on the basis of deductive error, apparitions presented in the course of dreams or hallucinations, attributions of true consequences to the operation of divine and mystical agencies, and the like. If, starting from the premise that ice is frozen milk, I conclude by expecting that ice will melt at room temperature; if in a dream I am convinced that

---

10. In fact, the equivocation need not be seen as specially tendentious. From the standpoint of phenomenology our perception of (into) our minds has a greater claim to veridicality than do our perceptions of phenomena. If the object of consciousness is a mental experience, it is of something immanent (in the mind); if it is a phenomenon, it is of something transcendent (to the mind). Now Husserl says, 'Every immanent perception necessarily guarantees the existence of its object' ('object' here meaning a mental experience). This guarantee of existence does not apply to transcendent perceptions, since such perceptions may be formed while under an illusion. If by contrast an immanent perception should be illusory, the perception would be *of that* illusion and thus not itself illusory. Immanent perceptions, therefore—reflections on the contents of one's consciousness—are more reliable than are the perceptions of objects in the world around us. There is thus a sense in which the knowledge we have of our minds is more trustworthy than the knowledge we have of the world. Indeed, Husserl contrasts the primordial and absolute existence in which my thoughts stand to me with the fragmentary and contingent mode of existence which holds for empirical objects. So that when I recollect, say, a particular melody, I 'know' that recollection more indubitably than I know the melody that I actually hear (again). Moreover, even should the melody be heard under legitimate conditions (i.e. nonillusorily), it is still always heard under an aspect, thus partially and incompletely; in recollection, on the other hand, it appears full-bodied and free of 'perspective' (see *Ideas*, pp. 143f. for discussion of these points).

Mars rotates around the sun; if I thoroughly understand the ebb and flow of the tides but believe that the movement is caused by the exertions of a supernatural demon—if in all such cases my belief corresponds with the facts, hence is true, I cannot be said to have knowledge of those facts. Justification thus imposes a condition on our *reasons* for holding a true belief, and unless those reasons are of the appropriate sort, I cannot be said to have the corresponding knowledge. This is thus a very strong doctrine. It defines 'true' in such a way that we can only have knowledge where there is a fact of the matter for the belief to be true *of*, and then restricts belief to a conviction that is attained by the correct employment of our rational faculties. If we grant that this formulation defines knowledge, we must conclude that a great deal—perhaps the bulk—of what we experience is unknowable.

But there are many modes of 'knowing'. The literature is full of references to innate knowledge, personal knowledge, tacit knowledge, spiritual knowledge, declarative and procedural knowledge, knowing *that* and knowing *how*, certitude (as well as certainty), and many other varieties. I am claiming that there is such a thing as conceptual knowledge and that it may be achieved if we take poetic language literally. We may begin our argument in support of this contention by asking what a poem consists of. Fundamentally, it consists of thoughts expressed in language. In this respect it is no different from other uses of language. Now we may certainly gain knowledge on the basis of language. If I know that there is ice at the North Pole, I know that exclusively through report; if I know that bear meat is nutritious, it is by report; if I know that Caesar conquered Gaul or that Socrates was married, again it is by report. A great deal of what we can be said to know thus results from our hearing or reading reports in which certain thoughts are asserted in language. If we have reason to believe that the thoughts so expressed correspond to certain facts, then we are entitled to conclude that we have knowledge of those facts.

Everything turns of course on the nature of the 'facts' in question. Concerning the sort mentioned above, it is possible to carry out investigations that would terminate in confirmation: there is

a North Pole, there is bear meat, there was a Caesar and a
Socrates, and what was asserted of these entities can be confirmed
by investigating empirical conditions. In general, however,
where facts such as these are concerned, we are satisfied that we
have knowledge of them simply on the basis of reports, oral or
written; we feel no need personally to investigate the conditions
that would serve to confirm them. We place our trust, that is, in
the reporters. The conditions presupposed in an assertion to the
effect that trees are weeping are of course not empirical. We may,
however, regard this difference as irrelevant. In this case also we
may place our trust in the reporter, that is, the poet, feeling it
unnecessary to seek confirmation. In Levin, 1976 (p. 159) I wrote:

> A poem is like a report by a traveller from outer space or time.
> What he has seen is the reality of some other world. The poet,
> in his transport, is such a traveller. He has seen realities which
> have no earthly counterparts. His report on those realities
> embodies what for him are accurate and faithful descriptions of
> objects that actually exist and events that truly took place. For
> us, not having accompanied the poet on his sojourn and thus
> not having experienced the direct vision of this other reality,
> the descriptions are metaphors. Metaphors, through a distor-
> tion of our world, enable us to enter upon one that is different.
> They are makeshift means to the conceptualization of an other-
> worldly reality. But as long as we perceive the poet's descrip-
> tions as metaphors, our suspension of disbelief is not total and
> we do not share fully in the poet's vision. True poetic faith
> would consist in our perceiving, with the poet, his descriptions
> as literally true.

Where in the passage above I spoke of 'perceiving', I would now
say 'conceiving of [the poet's] descriptions as literally true'. The
essential point of the passage, however, lies in the crediting of the
poet with being veracious. It follows that deviant expressions are
to be read as conceptual, not linguistic, metaphors. If we effect
the conceptual construals, then what the resulting conceptions
are true of is the poet's vision of reality—a reality that is strange
and exotic only to minds locked into a conventional ontology.

What justifies our belief in the truth of this reality is the sympathetic employment of our empathic faculties. If we give ourselves up to this experience, we have certainly learned something in reading the poem. And there is no reason to deny that what we learn counts for us as knowledge.

To recapitulate the interpretive strategy that we have been developing, we assume that the poet attempts to represent in his poem mental and emotional exertions of an unusual power and range. As an issue of these exertions the poet is transported phenomenologically into a realm of his own making, an otherwordly reality in which the empirical conditions of this world do not necessarily obtain. In order to represent faithfully his vision of that reality, the poet (by constraint) employs language that is semantically deviant. The reader, then, to have any chance of mentally reconstructing and participating in that reality, must attempt a conceptual construal of that language. This means that as the interpretation of a metaphor the reader will produce a schema; in the attempt to 'flesh out', to render substantive, that schema, he will countenance it as a possibility that the conditions described by the language taken literally might somehow obtain. The recognition and serious countenancing of this possibility, I am claiming, represents a type of knowledge.

One More Comparison of Science and Poetry

Before I conclude this chapter, it will be worthwhile to reconsider the conclusions that we have arrived at in our analysis of metaphor and compare them with the ones reached in our discussion of science.[11]

In our discussion of the expression *conservation of energy* we pointed out that the new meaning gained for the notion of conservation was established only with the thinking out and formation of a comprehensive theory of thermodynamics. Once the theory is formed the extended or modified meanings of the

11. We shall not discuss in this connection the 'entropy'/'pandemonium' opposition, as it presents little theoretical interest in this context.

words assume fixed, well-defined positions in the semantic field. But behind this process there typically lie a series of experiments and the testing of various hypotheses. During the course of these procedures the new meanings are inchoate and tentative. It is only with the formation of the theory that the shifts of meaning are actually accomplished. And once this state is achieved, the words in their modified meanings take standing positions in the semantic and, correlatively, in the conceptual field. As such, they represent new concepts. The theory then defines relations between these concepts. All this is unlike what occurs in metaphor. In the first place, on my analysis of metaphor there is no extension of meaning. The novelty of the expression consists in the hitherto unconceived of relation that it projects between preexisting concepts. The novelty is thus in the conception, not in the concepts. This is the essential difference between the new knowledge produced in science and that achieved by metaphor. Both types reveal a new relation between terms. But in science the terms, that is, the concepts, are new, the novelty of the relation being a concomitant and automatic consequence. In metaphor the relation is new, but since the concepts related belong to different conceptual subspaces, there is nothing automatic about the relation. Moreover, with metaphor there is no mediation of a conceptual change by a lengthy process during which extended meanings of words are hypothetically assumed. In metaphor the entire process is telescoped in the instant of conception (both for the poet and the reader). No preliminaries, in the form either of prior experimentation or hypotheses, precedes or accompanies the metaphoric act.[12] The metaphor is an immediate expression of the new conception. Where in science the new trajection results from prior ground laying—in the form of defining new concepts—in metaphor it is instantaneous. We might say that in science the new trajection is based upon and made possible by a

---

12. If it should be suggested that for the poet too there might intervene a process of trial and experimentation before arriving at the precise form for the metaphor, it would have to be pointed out that no trace of this process appears in the metaphor, unlike the situation in science, where records of the experiments exist and may be adduced in support of the theory.

series of preparatory steps, in metaphor it is invented on the spot. From this it follows that the knowledge embodied in a metaphor is entrained immediately, at the actual point of expression, by the conception of the (new) relation which is asserted in the linguistic collocation. It is in this conception that the poet's new trajection is realized by the reader.

5

Vico and the Language of the 'First Poets'

On the approach that I am taking in this study, there is in poetry no metaphor of the conventional sort; the language functions on a single plane, the literal, and the resulting interpretation is conceptual, not linguistic. This approach thus differs fundamentally from the rationalization of metaphor that has prevailed since at least the time of Aristotle. At the same time it bears a prima facie similarity to the views of certain thinkers who have treated metaphor not so much as a problem in its own right but in the context of theories concerning the origin of language. The views I refer to here are not those of linguists who have dealt with this question and to whom we owe explanations embodied in the so-called bow-wow, pooh-pooh, yo-he-ho, and ding-dong theories of language origin. In the explanations that these theories provide, it 'occurs' to man that he can call a natural object by the sound it characteristically emits (bow-wow), a strong emotion or physical effort by the involuntary sound it evokes (pooh-pooh, yo-he-ho, respectively); as to the ding-dong theory, based on a mystical affinity or harmony held to exist between man and things, such that emanations from the latter cause vocal impulses in the former, it is too fanciful to merit serious consideration (for a discussion of these explanations, see Jespersen, 1964). In all such theories man is seen basically as a reactive agent, his powers of imagination being essentially dormant or inert and his feelings and passions left largely out of account; no consideration, in other words, is given to the possibility that language developed as a result of *projections* from man *onto* the elements in his environment. One thinker who did try to explain the origins of language in the latter way was Giambattista Vico. And in his account metaphor plays a fundamental and characteristic role. In this chapter I show how in a fundamental respect Vico's views on conceptual metaphor differ from my own.

Early Man's Metaphysical Outlook

Vico's views on the origin of language are presented at various places in the *New Science*.[1] The critical exposition for our purposes, however, occurs in the section entitled 'Poetic Metaphysics'. Here Vico argues first that the accounts which have come down to us give a distorted and false picture of the conditions under which early man lived and the manner in which he related to his environment. The distortion results from the fact that the picture was fashioned by latter-day philosophers who used the evidentiary materials—the myths and fables—to construct for early man a system of metaphysics which consisted with their own notions of what a world outlook should be. The mistake consists in applying to the construction of that system principles of rationality, principles which, given the nature of the men to whom they were attributed, could not but lead to an inappropriate picture. Vico, on the other hand, proceeding according to his dictum that 'Doctrines must take their beginning from that of the matters of which they treat', attempts first to reconstruct the actual conditions under which early man apprehended his universe and then constructs a worldview, or metaphysics, consistent with those conditions.

The first men were 'stupid, insensate, and horrible beasts'. Since in their development these men were practically at the level

---

1. Thomas Goddard Bergin and Max Harold Fisch (trs.), *The New Science of Giambattista Vico* (Ithaca and London: Cornell University Press, 1968); references to this work are to paragraphs.

of animals, their sole way of knowing things was through the senses (374–75):

> Hence poetic wisdom, the first wisdom of the gentile world, must have begun with a metaphysics not rational and abstract like that of learned men now, but felt and imagined as that of these first men must have been, who, without power of ratiocination, were all robust sense and vigorous imagination. This metaphysics was their poetry, a faculty born with them (for they were furnished by nature with these senses and imaginations); born of their ignorance of causes, for ignorance, the mother of wonder, made everything wonderful to men who were ignorant of everything. Their poetry was at first divine, because . . . they imagined the causes of the things they felt and wondered at to be gods; . . . they gave the things they wondered at substantial being after their own ideas, just as children do, whom we see take inanimate things in their hands and play with them and talk to them as though they were living persons.

'They gave the things they wondered at substantial being after their own ideas'. These ideas were such that a nature unlike their own, that is, one disposed by purely physical forces, was beyond their capacities to conceive. In his attempt to 'rationalize' nature, therefore, man makes himself the measure: 'When men are ignorant of the natural causes producing things, and cannot even explain them by analogy with similar things, they attribute their own nature to them. The vulgar, for example, say the magnet loves the iron' (180; see also 120, 122). In this way the sky, the earth, the sea, were all animated. And because early man was awed by the physical manifestations of these natural forces, he endowed the animated entities with superhuman powers and worshipped them as gods. The first men who attempted to render this view of the world, therefore, were necessarily theological poets, and the first language, that spoken by these poets, 'was not a language in accord with the nature of the things it dealt with (as must have been the sacred language invented by Adam, to whom God granted divine onomathesia, the giving of names to things according to the nature of each), but was a fantastic speech making use of physical substances endowed with life and most of them imagined to be divine' (401). In the last clause of this quotation we can see the basis upon which Vico feels himself justified in calling these first speakers (or singers) 'theological poets'.

Vico continues (402):

> This is the way [that is, as animated physical substances imagined to be divine] in which the theological poets apprehended Jove, Cybele or Berecynthia, and Neptune, for example, and, at first mutely pointing, explained them as substances of the sky, the earth, and the sea, which they imagined to be animate divinities and were therefore true to their senses in believing them to be gods. By means of these three divinities . . . they explained everything appertaining to the sky, the earth, and the sea. And similarly by means of other divinities they signified the other kinds of things appertaining to each, denoting all flowers, for instance, by Flora, and all fruits by Pomona. We nowadays reverse this practice in respect of spiritual things, such as the faculties of the human mind, the passions, virtues, vices, sciences, and arts; for the most part the ideas we form of them are so many feminine personifications, to which we refer all the causes, properties, and effects that severally appertain to them. For when we wish to give utterance to our understanding of spiritual things, we must seek aid from our imagination to explain them and, like painters, form human images of them. But these theological poets, unable to make use of the understanding, did the opposite and more sublime thing: they attributed senses and passions . . . to bodies, and to bodies as vast as sky, sea, and earth.

In this passage Vico very pointedly contrasts two opposed ways of rationalizing the ontological status of entities that exceed what our experience provides a warrant for. Where in the subsequent tradition poets personify abstractions and attribute to those personifications all the properties that pertain to the abstract qualities (love, avarice, music, and so on), the theological poets animated insentient substances (the sky, the earth, the sea) by attributing to them human senses and passions. On the face of it, the difference might not appear to be so radical; we might see in both cases the importation and attribution of human characteristics to inanimate entities. The reason that for Vico one of these practices is more 'sublime', however, is that the theological poets, in their intellectual naiveté, were expressing a direct and unmediated vision of their universe as they 'felt' it. As soon as man became sophisticated about his world, this innocent and artless response to the features of his universe was no longer possible. Overlaid on his sensuous and imaginative faculties is the 'rectifying' function of reason. To a poet working in an intellectual tradition of this sort the simple, childlike apprehension of his universe is foreclosed. When such a poet, therefore, casts an abstract quality in a personified form, there is no pretense that the universe is as pictured in the poem; what we have, rather, is a mannered and calculated elaboration of the conventional universe. One consequence of this difference in metaphysical outlook is that where the rational poetic 'strategy' effects on the original abstract quality a *reduction*, the imaginative strategy imparts to the original substance an *augmentation*. In the one a quality, say love, is represented by a woman; in the other a physical entity, the sky, is infused with divinity. There our attention is diverted from the abstraction love, here it remains on the substance sky. Beyond this, moreover, is the question of how much surety the poet goes for the description of the world he has proffered. No subsequent poet would say that he thinks that love is a woman, but the first poets would insist that the sky was a god. The phrase of Tacitus concerning frightened men which Vico instances earlier (376) can thus be applied with equal justice to the first poets: they 'no sooner imagine than they believe'. It is in this unreasoning conviction that what they are describing is real that their greater sublimity lies.

The first divine fable, that of Jove, is informed by and manifests the callow metaphysics and naive credulity of early man. It expresses the awe and wonder with which men responded to the thunder and lightning that descended from the sky. Ignorant of their own nature, 'and because in that state their nature was that of men all robust bodily strength, who expressed their very violent passions by shouting and grumbling, they pictured the sky to themselves as a great animated body, which in that aspect they called Jove . . . who meant to tell them something by the hiss of his bolts and the clap of his thunder' (377).

Early man's primitive cast of mind, which determined him to see nature in his own image, is then contrasted by Vico with the nature of our civilized minds, which are

> so detached from the senses, even in the vulgar, by abstractions corresponding to all the abstract terms our languages abound in, and so refined by the art of writing, and as it were spiritualized by the use of numbers, because even the vulgar know how to count and reckon, that it is naturally beyond our power to form the vast image of this mistress called 'Sympathetic Nature'. Men shape the phrases with their lips but have nothing in their minds; for what they have in mind is falsehood, which is nothing; and their imagination no longer avails to form a vast false image. It is equally beyond our power to enter into the vast imagination of those first men, whose minds were not in the least abstract, refined, or spiritualized, because they were entirely immersed in the senses, buffeted by the passions, buried in the body [378].

Only men capable of this 'vast imagination' could have produced the first poetry, in which, inspired by a fear and wonder whose causes lay beyond their powers of comprehension, the first poets saw in the physical forces of nature manifestations of informing deities. In such conceptions we find the proper material of poetry, namely, a 'credible impossibility'. Thus, even though 'it is impossible that bodies should be minds, yet it was believed that the thundering sky was Jove' (383).

Rationalization of the First Fables

As part of his overall endeavor Vico gives an account of how the first fables are to be understood. The account, naturally, grows out of and is consistent with Vico's rationalization of the primitive metaphysical outlook. The specific question that concerns Vico is how early man dealt with what today we understand as abstractions. Limited as he was in the formation of his reasoning powers, early man had not developed universal concepts. For him everything was particular. At the same time it is axiomatic that 'The human mind is naturally impelled to take delight in uniformity' (204). The notion of universal concepts being unavailable to them, the first poets apotheosized particulars into poetic characters:

> that is, imaginative class concepts or universals, to which, as to certain models or ideal particulars [they reduced] all the particular species which resemble them. Because of the resemblance, the ancient fables could not but be created appropriately. Just so the Egyptians reduced to the genus 'civil sage' all their inventions useful or necessary to the human race which are particular effects of civil wisdom, and because they could not abstract the intelligible genus 'civil sage', much less the form of civil wisdom in which these Egyptians were sages, they imaged it forth as Thrice-great Hermes. So far were the Egyptians, at the time when they were enriching the world with discoveries useful or necessary to the human race from being philosophers and understanding universals or intelligible class concepts [209].[2]

The rationalization given here for the import and function that Hermes had in the fables of the Egyptians is the same as that

2. Vico contrasts intelligible and imaginative class concepts. Intelligible would be such as are abstracted from the observation or experience of particular phenomena, the word expressing the generalization then signifying the characteristic properties of each and every particular object or experience that belonged to the general class. Thus, humanity, virtue, trade, as we understand these notions, would be intelligible class concepts. According to Vico the first speakers were incapable of forming such concepts. Imaginative class concepts, on the other hand, are arrived at by projecting onto a natural physical phenomenon characteristics of the human observer. This projection can take one of two forms: a class of identical phenomena can be represented by a titular divinity or hero, e.g. all flowers by Flora, all valorous men by Achilles, or a single, extensive phenomenon—the sky, the sea—can be represented by a divine being whose (attributed) sentient characteristics could be held responsible for the properties and activities of that phenomenon (viz., Jove, Neptune).

which we earlier saw given for those of Jove, Cybele, and Neptune, where it was said that 'by means of these three deities, they [that is, the Greek theological poets] explained everything appertaining to the sky, the earth, and the sea'. These gods were thus also poetic characters which stood generically for a variety of particulars.

Vico's analysis thus explains both the origin and the logical standing of the characters that appear in the first fables. On the basis of his analysis, Vico asserts further that the fables have univocal, not analogical, meanings. By way of assessing this significant claim, we must point first to a possible ambiguity in Vico's use of the word *fable*. We are accustomed to think of a fable as a story or narrative, and this indeed seems to be the sense in which Vico sometimes uses the word. But when Vico says that fables have univocal meanings, he is using *fable* in a different sense. A fable in this sense is to be equated with the imaginative class concepts that we have seen the poetic characters to represent. Thus Jove and Hermes, and not the stories in which they appear, are fables. Moreover, when these fables (fabulated characters) occur in the mythologies, their proper interpretation is as allegory. This is described in paragraph 403:

> Thus the mythologies, as their name indicates, must have been the proper languages of the fables; the fables being imaginative class concepts, as we have shown, the mythologies must have been the allegories corresponding to them. Allegory is defined as *diversiloquium* insofar as, by identity not of proportion but (to speak scholastically) of predicability, allegories signify the diverse species or the diverse individuals comprised under these genera. So that they must have a univocal signification connoting a quality common to all their species and individuals (as Achilles connotes an idea of valor common to all strong men, or Ulysses an idea of prudence common to all wise men); such that these allegories must be the etymologies of the poetic languages, which would make their origins all univocal, whereas those of the vulgar languages are more often analogical.

This passage requires some discussion. To begin with, we observe that the word *allegory* is subject to the same (systematic) ambiguity as we noted earlier in the case of *fable*. Moreover, some explanation is in order regarding the manner in which the two notions are related. In addition to all this, there is a problem connected with Vico's usage as regards analogy and its relation to univocality.

A name like Jove or Achilles, normally construed, refers to the god or hero who bears that name. In a standard reading of *The Iliad*, for example, one which approaches it as a fictive product, a work of the poetic imagination, such would be the signification of the names. On such a reading, we might say, the names are taken 'literally'—simply as referring to the individual entities which they designate—and the descriptions of the events in which those individuals figure, we might then say, are regarded as 'factual'. It is on the basis of this kind of reading that Plato in *The Republic* (Cornford, 1945, 75ff.) deplores those episodes in Homer where the gods are said to lie, where heroes engage in lamentations and, generally, where he deems the behavior unseemly. For Vico, a reading of this sort, in which 'Jove' names a particular god and 'Achilles' a particular hero, grossly mistakes the purport of those names. According to him the Homeric tales are to be seen not as poems but as mythologies. In this light the names (the fabulated characters) refer not to individuals but to imaginative class concepts, and the mythologies are then the allegories corresponding to them. Unlike a poem, therefore, which narrates the experiences of individual gods and heroes, a mythology, by the incorporation in its fables of a people's cultural development and outlook, embodies the history of a nation ('the fables were true and trustworthy histories of the customs of the most ancient peoples of Greece' [7]; 'the first fables must have contained civil truths, and must therefore have been the histories of the first peoples' [198]).

Vico's discussion contains an echo of the distinction drawn by Plato in the *Cratylus* between the analogical and the anomalistic basis of the first language. In paragraph 401 Vico says, '*Mythos* came to be defined for us as *vera narratio*, or true speech, the natural speech which first Plato and then Iamblichus said had been spoken in the world at one time. But this was mere conjecture on their part, and Plato's effort to recover this speech in the *Cratylus* was therefore vain, and he was criticized for it by Aristotle and Galen'. Vico then goes on, as we saw above,

> For that first language, spoken by the theological poets, was not a language in accord with the nature of the things it dealt with (as must have been the sacred language invented by Adam, to whom God granted divine onomathesia, the giving of names to things according to the nature of each), but was a fantastic speech making use of physical substances endowed with life and most of them imagined to be divine.

The natural speech which Vico alludes to here is, in Plato's terms, analogistic, that is, a speech in which the signs stand in a motivated, not an arbitrary, relation to the things they signify. This type of speech Vico allows for the sacred language of Adam but denies for the theological poets. At the same time, however, the language of these poets is not anomalistic, that is, arbitrary; the signs in their 'fantastic speech' may also be said to be motivated, only the motivation is not a function of any natural accord between the signs and the things they represent, it is a function of early man's metaphysical outlook. When 'Jove' is used to refer to the heavens, it is because the heavens were seen as animated. Thus the association of the sign and thing was not *determined* by a natural accord held to subsist between them; it was, instead, *prompted* by a projection from the imagination onto the thing. Neither term of Plato's dichotomy, therefore, comprehends Vico's idea of this early language.

Vico asserts that the ancient allegories have univocal signification, and he contrasts such allegories with those of the vulgar languages, where, he says, the signification is analogical. In order to assess this claim it is necessary to refer briefly to the writings of Aristotle, where these notions first make their appearance. At the beginning of the *Categories* Aristotle describes two semantic modes in which a word may signify—or, as he puts it, in which things may be named. A word has univocal signification when it

applies to more than one thing each of which has a nature conforming to the word's definition: thus 'animal' applies univocally
to a man and an ox, both being animate substances capable of
sensation (the definition of 'animal'). A word has equivocal signification when it applies to more than one thing, each of which
has a different nature (thus conforming to a different definition),
and the things agree only in being called by that word: 'dog' is
applied equivocally to a barking animal and a stellar constella-
tion. Words that signify univocally are called synonyms and
those that signify equivocally, homonyms.[3]

In the *Metaphysics* (1968, 61f., 137) Aristotle introduces an
additional way in which a word may signify. The word *medical*,
he says, relates in a variety of ways to the art of medicine:
'anything is said to be "medical" because it possesses the art of
medicine, or because it is naturally suited to the art, or because it
is what medicine does'. The mode of signification here, Aristotle
suggests, is analogical; 'medical' is said analogously of a physician, a scalpel, and an operation. If the relation involved here
should be set out in the form of a proportion, it would comprise
only three different terms: *medical : physician :: medical : scalpel*. If
we compare the proportion containing 'medical' with one that
we might construct using a univocal signifier, namely, *animal :
man :: animal : ox*, we again have but three different terms. There
is the difference, however, that 'animal', as being their genus,
categorially subsumes both man and ox; it therefore signifies
univocally, that is, with the same sense, and directly, of both
objects. With 'medical', on the other hand, the case is different. It
cannot signify physician and scalpel univocally, since its sense is
different on the two applications; there is no relation of species to
genus. At the same time, its signification is not equivocal, inasmuch as the relation of physician and scalpel to 'medical' is not
fortuitous; there does obtain an indirect relationship between
each and the signification of 'medical'. As Aristotle says,

> In truth, we use [such] terms neither in an equivocal nor in the
> same [that is, univocal] sense, but as "medical" may refer to a

3. See Aristotle (1973), pp. 13ff.

single object by various relations which are neither identical nor ambiguous; thus a patient, an operation, and a surgical instrument are all called "medical", not equivocally or to denote a single subject, but because all have some relation or other to a common point of reference.

Analogous signification thus has an underpinning of relations. The relations are not abstract, however, as are the categorial relations that underlie univocal signification; they are, instead, factual or empirical, resting on connections that exist in the world of experience.[4]

Now the Achilles (or Jove) of the mythologies is an imaginative class concept—or, as such concepts are otherwise called, a concrete universal. As such, the name assumes a mode of signification lying somewhere between (strict) univocity and (mere) analogy. It is not univocal in the strict sense, since no relation of generic subsumption holds between Achilles and other strong men. At the same time, its mode is not analogical. Unlike what obtains with 'medical', where the objects analogously related to that term are among themselves totally disparate (physician, scalpel, operation), both Achilles and a strong man are men. They may thus bear the *same* relation to a third term. We recall Vico's formulation,

> Allegory is defined as *diversiloquium* insofar as by identity not of proportion but (to speak scholastically) of predicability, allegories signify the diverse species or the diverse individuals comprised under these genera. So that they must have a univocal signification connoting a quality common to all their species and individuals (as Achilles connotes an idea of valor common to all strong men, or Ulysses an idea of prudence common to all wise men).

Rendering one of Vico's examples, we might put *valor : Achilles :: valor : strong man*. So that, since valor is common to (and hence predicable of) both strong men and Achilles, the name Achilles, as the universal class concept, signifies univocally; it stands not simply for an individual Greek warrior but for the genus.

4. For discussion of this difference see Levin, 1982b.

The difference between what Vico calls identity of proportion and identity of predicability stems from the fact that in the former the focus is on the analogous term (the analogon), in the latter on the analogates. In the former there is no similarity between the analogates; there is an identity in the proportions by which each analogate stands to the analogous term (the predicate). In identity of predicability, since the analogates are members of a common genus (or species), a similarity holds between them, and it is because of this similarity that they take the same predicate. Thus 'medical' is predicated proportionally of a physician and a scalpel, but 'valorous' is predicated identically of Achilles and a strong man. Achilles becomes the bearer of an attribute common to diverse species and individuals, an attribute which, from having been predicated distributively of all strong men, he, as the name of a universal class concept, comes to epitomize. In this way also, the meaning of the allegory is univocal, the diversity of specific origins being united in and identified with the eponymous bearer.

As opposed to this—their univocal status and function in the heroic language of the mythologies—Vico says that in the vulgar languages the allegories are 'more often analogical'. What he probably means by this is that in such languages the allegories have a background like that of 'medical', that is, one in which a single predicate comes to be used as representative for a set of objects and properties which, though not similar among themselves, stand each in an analogous relation to that term. If this is his meaning, however, he does not express it in so many words. The nearest he comes to an explanation occurs in paragraph 935, in which, after describing the characters used in the theological and heroic poetry, that is, the types of imaginative class concepts represented respectively by Jove and Achilles, Vico continues, 'Finally, there were invented the vulgar characters which went along with the vulgar languages. The latter are composed of words, which are genera, as it were, of the particulars previously employed by the heroic languages; as, to repeat an example cited above [460], out of the heroic phrase "The blood boils in my heart" they made the word "I am angry" '. In the paragraph (460) which Vico mentions, he deals with the same theme, this time in the course of discussing the transition from poetic language to prose:

> For after the poets had formed poetic speech by associating particular ideas, as we have fully shown, the people went on to form prose speech by contracting into a single word, as into a genus, the parts which poetic speech had associated. Take for example the poetic phrase "The blood boils in my heart," based on a property natural, eternal, and common to all mankind. They took the blood, the boiling, and the heart, and made of them a single word, as it were a genus, called in Greek *stomachos*, in Latin *ira*, and in Italian *collera* ['I am angry']

The process that Vico here describes compares in a significant way with poetic allegory in that here too one term is made to stand generically for others. The difference is that in the poetic allegories the sense of the term is univocal, in the vulgar allegories it is not. Vico thought it was analogical; thus as 'medical' stands to (comprises) physician and scalpel, so 'angry' stands to (comprises) blood and boiling (in the heart).

This concludes our examination of Vico's 'Poetic Metaphysics'. The aspect of his account that is for us of primary importance springs from his recognition that for early man the relation between language and reality was fundamentally different from what that relation consists in for us. For us (as for those generations that succeeded early man) what we think the world is like consists essentially with its actual nature. This consistency developed as man came more and more to know the properties and principles of physical reality. Our language reflects the historical process whereby fact and our understanding have been brought into conformity. The mistake of those philosophers and scholars who speculated on the origin of language lay, according to Vico, in their unexamined assumption that early man was equipped with the same capacities for understanding his world as were men of subsequent eras. All such accounts are therefore *rational* accounts, presupposing that early man possessed an understanding of the physical world much like the one possessed by us.[5] This for Vico is a fundamental mistake. The 'master key' to his *New Science*, 'which cost [him] the persistent research of almost all [his] literary life', lay in the discovery that the early gentile peoples 'were poets who spoke in poetic characters' (the class concepts) and this 'by a demonstrated necessity of nature' (34). The demonstration proceeds from Vico's explanation of early man's metaphysical outlook. From this outlook there necessarily follows the 'poetic' vision of the outer world. So that what to us are 'fantastic' conceptions were for early man straightforward descriptions of the world as he naturally understood it.

It follows from all this that the poems of early man, 'fantastic' as they might appear to us, were intended (and were taken) literally. This is the position we have adopted in this study as regards the interpretation of certain poets. The difference, of course, is that for early man his response was the natural one. To him his poetry was 'factual'; the need to construe was unimaginable, there being no conceivable basis for him to do so (a corollary being that in the context of early poetry the notion of linguistic deviance makes no sense). For us today to read poetry in this direct, unmediated fashion requires, as we have seen, the overcoming of deep and powerful linguistic and conceptual conventions that have grown up in the subsequent historical development.

Metaphor in the Vichian Context

Vico's treatment of metaphor is presented in the section entitled 'Poetic Logic', a section which deals with the question of tropes in general and which immediately follows the 'Poetic Metaphysics'. The relationship between the two discussions is described by Vico in the section's opening paragraph:

> That which is metaphysics insofar as it contemplates things in all the forms of their being, is logic insofar as it considers things

5. Compare Rousseau's remark (1966, 11): 'The language of the first men is represented to us as the tongues of geometers, but we see that they were the tongues of poets'.

in all the forms by which they may be signified. Accordingly, as poetry has been considered by us as a poetic metaphysics in which the theological poets imagined bodies to be for the most part divine substances, so now that same poetry is considered as poetic logic, by which it signifies them [400].

We have already described a fundamental aspect of poetic logic in our discussion of the poetic characters, where the names of certain gods and heroes are used as designations of imaginative class concepts. Looked at as *expressions*, these names are the logical outcome of the underlying metaphysical outlook. Vico proceeds now to describe other forms of expression which assume tropological value for the same underlying reason. Before moving to his discussion of the tropes, however, we shall look briefly into the general background for the production of metaphors.

In the tradition of classical rhetoric two fundamental motivations are advanced for the employment of metaphoric terms. The chief motivation of course is to make the description vivid and arresting; the other motivation arises from a gap, or lacuna, in the lexicon and is referred to as 'catachresis'. In the former use the metaphor is a substitute means to describe a condition for which a proper term is available; in catachresis it is an expedient means to describe a condition for which no proper term exists. Catachresis is thus metaphor by default—compare Quintilian (1953, III, 303) where he says, 'As an example of a necessary metaphor I may quote the following usage in vogue with peasants when they call a vinebud *gemma*, a gem (what other term is there which they could use?)'. Now as Vico describes the origin and nature of the tropes they are all catachretic in their motivation. As we might expect, however, the principle behind the notion of catachresis must be modified in the context of Vico's assumptions. At the stage of which Vico writes, the lexicon available to man is an outgrowth of his metaphysical outlook. The words it contains reflect his primitive, unelaborated mentality. He has a complete set of words describing his corporeal and emotional natures and, perhaps, the natural objects in his environment. He lacks words for abstract qualities and for any physical properties that govern the life and activities of those objects. His lexical gaps are therefore extensive and systematic. So that where later uses of cata-chresis are more or less unsystematic, being essentially a matter of linguistic accident, his are indexical, pointing by implication to a characteristic orientation toward his world.

Thus, as opposed to the *lexical* gaps which are the motivation for the standard variety of catachresis, the catachreses of the first poets served the purpose of filling *cognitive* gaps. Consider in this connection an expression like 'mouth of the river'. Viewed as a standard example of catachresis, the use of 'mouth' would be seen as motivated by a similarity between the opening of the human mouth and the widening contours of a river as it enters the sea. Should a first poet have used the same expression, it would also have been catachretic; but the motivation in this case would have been the apprehending of the river as an animated being, thus as in fact having a mouth. Of course, as we have seen, this ap-prehension of the river was a natural consequence of the first metaphysics. At the same time, the use of an expression like 'mouth of the river' would have grown out of a *projection*—consistent or natural as it may have been metaphysically—from properties that early man knew of in humans to a natural body of a different kind. The gap that the catachretic use had to fill was thus a cognitive gap. In the one case there is extension of a *word* into a new linguistic context, in the other the extension of *cognition* to a different empirical phenomenon. It was not as though men saw rivers as rivers and asked themselves for the word that would express the similarity they saw between such bodies of water and human beings; it was rather that men saw rivers as sentient entities and asked themselves what organ was common to both types of being; not 'It is like a human mouth', rather 'It is a river mouth'.

Later in this chapter we shall have to compare the cognitive extensions that we have posited as the basis for the met. phors of early poetry with the different basis upon which operate the conceptual metaphors that we have postulated for modern po-etry—as also the degenerate (that is, catachretic) function of the one with the full-fledged function of the other. At this point, however, we must raise and consider another question. In what light would the first poets themselves have viewed their descriptions; that is, if they *necessarily* or naturally saw physical bodies as animated, in what sense were their descriptions of those bodies metaphorical at all? Vico is of course aware of this problem, even if he does not raise it explicitly. Although, as we shall see below, he describes metaphor, metonymy, synecdoche, and irony (the four tropes to which he says all others are reducible) and finds them (all but irony) operative in the first poetry, he makes clear that his analysis is retrospective—approached from the standpoint of later development. He writes:

> All the tropes—which have hitherto been considered ingenious inventions of writers, were necessary modes of expression of all the first poetic nations, and had originally their full native propriety. But these expressions of the first nations later became figurative when, with the further development of the human mind, words were invented which signified abstract forms or genera comprising their species or relating parts with their wholes [409].

So that, as Vico here makes plain, tropes are reasonably seen as such only when they can be read off against another, proper mode of expression. In the absence of any such expression, the tropes *are* the proper mode. And just as these first descriptions become linguistic metaphors only from the perspective of the subsequent linguistic development, so they become conceptual metaphors only from the perspective of the subsequent metaphysical development.

The tropes that Vico specifically discusses are metaphor, metonymy, synecdoche, and irony. He writes: 'All the metaphors conveyed by likenesses taken from bodies to signify the operations of abstract minds must date from times when philosophies were taking shape. The proof of this is that in every language the terms needed for the refined arts and recondite sciences are of rustic origin' (404). He then continues:

> It is noteworthy that in all languages the greater part of the expressions relating to inanimate things are formed by meta-

phors from the human body and its parts and from the human senses and passions. Thus, head for top or beginning; the brow and shoulders of a hill; the eyes of needles and of potatoes; mouth for any opening; the lip of a cup or pitcher; the teeth of a rake, a saw, a comb; . . . the flesh of fruits; a vein of rock or mineral; the blood of grapes for wine; the bowels of the earth. Heaven or the sea smiles; the wind whistles; the waves murmur; a body groans under a great weight. The farmers of Latium used to say the fields were thirsty, bore fruit, were swollen with grain; and our rustics speak of plants making love, vines going mad, resinous trees weeping [405].

In the above collection of examples we can separate two distinct types of metaphor. All, according to our analysis, are (cognitively) catachretic. The examples of the first type, however (up to 'bowels of the earth'), seem somewhat less interesting than those of the second ('heaven smiled', et seq.). The metaphors of the first set are formed by attributing to inanimate things properties of 'the human body and its parts', those of the second by attributing to them properties of the 'human senses and passions'. A consequence of these two varieties of attribution is that the former yields a description of a body, the latter a proposition involving a body; in the first case a body is more fully characterized as to its physical makeup, in the second it is accorded life and vitality. The first type of attribution would be reckoned catachretic on any account of the process, including that of the classical tradition, but the second would in that tradition be reckoned a full-fledged metaphor. This distinction emerges only when the matter is looked at retrospectively, however; looked at synchronically there is no such distinction to be drawn between the two types of metaphor—both are consistent with the constrained metaphysical outlook. As Vico says,

> All . . . is a consequence of our axiom that man in his ignorance makes himself the rule of the universe, for in the examples cited he has made of himself an entire world. So that, as rational metaphysics teaches that man becomes all things by understanding them (homo intelligendo fit omnia), this imagina-

tive metaphysics shows that man becomes all things by *not* understanding them (*homo non intelligendo fit omnia*); and perhaps the latter proposition is truer than the former, for when man understands he extends his mind and takes in the things, but when he does not understand he makes the things out of himself and becomes them by transforming himself into them [405].

Given a logic based on such a metaphysics, 'the first poets had to give names to things from the most particular and the most sensible ideas'. Synecdoches are names springing from the former (that is, particular) ideas, metonymies names springing from the latter (sensible) ideas. 'Metonymy of agent for act resulted from the fact that names for agents were commoner than names for acts. Metonymy of subject for form and accident was due to inability to abstract forms and qualities from subjects. Certainly metonymy as cause for effect produced in each case a little fable, in which the cause was imagined as a woman clothed with her effects; ugly Poverty, sad Old Age, pale Death' (406). The treatment of metonymy is again based on the conceptual poverty that Vico postulates for early man. Today we explain metonymy as deriving from a relation *that we are conscious of* which holds between the thing to be designated and features that in some general way are associated with it: we use 'a Cicero' for an orator, 'Homer' for his works, 'crown' for a king, and so on, in all cases aware of the grounds for doing so. As Vico suggests by his examples, however, the first metonymies resulted largely from ignorance. The metonymic expression was not a form that registered a link between a designatum and one of its known referential accompaniments; it was rather a necessary makeshift—a retraction from the unknown to the known.

Since the synecdoche here in question is a transference from particular ideas, Vico treats only of the part-whole and the species-genus relationships. He instances the shift of 'mortals' from designating only men to comprising persons in general, the use of 'head' for person, 'roof' for a house, 'poop' for a ship, and so on (407). All these examples—of both metonymy and synecdoche—are catachretic in our terms, following from the projection of known quantities onto quantities (qualities) which in their abstractness lay beyond the power of early man to rationalize as such. Vico points out in passing that the word *man* is in fact abstract, 'comprehending as in a philosophic genus the body and all its parts, the mind and all its faculties, the spirit and all its dispositions' (407).[6] The use of a word with such a signification was foreclosed to early man. Thus even the word *mortals*, which Vico has cited earlier as instancing synecdochic extension, must originally have been a metonymy for man.

Vico's treatment of irony is in the present context of considerable interest. Although he had included irony as one of the four tropes to which all others can be reduced, he takes it up now only to show that it has no applicability in the context of the early poetry. Nor should this be a surprising conclusion. He writes,

> Irony certainly could not have begun until the period of reflection, because it is fashioned of falsehood by dint of a reflection which wears the mask of truth. Here emerges a great principle of human institutions, confirming the origin of poetry disclosed in this work: that since the first men of the gentile world had the simplicity of children, who are truthful by nature, the first fables could not feign anything false; they must therefore have been as they have been defined above, true narration [408].

The status of irony in the tropological field is somewhat compromised. In the ancient rhetorics it is both reckoned one of the (four) major tropes and assigned also to the category of figures of thought (cf. Quintilian, 1953, III, 349). Although Vico includes irony among the tropes, his discussion of it above is best understood if we approach it as a figure of thought. Without exercising ourselves over questions of detail, we may define a figure of thought as comprised in the intention that our expression should be interpreted otherwise than as what it explicitly says. The

---

6. Compare Rousseau (1966, 33): '[Primitive men] had the concept of a father, a son, a brother, but not that of a man. Their hut contained all their fellow men'.

difference between a figure of thought and metaphor (which agree with each other in the above respect) is that what the expression explicitly says has in a figure of thought a perfectly respectable meaning taken literally. To interpret it figuratively requires not a modification of the express meaning, as in metaphor, but a recoil from that meaning in favor of another, frequently its opposite. 'Our life is but a dream' requires us to construe the meaning, since the words in the expression are semantically incompatible with one another. By contrast, for a sentence like 'My professor is a prince' to be taken ironically, the interpretation, inasmuch as the sentence has a perfectly straightforward meaning taken literally (it could even be true), must be arrived at by first rejecting that meaning. Like other figures of thought, then, irony is a form behind which there lies an indirect or devious intent.[7] It thus implies a sophistication of mind that was completely foreign to early man. Neither irony nor any other figure of thought lay within his expressive capabilities. We might note here that figures of speech, as later rhetoricians understood the notion, likewise played no role in his poetic exposition. Given his intellectual orientation, everything that he said in his poetry was meant as stated and was expressed as was necessary. The first poets were no rhetoricians.

Vichian and Conceptual Metaphor

We began this chapter by indicating that there exist certain similarities between the view of metaphor that I have been advocating, that is, as conceptual rather than linguistic, and the views of certain thinkers who have treated metaphor in the context of language origins, and we used the account given by Vico as an example of the views advanced by those thinkers. The similarity of the two approaches consists essentially in their agreement that metaphors are intended as literal descriptions of some reality and should so be understood. Their dissimilarity

7. For some discussion of this aspect of irony and other figures of thought see Levin, 1982a.

derives from the different metaphysical outlooks prevailing at the two stages for which they respectively give an account—the different notions, that is, of what reality consists in.

In discussing the metaphoric practice of the first poets we introduced the notion of catachresis and characterized it as a degenerate form of metaphor. It is metaphoric in the sense that a word is transferred from its proper range of use into another context. But since it does not in this process of transfer replace a customary or proper term (there being none), it does not serve to activate the kind of intellectual play associated with true metaphors. We may consider catachresis degenerate, further, in that the function it performs could be managed more efficiently by other means. A catachresis ekes out the language. Its function would be better served if a proper term for the use already existed in the language or, failing that, by a new coinage explicitly designed to fill the lexical gap. Seen in this way, catachresis implies a deficiency. In the standard case this deficiency is a matter of the language. For early man, however, the deficiency was of a different kind, a function of his underdeveloped cognitive capacities. It was this latter type of deficiency that the first metaphors were designed to eke out. To the extent that they manifest uses of the language, the two types of catachresis stand on the same footing. Yet what the metaphors of the first poet implemented was not the mere extension of a word's privileges of occurrence; it implemented an extension of his cognitive range. The deficiency in his case was made good not by plugging a word into an unaccustomed slot but by projecting the properties that he felt characterized his own constitution onto nonhuman objects, in this way endowing them with his own sensibilities. The first metaphors, therefore, for all their being catachretic, have a profound substantivity. At the same time, however, they have a radically different grounding from conceptual metaphors.

According to Vico, early man saw the universe in his own image. Thus the descriptions of the first poets, in particular as applied to physical nature, were anthropomorphic. Ignorant of the real forces that vitalized and activated the natural objects in their environment, they subsumed those forces under animate beings, in some cases adding divinity to the bodies thus animated. From the standpoint of their primitive metaphysics, there was nothing in this process that was strange, inappropriate, or irregular. In projecting features and attributes of their own human natures onto those of outward physical phenomena, they were merely being consistent with their notions of how the world was ordered. We must remember that, as Vico repeatedly states, these early men were as yet incapable of abstraction—to which should be added that they were ignorant also of the forces that governed physical nature. In the light of these intellectual limitations, the (fanciful) descriptions that occur in the first poetry must be taken at face value, as literal descriptions of a felt reality. If we see these descriptions as metaphors, therefore, it is only in the catachretic sense that we have described above.

In the course of man's subsequent development the cognitive deficiencies under which early man labored in respect to his comprehension of the physical universe have for all practical purposes been made good. In addition, the inability to form abstractions has long since been superseded by a noteworthy development of just that ability. The entire metaphysical picture has changed. Thus when we now encounter in poetry an expression that is singular in that the factual claim it appears to make is outlandish or bizarre, we have to approach the question of its corrigibility according to a different set of ground rules. We cannot appeal to cognitive limitations, as was done in the case of the first poets. We do not now labor under those limitations. So that today, as has been indicated, the problem posed by such an expression is generally seen as one of semantic adjustment. On this approach the question of metaphysical outlook does not arise—except in the sense of an implicit limit which cannot be transgressed. Metaphor is therefore seen as an essentially semantic problem. This is true even though factors of reference and background knowledge and beliefs may also come into play, since these factors are entertained as part of the 'meaning' of the words involved. All this follows of course from the implicit assumption that the world is a constant and that the language, if it makes any factual claim at all, makes it about that world.

As soon as we free ourselves from the tacit assumption that the world is a fixed quantity and thus that it is the expression that must be adjusted in any lack of fit between that quantity and what an expression says, we open up an entire range of new possibilities. Where the first poet, on hearing thunder, would look at the sky and say, 'Jove is angry' and conceive of the sky as an animated being, we, on reading the sentence 'The sky is angry', will conceive of a world in which the sky may be angry. The attribution of divinity apart, there is a profound difference between the two responses. The first poet simply projected what he knew further into the world in which he lived; he believed that Jove was a part of that world. But in order for us from our metaphysical vantage point to conceive of the sky as angry, we have to transcend our world. For us, therefore, the status of the expression is not a mere (cognitive) catachresis; it evokes an act of construal, an act in which the state of affairs described by the expression is conceived of as a possibility. The locus of such 'possibilities' is a metaphoric world.

6

Expressibility and Aquinas' Theory of Analogy

One characteristic that most commentators attribute to language is an extreme resourcefulness. There is nothing we can think of, it is maintained, that we cannot express. Searle (1969, 88) formulates this condition in his 'principle of expressibility': 'whatever can be meant can be said'. Katz (1972, 19) finds a suggestion of the principle in Frege and explicates it as 'anything which is thinkable is communicable through some sentence of a natural language (because the structure of sentences mirrors the structure of thoughts)'. In these (and similar) characterizations the focus is on language, on its expressive power. If anything is thinkable, the argument runs, it can be expressed in language. Logically equivalent to this is the argument that anything that cannot be expressed in language is not thinkable. Thus, proof that one is disposing of a thought is provided by its verbal expression, and there can be no other proof. The possibility that there might be thoughts which are unexpressible, or expressions of less than or other than fully-formed thoughts, is supererogated by the principle. In conditioning thoughts on expressibility, the principle abstracts from and simply neutralizes the problematic status of thinkability.

It should be mentioned that most assertions of the expressibility principle add a codicil. It is conceded that a speaker may have a thought for which his language does not provide the precise means of expression. In such cases, however, it is held to be possible—through neologism, borrowing, or new word formation—to augment the language and so make it capable of expressing that thought (see Searle, 1969, 19–20). This ability to eke out the language, which in the context of the expressibility principle seems to render it utterly indefeasible, will be seen later, in a different context, not as a mark of language's resourcefulness but as a measure of its inherent limitations. In the new context the emphasis will be not on what can be expressed but on what can be thought. That question, as we have seen, is not really addressed by the expressibility principle, that is, it is not treated as a question in its own right; the focus, as mentioned above, is on language, on its expressive power. What interests us about the principle, however, with its implied claim of universal applicability, is precisely the extent to which it may, or may not, be relevant when the 'thoughts' in question are such as are associated with deviant sentences.

Thinkability

The question of what is thinkable has not been ignored by philosophers, however. But the answer to that question has taken the form not of a principle but of a limit. It is maintained that we cannot think of (in the sense that we cannot have the intuitive grasp of) anything that involves a contradiction. We recall that for Husserl (chapter 2) notions like square circle and wooden iron could be entertained by the mind only as 'mere' concepts, the possibility that they might be *presented* as intentions being foreclosed on a priori grounds. By way of reformulating Husserl's discussion in the context of thinkability, we might say that notions involving contradictions can be thought *about* but cannot be thought.

Another discussion of thinkability is presented in an essay by Hanson entitled 'Imagining the Impossible' (1971, 215–21). Hanson's purpose in this essay is to examine the logical status of statements like ' "X is a quadrilateral triangle" is impossible (i.e. of the form P.~P)' and 'It is impossible to imagine (or think) a quadrilateral triangle' (my paraphrase). The first statement is necessarily true in that its denial would not merely be false but self-contradictory. The second statement is also necessarily true, he argues, but in a different sense—not in that its denial is self-contradictory but in that there is no conceivable way to show that it is false. Hanson takes it as axiomatic that 'it is of the essence of imagining, thinking, and picturing that we cannot imagine, think, or picture what is logically impossible', and even though this axiom is not a tautology but is based on our experience, it is necessarily true. Its truth is determined for us by the way we in fact think; in fact, 'what is logically impossible is never discovered to be either thinkable, imaginable, or picturable'.

What the views discussed above have in common is that they tell us what we *cannot* think—what stands at the limit of our powers of thought. And that limit, as we have seen, is represented by notions like square circle and quadrilateral triangle, that is, notions that are internally contradictory. So far as the question goes of what we *can* think, we are left by inference with the expressibility principle (amended by the exclusion of contradictions): we can think only what we can express. In what follows, the shortcomings of that principle for the type of 'thoughts' that concern us will become clear.

Before embarking on that discussion, however, I shall comment briefly on another philosopher who, I believe, reflected on the question of what can be thought. I refer to Wittgenstein. That that question preoccupied him may be inferred from his assertion (1961, 5.6.) '*The limits of my language* mean the limits of my world'. The limits that in this assertion are presupposed for our language impose a corresponding limitation or boundary on our world. Wittgenstein does not spell out the implications of this assertion, but it is fair to assume that he understood something to lie beyond that boundary. Whether we can in some sense think about this beyond is a question left open by Wittgenstein; all he says is that we cannot speak about it. To be sure, a region of this sort—one beyond the reach of our language—has a highly problematic if not indeed a dubious ontological status. And, of course, Wittgenstein also said, 'What we cannot speak about we must pass over in silence' (1961, 7).[1] Now unless this statement is to be seen as a tautological banality, we must here also take Wittgenstein to be implying some further region of being—one which comprises elements that may impinge upon and affect our consciousness even though those affections cannot be translated into thoughts and thus be expressed. We may, in other words, have an awareness of things for the expression of which our language is not an adequate or appropriate vehicle. These 'awarenesses' may not, in the strict sense, be thoughts. They are more like intimations, promptings of the spirit which enter our consciousness even if they do not crystallize into conceptual constructions. They are 'thoughts' that, as we might say, lie too deep for words. I shall argue that thoughts like these are expressed in poetry but that, the nature of these thoughts being what it is, the language, in expressing them, is strangulated, twisted, and decentered from its normal mode of expression and rendered 'metaphoric', that these metaphors, in consequence, occupy that status not in virtue of their linguistic construction but in virtue of the mental exertion that lies behind and actuates them.

Limitations on the Expressive Power of Language

Generally speaking, a natural language is calculated to serve the needs of its speakers. As those needs change, the language too will change, dropping words whose usefulness has been outlived and adding words for which developments have

1. If we look at what precedes this statement (the last one in the *Tractatus*), we see it properly, I believe, as an expression of resignation or defeat. The statement is indeed a fitting close to the *logical* enterprise of the *Tractatus*. But the note of defeat emerges from considering what Wittgenstein seemed to feel was the little which that enterprise accomplished. What really counts, he seems to imply, is not what we can regiment of the world but how much is left out of that regimentation, how much more there in some sense is that lies beyond our power of comprehension For an attempt at a different explanation of this statement see Black (1964, 378ff.) It should be added that the meaning of '*The limits of my language* . . . ' would require a different analysis in the context of the *Philosophical Investigations* (1968), in which it would have relevance for the problem of 'other minds' and their accessibility.

created the need. These developments may be in the field of technology and science or in such cultural areas as religion, custom, or political institutions. All such developments are broad based, affecting the generality of a linguistic population or some sizable segment thereof. So far as the general problem of communication is concerned, such developments leave the situation in principle unchanged; the language continues adequate to communicative needs, speakers remain able to talk about the (evolving) world.

There are, however, communicative needs for the expression of which the language is not so accommodating. These needs are not broad based but pertain essentially to an individual, one who wishes to express an aspect of the world which may be 'real' only for that individual and for which, that being the case, his language has not developed appropriate means. This predicament is a commonplace for religious mystics and other subjects of divine inspiration. It is part of my argument that certain poets, at times of poetic inspiration, find themselves in the same predicament— that the insight they have into the world's phenomena leaves them with a vision which the language at their disposal is ill-equipped to express, and that consequently their poems must be seen as imperfect renderings of that vision. And, as I have been arguing, to regard this 'imperfection' as an artistically indirect way of describing something which could be 'perfectly', if unartistically, described is to mistake and demean the problem.

All of us speak quite naturally of flowers, birds, rivers, horses, and rocks. We say that the flower is fragrant, the bird is singing, the rock is cracked, and so on. We are able also to describe features that are specific to these phenomena: we say of a flower that it is axillary, of a bird that it is seed-eating, of a rock that it is igneous. Observations of both these types are made on the basis of features that these natural objects actually present to us. In this respect our observations about the objects of nature correspond to observations that we make about human beings, whose characteristics we likewise describe on the basis of features that they present to us—we say that a person is well-groomed, or laughing, or pale, the evidence for these judgments being primary and direct appearances. Where human beings are concerned, however, we speak also of states or conditions for whose existence the evidence is only indirect. We say, for example, that a person is happy or sad. Even if we are led to these judgments after the person tells us that he is in this condition, we have only his report—which for a variety of reasons may be false or incorrect. In most cases, however, our judgment is made on the basis not of report but of observed, secondary behavior. And even though the possibility of error is here also present, we use words like *happy* and *sad* with a large measure of confidence that they fairly describe the mental or emotional state of other humans.

According to Russell (1976, 485), the basis for this confidence is a projection from our own experience onto that of another human being. If we observe in another person a form of behavior which in our own case is caused by a certain mental or emotional state, we attribute that state to the other person.[2] I would argue that with so-called insentient or nonhuman objects these outward appearances may also be regarded as manifestations of inner states. It is true that it rarely occurs to the average person to consider what the flower's inner state may be when it gives off fragrance, the bird's when it is singing, the rock's when it is cracked. We do not, in short, try to see into the life of things. But this empathic penetration is the very impulse and ambition of the poet. As Keats put it in his little poem 'Where's the Poet?':

> 'Tis the man who with a bird,
> Wren or eagle, finds his way to
> All its instincts; he hath heard
> The lion's roaring, and can tell
> What his horny throat expresseth.

2. Russell writes:

I am, of course, not discussing the history of how we come to believe in other minds. . . . What I am discussing is the possibility of a postulate which shall establish a rational connection between this belief and data, e.g. between the belief 'Mother is angry' and the hearing of a loud voice.

The abstract schema seems to be as follows. We know, from observation of ourselves, a causal law of the form 'A causes B', where A is a 'thought' and B a physical occurrence. We sometimes observe a B when we cannot observe any A; we can then infer an unobserved A.

It is into this *inner* life that the poet tries to project himself, and it is of this inner life that he tries to communicate his vision. The question is how the poet is to accomplish this. If we consider the matter carefully we may conclude that the inner life of natural things is closed to us not by any necessity deriving from our affective powers but by limitations imposed on us by our language. If we are affected by natural objects we find ourselves in a state of mind which we cannot adequately express. Suppose that, on seeing a rose blooming, I feel that bloom to be an outward manifestation of its inner state. How would I express that feeling? I might say, 'The rose is happy'. On the face of it I am proceeding just as I would if I made such a comment of a friend on noticing certain of his outward manifestations. At this point the problem emerges: in the absence of a predicate that specifically describes the inner state of a nonhuman object we use one that is defined for humans. It is a fact about our language that for the description of inner states we have, almost exclusively, only such as apply to humans. When, therefore, we wish to remark such a state of nonhuman objects we are forced to use predicates defined for a different sort. In theory, there is no reason why we could not have added to our language whole classes of words defined for the inner states of natural phenomena. The need for such terms has not been felt, however, since most people have no reason to use them. But for poets I believe there is such a need. Yet poets are not in the business of language reform; they use the language at their disposal. In order to express what they see and feel, however, they strain that language to the utmost. This of course is a claim commonly made for poets. In its usual form, though, it amounts to saying that for the proper expression of his thought the poet exploits the rich and varied resources of his language, plumbing its lexicon to find the exact word and stretching to novel limits its syntactic forms. Poets certainly do this. But such linguistic exercises are compatible with the expression of ordinary thoughts. The thoughts that we are concerned with are extraordinary and such as the language is not really equipped to express. Seen in this light, an expression like 'The rose is happy' reflects not the artistic or felicitous play of language but its great laboring—a striving after expression that is doomed to failure by the build of the language.

The question of how adequate our language is to express the facts of our experience is not restricted to the problem posed by the inner states of natural objects (assuming of course that this constitutes a problem). The question arises also in respect to theological discourse. It is from this angle that Kenneth Burke approaches the question in *The Rhetoric of Religion* (1970, 14f.). He declares that there are 'four realms to which words may refer'. There are words that refer to the natural realm, the sociopolitical realm, and there are words that refer to words. These three orders of words cover the world of everyday experience. In addition, however, we use words that refer to the 'supernatural'. Concerning the latter he writes:

> The supernatural is by definition the realm of the 'ineffable'. And language by definition is not suited to the expression of the 'ineffable'. So our words for the fourth realm, the super-natural or 'ineffable', are necessarily borrowed from our words for the sorts of things we can talk about literally, our words for the three empirical orders (the world of everyday experience).

Burke says earlier of this borrowing that it is 'by analogy from our words for the other three orders'. Later in this chapter I shall take up the question of theological discourse and the role that analogy has been held to play in such discourse. Here I wish only to indicate the parallelism between Burke's conclusion about the unsuitability of our language to express the 'ineffable' and the corresponding conclusion that we have arrived at regarding our responses to the inner states of natural objects. It should now also be apparent that our language is not an ideally efficient mechanism, one perfectly suited to the expression of all our needs—and, moreover, that the expressibility principle can only be maintained by the allowance of various shifts and ad hoc devices, and that these shifts and devices may produce linguistic concoctions that are at best compromises and at worst totally inadequate expressions of what we may wish to communicate.

A Proposal for Augmenting the Language

To bring into sharper focus the linguistic limitations under which we labor, let us experiment with a means to augment our language. Suppose that instead of saying 'The rose is happy' we introduce for our purpose a new predicate—say, 'oobis'. We could now say 'The rose is oobis', where 'oobis' might be defined as 'happy, *sp.* of flowers'. This definition, we notice, is tendentious, evincing in its form the tyranny that human states and conditions exert over our responses to objects in other domains. By way of ameliorating that tendentiousness we might modify our definition of 'oobis' to read 'a state in flowers that corresponds to happiness in humans'. This is an improvement, since the meaning of 'oobis' is now given not as a species of human happiness but as a nonhuman counterpart of it. Of course, from the introduction of a word and its definition it does not necessarily follow that we know what the word means. We know what 'happy' means because we have experience of that state in ourselves and others. It is, on the other hand, not clear that we have experienced 'oobisness'. Certainly we have not experienced it in ourselves. The question is whether we have ever empathized with that condition in a flower. This is a question that each one must decide for himself or herself. The point of our experiment, however, is not to facilitate apprehension of a flower's inner state but to bring into relief the extent to which the limits of our language constrain our view of the world. In the absence of words specifically defined for conditions that we may wish to attribute to certain phenomena, we have difficulty not merely in describing those conditions but, also and more important, we find it difficult to bring those conditions to mental awareness.

I said above that introduction of the word *oobis* along with its definition would not necessarily facilitate our apprehension of a flower's inner state. I wish now to suggest that it might serve, nonetheless, to prime our readiness for such apprehension. Let us notice first that an utterance like 'The rose is happy' is quite ineffectual for this purpose. If we take it as a standard metaphor, we simply preclude the possibility of any such apprehension. If on the other hand we take it literally, the entire burden of application rests on us; we have mentally to process and formulate the meaning of 'happy' as pertaining to flowers. In other words, the language is not serving our needs; it is simply presenting us with a problem. With 'The rose is oobis', again, the language is working for us. Part of the mental calculation has already been coded into the language, and the reader's task is to that extent lightened. We should notice that introduction of 'oobis' has implications also for the meaning of 'rose' (and the names of other flowers). Roses would now be seen as subject to the inner state defined by 'oobis'. Thus the entire utterance of 'The rose is oobis' would be semantically transmuted.

Needless to say, there is about this entire discussion an element of factitiousness. It will be said that if we as speakers really had a need for a predicate like 'oobis' it would be in the language; the absence of such a predicate is proof that we have no need for it. I have, however, not introduced this discussion of 'oobis' in order to show that we need such a predicate. My object has been simply to approach from a different angle the problem attendant on the literal interpretation of an utterance like 'The rose is happy' and attempt to show thereby how great is the semantic and epistemological distance that such an expression is used to close.

We can now see, I believe, that the expressibility principle is quite problematic—it might even be said that there is about it an air of banality. It amounts to saying that in a natural language there is an expression for everything that is expressed. If we ask, however, whether the language enables us to express everything that we may wish to express, the principle is unhelpful. For someone who is affectively responding to what he believes is an inner state in a flower and wishes to verbalize that response, the language is not forthcoming. For such a response an expression like 'The rose is happy' is simply inadequate. It is not an eking out of the language, such as is countenanced by the codicil to the expressibility principle; it is, rather, a collapse into its preexistent form. It is not an advance but a retreat. In this connection the role of analogy is sometimes invoked to mediate between the face of an expression and its intended meaning. From our present vantage point such an invocation is a mark of language's surrender, a handing over of its responsibility to its users. It is they who must read a sense into an expression which conveys—by the default of language—an indirect and imprecise impression of a certain phenomenon or experience. 'The rose is happy' is disassembled *by the reader* into four terms, of which one, the rose's counterpart to human happiness, is left floating in a semantic limbo. Granted, there may be in such an exercise an access of suggestiveness. But it yields no insight into the nature of the experience that might lie behind the utterance.

The problem we are dealing with is fundamental. It is a question of whether the language is the servant of our needs or we are the slaves of our language. Goethe once said (Eckermann, 1930, 414):

> All languages have arisen from surrounding human necessities, human occupations, and the general feelings and views of man. If, now, a superior man gains an insight into the secret operations of nature, the language which has been handed down to him is not sufficient to express anything so remote from human affairs. He ought to have at command the language of spirits to express adequately his peculiar perceptions. But as this is not so, he must, in his views of the extraordinary in nature, always grasp at human expressions; with which he almost always falls too short, lowering his subject, or even injuring and destroying it.

We do not command the language of spirits; we must, as Goethe said, make do with the language of mortals—deficient as that language may be. And the ones affected most acutely by that deficiency are poets. Poets are par excellence those 'superior' beings who gain insight into the secrets of nature and who find the language inadequate to the expression of those insights. That being the case, a heavy interpretive responsibility falls on the reader. I have already said that this responsibility is not properly discharged by the standard move to analogy. The reader must start from the actual utterance but then, in awareness of the poet's linguistic straits, he must negotiate through that utterance to the poet's original insight. This negotiation on the part of the reader represents not so much a semantic construal as it does a phenomenological or conceptual construal. In processing an utterance like 'The rose is happy' he does not try to figure out what sense to give to 'happy'; he tries to understand what it would be like for a rose to be happy.

I have described elsewhere (Levin 1977, 1979) what is to be understood by phenomenological construal.[3] Given a deviant utterance like 'The rose is happy', there are fundamentally two interpretive strategies that we may elect to adopt. On the first strategy we try to rationalize its meaning. We interpret the utterance to mean 'The rose is blooming, fragrant' or some such. It is important to recognize that in adopting this strategy we tacitly assume the world as a constant factor; that is, in the incompatibility between what the utterance says and the 'facts' of the world, we assume that the latter are fixed, determined by natural laws and the results of our ordinary experience. On the second strategy we take the language (of the utterance) as fixed. We then must construe the world, construe it in such a way as to admit for it the possibility that a flower can be happy. A world that admits of such possibilities is a metaphoric world and, in the face of a 'deviant' expression, it is only by the conceiving of such possibilities that a reader can approximate to the insight or vision that the poet has achieved and (imperfectly) expressed.

Aquinas' Theory of Analogy

If our assumption is granted that the feelings a poet has the need to express are such as exceed the resources of his language, the poet is thereby placed in the company of another class of writers who labor under the same difficulty. I refer to those whose profession it is to discourse about God. In this case also feelings are involved for the expression of which the language is a poor and inadequate vehicle. St. Augustine said: 'You are my God, my Life, my holy Delight, but is this enough to say of you?

---

3. I there mistakenly referred to this type of construal as phenomenalistic.

Can any man say enough when he speaks of you? Yet woe betide those who are silent about you. For even those who are most gifted with speech cannot find words to describe you' (*Confessions*, I, 4). And yet the need for such description continues to be felt. Unequal as it may be to the task, the language must be pressed to serve this need. This is particularly true for those theologians who assume the responsibility of explaining the ways of God to man. In this regard one theologian who stands out is St. Thomas Aquinas, who developed his doctrine of analogy by way of dealing with this problem. To call his production a theory would be to make too strong a claim since, as is pointed out by Klubertanz (1960, 3), although Aquinas speaks of analogy in almost every one of his works, 'he nowhere gives a thorough *ex professo* treatment of the problem'. For this reason also it is not easy to present in summary form exactly what Aquinas' doctrine of analogy amounts to. There is, however, so substantial a discussion of the question in his works that a résumé of its chief characteristics is entirely feasible.[4] In discussing his doctrine I hope to show the parallelism that exists between the problem faced by Aquinas and our own and also the light that his solution throws on the general question of 'expressibility'.

The problem faced by Aquinas was this: how is it possible to speak of God and man in the same language? Aquinas could not indulge the expedient of entertaining a separate, a divine language for discoursing about God, since Scripture uses human language to make statements about God (for example, 'God is wise', 'God is good'), and such statements, as revelation, must be taken as true assertions. He therefore had to devise a scheme in which such predicates as 'wise' and 'good', the very predicates whose normal employ is for human beings, could be understood also as applying to God. It was to meet this problem that Aquinas developed his doctrine of analogy.

Before undertaking a systematic exposition of Aquinas' doctrine, I shall summarize informally its salient characteristics and

---

4. I have consulted the following texts, among others: Burrell (1973); Copleston (1955); Klubertanz (1960); Phelan (1948); Ricoeur (1977); Ross (1976).

the implications that they have for the study of metaphor. 'Wise' and 'good', the kind of predicates for which the analogical doctrine was developed, are those that signify 'pure perfections', that is, such as are not associated with specific beings on the basis of their proper natures. We are thus not concerned with predicates like 'laughing' or 'happy', predicates peculiar to humans, or 'lion' or 'rock', predicates that refer to specific substances. When, as sometimes, such predicates in fact are used of God, they function metaphorically. Because such predicates are defined for and apply properly to created things, it is by extension that they are predicated of God. This extension is analogical, to be sure, but it is a defective analogy, the so-called analogy of improper proportionality. The proportionality is improper for the reason that 'lion', say, applies properly, that is, univocally, to creatures of that species, but improperly, thus metaphorically, to God. All this follows from the fact that 'lion' is a predicate defined for a specific nature. Where predicates signifying the 'pure perfections' are concerned, however, the so-called transcendental predicates, there is no such proper definition restricting their use to an order of created things. Such 'pure perfections' exist in God essentially and flow from Him to His creatures. They can therefore be predicated of both God and man. Not, to be sure, so that the predicate has univocal signification in the two applications, God being the exemplar of those perfections, man only participating in them. However, neither is the signification merely equivocal. There is a shared, a distributed, component of meaning. This meaning can thus apply analogically to God and to man. God being simple, comprising all His attributes in His being, a predicate like 'wise' applies to Him directly and immediately. Aquinas calls this mode of application *res significata*; the predicate designates not an attribute of God but His very essence. But the same predicate applied to man signifies only one of his attributes. Here the predicate applies in its *modus significandi*, that is, by way of its normal signification. This shared but ontologically (and epistemologically) divided signification underlies the appropriate analogical relation between God and man, that of proper proportionality.

Formal discussions of Aquinas' doctrine of analogy generally start from the commentary of Cajetan who, in his *De nominum analogia* (1498), attempted to sort out the various types of analogy that are discussed in Aquinas' writings and nominated one of those types as that proper to metaphysical discourse and statements about God. Cajetan divided analogical usages into three types, of which the last comprises two subtypes. He labeled these analogy of inequality, analogy of attribution, and analogy of proportionality (proper and improper). His analogy of inequality is generally left aside as being largely irrelevant to Aquinas' designs (in fact, Cajetan himself, after describing it, concludes that it is not even a form of analogy; see Klubertanz, p. 8). In any case, it amounts to little more than what ordinarily would be termed univocal or generic predication—where, for example, 'animal' would be used of both a horse and a cow.[5] The analogy of attribution (or reference) occurs when a predicate which is defined in its proper or intrinsic use for a certain class of objects is used not of such an object but of some property or aspect that is related to that object. Thus the predicate *healthy* is primarily and properly defined as applying to animal bodies. If now we say that urine or a certain diet is healthy, we use 'healthy' analogically, by way of attributing health to an aspect (a sign in the case of urine, a cause in the case of diet) that is related to the primary object to which health pertains. To cast this in the terminology generally employed, 'healthy' is the analogon or analogated term, 'animal' and 'urine' the analogates, with 'animal' being the primary analogate, 'urine' the secondary. As we see, the analogon, 'healthy', is applicable to both analogates, but principally or intrinsically to one ('animal') and only secondarily (via a metonymic relation) to the other.[6]

In the analogy of proper proportionality (Cajetan's nominee) there is not the type of relation between the analogates that we find in the analogy of attribution; instead, the relation is one of a proportionality between the proportions (ratios). If we take A : B

5. His reasoning was that although there might be a unitary signification for 'animal' taken as the name of a genus, there was an inequality in its application to different species.
6. The same type of analogy—by attribution—was described in chapter 5; the analogon there was 'medical'.

:: C : D as the schema for this type of analogy, no (critical) relation exists between B and D, the analogates; there is instead a proportionality, in that the relation of A to B is proportional to that between C and D. This relation, however, may be of two types, one in which the relation is proportional in that the same analogon is predicated of both analogates, the other in which a different analogon is predicated of each analogate. The former arrangement is that of proper, the latter of improper, proportionality. An example of proper proportionality would be *wise : man :: wise : God*; an example of improper proportionality might be *stubborn : man :: difficult : problem*.

On the face of it, the analogy of proper proportionality resembles analogy of attribution, in that one predicate (analogon) 'covers' both analogates. The difference lies in the intrinsic natures of the predicates and their consequent relations to the analogates. 'Healthy' is a predicate that applies to a homogeneous denotational realm, if in various ways. Although its relation to its analogates is different in the two proportions—primary in the one and (for whatever reason) secondary in the other—its entire realm of denotation is mundane; in any of its analogous applications it refers to (aspects of) an animal body. The case is different for proper proportionality. This type is defined for predicates that have application in different realms—the mundane and the supernatural. They thus have a heterogeneous application. Such predicates ('wise', 'good', and so on) are termed 'transcendental'.[7] It is because of the presence in our language of these transcendental terms that the problem of analogy assumes its importance in theological discussion.

7. Burrell (1973, 95) says that expressions like 'one', 'good', and 'being' are 'transcendental in the sense of pervading every category and hence defying definition'. Terms like the above, to which is sometimes added 'true', are frequently also referred to as 'transcategorical'. It would seem to be advisable, however, to reserve 'transcategorical' for terms like 'one', 'being', and 'true', which really are applicable to all categories ('true' of statements), and restrict 'transcendental' to terms like 'good', 'wise', and 'just', which apply only to God and human beings (although 'good' for certain metaphysical reasons is transcategorical as well). For our purposes, however, we may disregard the above distinction (it does not seem to be upheld in the literature in any case) and speak simply of transcendental terms.

A representative text of Aquinas that serves as a key for the foregoing analysis occurs in *De veritate* (question 2, article 11). I cite it from the translation of Mulligan (1952):

> Since an agreement according to proportion can happen in two ways, two kinds of community can be noted in analogy. There is a certain agreement between things having a proportion to each other from the fact that they have a determinate distance between each other or some other relation to each other, like the proportion which the number two has to unity in as far as it is the double of unity. Again, the agreement is occasionally noted not between two things which have a proportion between them, but rather between two related proportions—for example, six has something in common with four because six is two times three, just as four is two times two. The first type of agreement is one of proportion; the second of proportionality.
>
> We find something predicated analogously of two realities according to the first type of agreement when one of them has a relation to the other, as when being is predicated of substance and accident because of the relation which accident has to substance, or as when healthy is predicated of urine and animal because urine has some relation to the health of an animal. Sometimes, however, a thing is predicated analogously according to the second type of agreement, as when sight is predicated of bodily sight and of the intellect because understanding is in the mind as sight is in the eye.
>
> In those terms predicated according to the first type of analogy, there must be some definite relation between the things having something in common analogously. Consequently, nothing can be predicated analogously of God and creatures according to this type of analogy; for no creature has such a relation to God that it could determine the divine perfection. But in the other type of analogy, no definite relation is involved between the things which have something in common analogously, so there is no reason why some name cannot be predicated analogously of God and creature in this manner.
>
> But this can happen in two ways. Sometimes the name

implies something belonging to the thing primarily designated which cannot be common to God and creature even in the manner described above. This would be true, for example, of anything predicated of God metaphorically, as when God is called lion, sun, and the like, because their definitions include matter which cannot be attributed to God. At other times, however, a term predicated of God and creature implies nothing in its principal meaning which would prevent our finding between a creature and God an agreement of the type described above. To this kind belong all attributes which include no defect nor depend on matter for their act of existence, for example, being, the good, and similar things.

In the above passage Aquinas distinguishes analogy of attribution from analogy of proportionality and divides the latter into its proper and improper subtypes. We may at this point expand somewhat on the latter distinction. It is clear, first of all, that proper proportionality, at least in its theological sense, involves the use of transcendental predicates ('good', 'being', and so forth).[8] When God is referred to as a sun or lion, on the other hand, the analogy is improper—metaphorical. We notice that such predicates are mundane, thus cross in their application to God from one realm or domain to another—in this respect, as was pointed out above, differing from the transcendental predicates. This difference underlies the theological distinction. Something more should be said, however, about the *structural* difference between proper and improper proportionality.

Both types of proportionality are based on a four-term schema. The difference between them derives from the number of *different* terms that appear in that schema. In proper proportionality these number three, the transcendental term appearing twice; in improper proportionality there are four. When God is called the sun, the statement is based on the (improper) propor-

---

8. The transition from mathematical proportionality to its use for theological purposes is not consistent. Mathematical proportions are equal in their proportionality, whereas those of ordinary language evince at best a similarity. For some discussion of this difference see Burrell (1973, 75).

tionality *heaven : God :: earth : sun*, God being the source of spiritual life, the sun of physical life.[9] This type of proportionality is familiar to us from the *Poetics*, where Aristotle presents it as his fourth type of metaphoric transfer—that by analogy. There Aristotle says that given such an arrangement, one can substitute D for B or B for D. Transferring in the former direction would give us 'sun of heaven' (not of the sky). This would then be a metaphor for God (in the same way as 'evening of life', one of the examples given in the *Poetics*, is a metaphor for old age). Now when Aquinas elucidates the biblical utterance 'God is the sun', his treatment has an implicit basis in Aristotle's metaphor by analogy.[10] There is, however, a difference between the procedures of Aristotle and Aquinas in that Aristotle was presenting a theory of how metaphors are formed; he thus presented the schematic *background* for the production or coining of metaphors.[11] Aquinas, on the other hand, started from metaphors that were already to hand in the Bible, and he thus had to reconstruct the schematic background.

Whether the schema is a priori or arrived at a posteriori does not, however, alter the critical fact that it contains four distinct terms. This fact is critical because from it there follows the impropriety of analogies involving God. Nothing that is properly proportionate to anything else can be properly proportionate to God. Whenever, on the basis of such a proportionality, something is predicated of God (sun, rock, lion), there will necessarily result a sort crossing; a predicate defined for one sort or category

9. Aquinas discusses this example in his commentary on book IV of the *Sentences* of Peter Lombard:

> Another [type of similitude] is that of proportionality. This is found in Scripture when figurative predicates are transferred from the corporeal to the spiritual realm. God, for instance, is called a sun because He is the source of spiritual life as the sun is the source of physical life . . . [cited in Klubertanz, 1960, 80].

10. Aquinas probably did not have recourse to the *Poetics*; however, Aristotle's doctrine of analogy was available to him from several sources, chiefly and importantly from the *Metaphysics*.

11. For a discussion of the distinctive role that analogy plays in Aristotle's theory of metaphor see Levin, 1982b.

will be applied to an object belonging to another. Of course, God does not belong to any category—He superordinates and subsumes all categories. But it is for this very reason that homogeneously mundane predicates cannot be properly applied to Him. When they are applied, they cannot be understood as making assertions true of God; they must be taken as metaphors.

The case is different when the predicate is one of the transcendentals. Since such terms are properly predicable of both God and creatures, the schema will contain only three different terms, the transcendental predicate appearing in each of the ratios. One instance of this schema will therefore be *wise : God :: wise : man*. At the same time, however, even though the predicate has a proper application on both sides of the proportion, it cannot be thought that it applies equally in both ratios. Man's wisdom cannot be of the same nature as God's. As Aquinas writes,

> When any name expressing perfection is applied to a creature, it signifies that perfection as distinct from the others according to the nature of its definition; as, for instance, by this term *wise* applied to a man, we signify some perfection distinct from a man's essence, and distinct from his power and his being, and from all similar things. But when we apply *wise* to God, we do not mean to signify anything distinct from His essence or power or being. And thus when the term *wise* is applied to man, in some degree it circumscribes and comprehends the thing signified; whereas this is not the case when it is applied to God, but it leaves the thing signified as uncomprehended, and as exceeding the signification of the name. Hence it is evident that this term *wise* is not applied in the same way to God and to man [*Summa theologiae*, I, question 13, article 5; in Pegis, 1948].

This difference in the application of transcendental predicates is explained further by Aquinas, in a more semantic fashion, in article 3 of question 13, where he introduces a distinction as to the manner in which a predicate may signify. A predicate like 'wise', when applied to God, signifies *res significata*; wisdom being of the essence of God, the predicate signifies that very thing. Applied to man, on the other hand, it signifies *modus significandi*, that is, according to its meaning.

The distinction in signification, according as it is to *res significata* or *modus significandi*, is just one of the ways in which Aquinas characterized the difference by which transcendental predicates apply to God and to man. At different stages of his writing he signalized it also as a difference of application to priority and posteriority, exemplar and likeness, first cause and effect, infinite and finite, perfection and imperfection, and participation (see Klubertanz, 1960, 35–76, and Ricoeur, 1977, 272–80, for some discussion). These shifts were actuated by certain problems that attended Aquinas' efforts to reconcile predication of the same attributes to God and man. One problem was the need to avoid any implication that the attribute possessed in different modes by God and by man existed as a higher genus—an inadmissible conclusion; another was the need to counter any suggestion of agnosticism that might be conveyed by attempts to indicate the meaning of the transcendental terms in their application to God—attempts which of necessity must always fall short; still another was the need to avoid the (anthropomorphic) impression that God was a kind of superman, and thus that the attributes possessed in common by God and man differed only in degree, not in mode. It was to deal with such problems that Aquinas, as he worked out his doctrine of analogy, was led to offer first one then another explanation for the manner in which the transcendental predicates applied. For our immediate purposes, however, these problems may be passed over; what it is important to bear in mind is that no matter how the difference in the application of transcendental terms is conceived, the schematic representation of proper proportionality comprises only three distinct terms.

In the respect that only three distinct terms appear in the schema, the analogy of attribution resembles, as we have seen, that of proper proportionality. However, as was pointed out above, the two types of analogy differ in that the repeated term (the analogon) has in proper proportionality a heterogeneous application, whereas in attribution the application is homogeneous, applying exclusively in the realm of the mundane. Founding this homogeneous application is the relation of one of the analogates to the other as its sign or cause. From this fact two important corollaries ensue. One is enunciated by Aquinas in saying that all such relations are determinate, by which he means that knowledge of the one implies knowledge of the other. This determination is sometimes demonstrated by showing that the definition of the secondary analogate contains the primary analogate. Thus the definition of 'urine' would be 'sign of health in an *animal body*'; the same procedure applies to 'diet'. The second corollary is that in analogy of attribution the analogon predicates of a single being. In the 'healthy' example, animal body is the being, urine or diet are aspects of that same being. Neither of these two characteristics holds for proper proportionality. First, as Aquinas says (see above), 'no creature has such a relation to God that it could determine the divine perfection'. So that from the fact that a man is wise it is not possible to comprehend God's wisdom. Second, wisdom is predicated of two beings, man and God.

Aquinas' Theory and Conceptual Construal

Paul Ricoeur has referred to Aquinas' doctrine of analogy as a 'magnificent exercise of thought' (1977, 280). In my exposition of that doctrine I may not have succeeded in conveying the grounds for such an impression. But anyone who reads Aquinas for himself and attempts to follow him as he struggles to extend the horizon of his language will find it difficult not to agree with Ricoeur's assessment. In any event, it is now time to consider the relevance of the preceding discussion to the concerns of this study.

As I see it, there is a similarity between the problem that faced Aquinas and the one posed by my view of metaphor. In both cases a single language, its stock of predicates designed to register the intellectual and affective states of a particular species is called upon to register those states in another order of being. The problems are obviously not identical (even setting aside the tremendous difference in their imports), but they do appear to present a certain symmetry of form. Aquinas was concerned to rationalize the sense of an expression like 'God is wise'; we are trying to effect the same result with an expression like 'The flower is happy'. On standard approaches to metaphor, 'The flower is happy' would instance analogy of improper proportionality—'happy' has a univocal signification in its proper application to humans; its application to a flower, however, is improper and thus can only be construed metaphorically. On this approach, that a flower can in fact be understood as happy, is ruled out a priori; consequently, a semantic interpretation of the expression must be made, one that has the flower doing something that flowers are normally understood to do (such as, bloom). I am rejecting this a priori assumption and suggesting that the application of 'happy' to a flower be viewed as a proper application.

Now 'happy' is not a transcendental predicate; it is one that is specifically defined for a proper nature—man. From the standpoint of flowers, however, which have no language of their own, such predicates, if not transcendental, are at least superior. We can therefore say that when 'happy' is predicated of humans, it signifies that property 'primarily', but when it is predicated of a flower it signifies 'secondarily'. These are just labels. But they serve a purpose if they constrain us to think of 'happy' as actually predicable of flowers. If we acknowledge this possibility, there will be a difference in the mode in which 'happy' signifies in the two applications (to a man and to a flower), but it will have a proper signification in both cases; the relation between the two significations, while not univocal, will not be equivocal either. The relation between them will be analogical, and the analogy will be one of proper proportionality.

The validity of this claim can be demonstrated by an examination of its structural implications. If 'The flower is happy' is treated along standard lines for metaphoric construal, the proportional background is *happy : man :: blooming : flower*, that is, the proportion comprises *four* distinct terms. On this basis, 'flower' is substituted for 'man' to arrive at 'The flower is happy'. In interpreting this expression we reflect on the underlying proportion, recover the predicate 'blooming', and thus interpret 'The flower is happy' to mean 'The flower is blooming'. If, however, as I have suggested, we regard 'happy' as a 'superior' predicate, one comprehending both humans and flowers, the proportion implicitly behind our interpretation becomes *happy : man :: happy : flower*, the same term appearing twice. In interpreting 'The flower is happy' against this background, we take 'happy' to be a proper application to flowers, albeit in a manner differing from its application to humans. The former approach interprets 'The flower is happy' as an analogy of improper proportionality, the latter as one of proper proportionality.

Aquinas was both a theologian and a philosopher. For Aquinas the theologian there was no need to prove that God exists or that He is wise and good. These were truths that he accepted on faith. If he in fact did offer proofs of God's existence, it was simply to provide a support in reason for the certitude of faith. It was in a similar spirit that he developed his doctrine of analogy—to show that those qualities of God that the Bible revealed to us could be accommodated to our everyday language. In the intellectual effort that he expended in formulating, revising, and reformulating his doctrine of analogy (an effort that persisted throughout his lifetime) we have a powerful witness to the refractory nature of language—to the problem it poses when we must try by its means to express feelings or intimations prompted by a Being or beings that lie outside the range of the strictly human. The very fact that Aquinas had recourse to a doctrine of analogy is a measure of this limitation in human language. I would say that in the final analysis it was not the doctrine of analogy that enabled Aquinas to understand the wisdom and goodness of God; it was his implicit faith that He is wise and good which provided that understanding. Similar considerations apply, I believe, to the attitude I am advocating in regard to metaphoric construal. The fact that Aquinas' doctrine of analogy can be extended to the domain of natural objects will of itself convince no ʹne of its proper motivation or utility. For even though of flowers we know that they exist, we have no evidence for their having emotions, appetites, and desires. It is open to us, however, to make commitments in the absence of factual evidence. Wordsworth said,

> 'tis my faith that every flower
> Enjoys the air it breathes.

['Lines Written in Early Spring', 11–12]

For him, apparently, flowers could be happy. For any others who entertain such a possibility, the treatment I have suggested for 'The flower is happy' might meet with a hospitable response.

7

The Universe According to Newton

In the preceding chapters we contrasted two logically distinct approaches to the problem of metaphoric construal. The less obvious approach, the one I have been promoting, we may call the conceptualist approach, while the customary approach we may term, for convenience sake, the semantic. The question to which these two approaches provide different responses is how one should go about construing a linguistic expression whose elements are prima facie incompatible with one another. On the semantic approach we construe out of this incompatibility a meaning, on the conceptualist approach a (re)vision of reality. To the question now of whether the conceptualist approach can be employed on poems generally, our answer is that there is no reason in principle why it cannot. In practical terms, however, we must say that it will be most fruitfully employed on certain poems only, poems which by their nature are sympathetic to the conceptualist approach. The circularity in the preceding statement is deliberate. The mental or theoretical attitude with which we ought to approach a poem cannot be prescribed in advance. That attitude develops processually in the act of reading and rereading the poem. The conceptualist approach represents a variant of interpretive strategy which contemplation of the poem may evoke as the one appropriate and revealing for that poem. In short, the actual experience of reading a poem may motivate the exercise of this option.[1] At the same time, we may be justified for certain poems in adopting the conceptualist setting beforehand, on the basis of what we know about the poet's period and outlook. Thus there are in the history and development of English poetry certain epochs which, in the light of the 'philosophical' temper of the age, a temper manifested in various but symptomatic ways by the poets of that period, might reasonably predispose us to a conceptualist reading. For reasons to be discussed below, the chief epoch which might be expected to motivate such a reading is the Romantic period.

As has been indicated, expressions that comprise incompatible elements describe, if taken literally, conditions or states of affairs that exceed the bounds of our mundane experience. On our assumption that those expressions are to be credited with what they in fact say (our primary thesis), two corollary questions are raised: what view of reality lay behind and motivated such expressions, and what mental faculty stamped its personal impress on that view and informed those expressions? In his discussion of the Romantic development, Piper (1962) provides a compact answer to these questions. He writes (p. 2), 'The crucial point in the history of English Romanticism came when the concept of the "active universe" met the developing theory of the Imagination'. The developing theory of the imagination will concern us in the next chapter. At this point our interest lies in the formula 'active universe'. The phrase implies a conception of nature as sentient, instinct with a sensibility which needed only what Keats called 'a greeting of the Spirit' to be quickened for the human observer (Wordsworth's 'auxiliar light' of the mind performs the same function). The conception of an 'active universe' (*Prelude*, II, 266) developed as a reaction to the view of man and his relation to the natural world that prevailed in the eighteenth century, a view whose principal intellectual support came from the physics and metaphysics of Isaac Newton. In similar fashion the 'theory of the Imagination' (to quote Piper) had to *develop* out of the

1. Compare parodies, satires, and elegies, where similarly we are not apprised beforehand how they are to be read.

background of John Locke's sensationalist epistemology.[2] Since the Romantic outlook is in large measure a reaction against the principles promulgated in the work of these two men, the nature and significance of that outlook cannot be properly evaluated unless we understand just what those principles were and come to appreciate the kind of intellectual climate that resulted from their adoption. In the final chapter of this book I shall show how the approach to metaphor that I have been advocating in these pages enables us to rationalize in a theoretically satisfying manner the relation between the Romantic imagination and the 'active universe'—the two elements in Piper's formulation. In advance of that demonstration, however, it is necessary to examine in some detail the scientific and philosophical contributions made by Newton and Locke and assess the influence that their respective doctrines exerted on the thought and worldview of the eighteenth century. In the course of examining those doctrines we shall also gain some sense, particularly by adverting to the criticisms lodged against them by Coleridge, of the evolving intel-

---

2. In a letter written in 1801 Coleridge, discussing Locke, speaks of him as one 'whose Name runs in a collar with Newton's, as naturally as Milton's name with that of Shakespere' (Griggs, II, 679). The enormously influential *Observations on Man, His Frame, His Duty, and His Expectations* by David Hartley, published in 1749, begins,

> My chief Design in the following Chapter, is, briefly to explain, establish, and apply the Doctrines of *Vibrations* and *Association*. The First of these Doctrines is taken from the Hints concerning the Performance of Sensation and Motion, which *Sir Isaac Newton* had given at the End of his *Principia*, and in the *Questions* annexed to his *Optics*; the Last, from what *Mr. Locke*, and other ingenious Persons since his Time, have delivered concerning the Influence of *Association* over our Opinions and Affections. . . .

In the words of a modern commentator:

> Wherever we turn in assessing the intellectual climate of the time we encounter the authority of Locke and Newton. They shaped the legacy which the eighteenth century received from the seventeenth, and their influence was all-pervasive and supreme. The new direction given to philosophy and the strong interest awakened by science promised that new concerns would dominate the new period. The picture of the universe supplied by Newton and the interpretation of the human mind proposed by Locke rapidly modified the outlook of the educated man; they provided the presuppositions which governed the thought of the new era [Cragg, 1964, 5].

lectual and spiritual tension out of which the Romantic temperament and metaphysics developed.

Newton and Nature

For all the wonder and admiration with which his contemporaries greeted Newton's discoveries about the natural
order, and for all that the poets of the eighteenth century honored
and glorified his name, the physics that Newton proferred to the
world was really a cold and dispiriting affair. It is customary to
cite, as epitomizing the eighteenth-century reaction, Pope's lines,
'Intended for Sir Isaac Newton':

> Nature and Nature's laws lay hid in night;
> God said "let Newton be!" and all was light.

If one today reads the *Principia* and the *Opticks*, however, the
impression gained is that while Newton may indeed have
brought to light Nature's *laws*, he left Nature itself rather
shrouded in darkness. And there is nothing really remarkable in
this. Newton's work is after all a mechanics. It is a mechanics,
moreover, of a strongly mathematical cast. We might say that
Nature has several natures, and that the one systematized by
Newton's laws is mechanical nature, Nature taken in its objective, material aspect. There is of course a kind of austere beauty
in any system shown to be so finely regulated, particularly one
of such scope and magnitude. And there is a corresponding
beauty, or elegance, in the laws that Newton showed to govern
that system. Left largely out of account, however, in Newton's
magisterial regimentation, is nature in its aspect as vital, organic,
and, concomitantly, in its office as nurse of human affections.[3]

---

3. Compare Burtt (1954, 238–39):

. . . it was of the greatest consequence for succeeding thought that now the
great Newton's authority was squarely behind that view of the cosmos
which saw in man a puny, irrelevant spectator (so far as being wholly
imprisoned in a dark room can be called such) of the vast mathematical
system whose regular motions according to mechanical principles constituted the world of nature. The glorious romantic universe of Dante and

Newton's *Opticks*

The imbalance between the treatment of material and vital aspects of nature characterizes both of Newton's major works, but it is perhaps more remarkable in the less 'cosmic' *Opticks*.[4] The latter work, if we pass over the 'metaphysical' musings in some of the queries, is devoted to the analysis of light—its properties and its physical effects; it thus might be expected to have few implications for the question of how the human observer was affected by nature and its manifestations. But Newton's results, particularly as they concerned the relation between light and color, in fact had such implications—in conditioning a characteristic mental attitude to natural phenomena. For the student of nature, aware of those results, could assume the attitude of detached observer, his view of the natural world informed not so much with a feeling for its evocative power as with a knowledge of its physical mechanisms. What feeling was engendered in him was rather for the intellectual prowess that brought this knowledge to light. We find this attitude expressed in the work of many eighteenth-century poets. Akenside, for example, could write:

> Nor ever yet
> The melting rainbow's vernal-tinctur'd hues

Milton, that set no bounds to the imagination of man as it played over space and time, had now been swept away. Space was identified with the realm of geometry, time with the continuity of number. The world that people had thought themselves living in—a world rich with color and sound, redolent with fragrance, filled with gladness, love and beauty, speaking everywhere of purposive harmony and creative ideals—was crowded now into minute corners in the brains of scattered organic beings. The really important world outside was a world hard, cold, colorless, silent, and dead; a world of quantity, a world of mathematically computable motions in mechanical regularity. The world of qualities as immediately perceived by man became just a curious and quite minor effect of that infinite machine beyond.

4. Signalizing Newton's virtual disregard for nature in its vital aspect is of course not to suggest that Newton's work was deficient as physical theory or that he had any obligation to comprehend that aspect in his experiments and laws; we point to the imbalance simply in order to indicate the effect that his views had on the eighteenth-century poets and to establish the context against which the Romantic poets were led to react.

To me have shown so pleasing, as when first
The hand of science pointed out the path
In which the sun-beams gleaming from the west
Fall on the wat'ry cloud, whose darksome veil
Involves the orient; and that trickling show'r
Piercing thro' every crystalline convex
Of clust'ring dew-drops to their flight oppos'd,
Recoil at length where concave all behind
Th' internal surface of each glassy orb
Repells their forward passage into air;
That thence direct they seek the radiant goal
From which their course began; and, as they strike
In diff'rent lines the gazer's obvious eye,
Assume a diff'rent lustre, thro' the brede
Of colours changing from the splendid rose
To the pale violet's dejected hue.

[*Pleasures of Imagination*, II, 103–20]

Akenside's description of the sunbeams' passage through the drops of rain is, if we abstract it from the poetical garb in which it is expressed, a rendering in intelligent layman's terms of the geometrically exact account that Newton gives of the phenomenon in book I, part 2 of the *Opticks* (proposition 9, problem 4). The satisfaction that Akenside takes in the role of knowledgeable observer is expressed in the opening lines.

The rainbow serves as a paradigm case for the impact that Newton's analysis of light made on the eighteenth-century poets.[5] In *The Seasons* Thomson writes in a vein similar to that of Akenside and derives the same satisfaction that, 'sage-instructed,' his eye can see 'the white mingling maze' *unfolded* into the 'various twine of light':

Meantime, refracted from yon eastern cloud,
Bestriding earth, the grand ethereal bow
Shoots up immense; and every hue unfolds,
In fair proportion running from the red

5. This point is made by Prickett (1970, 8). Prickett in fact devotes his introduction to a discussion of 'The Rainbow and the Imagination'.

To where the violet fades into the sky.
Here, awful Newton, the dissolving clouds
Form, fronting on the sun, thy showery prism;
And to the sage-instructed eye unfold
The various twine of light, by thee disclosed
From the white mingling maze. Not so the swain.
He wondering views the bright enchantment bend
Delightful, o'er the radiant fields, and runs
To watch the falling glory; but amazed
Beholds the amusive arch before him fly,
Then vanish quite away.

[Spring', 203–17]

The newly won understanding of how the sun's rays in their refraction and reflection by raindrops were separated into their spectral components was to the poets of the eighteenth century a source of intellectual satisfaction, a measure of man's dominion over nature. At the close of her comments on the lines of Thomson cited above, Nicolson (1966, 32) writes of these poets, 'They delighted in their own intellectual maturity, feeling that they had outgrown the childlike attitude of the simple swain who seeks a pot of gold, or of Noah, to whom the rainbow was a miracle. They did not believe that Newton had taken beauty from poetry; he had added new beauty, because he had added truth'. John Keats, of course, writing some seventy years later, was not convinced of this and was to see in the *unweaving* of the same rainbow not an access of intellectual power so much as a suffocation of the spirit:

Do not all charms fly
At the mere touch of cold philosophy?
There was an awful rainbow once in heaven:
We know her woof, her texture; she is given
In the dull catalogue of common things.
Philosophy will clip an Angel's wings,
Conquer all mysteries by rule and line,
Empty the haunted air, and gnomed mine—
Unweave a rainbow.

[*Lamia*, II, 229–37]

Where for Akenside and Thomson the application of science yielded an enrichment of nature, for Keats that application produced only its impoverishment.[6]

Newton's *Principia*

If the effect of the *Opticks* was to interpose a theoretical screen between the observer and the manifestations of nature, the grander and metaphysically more pregnant *Principia* affected that relation in ways that were yet more profound. Since the findings of the *Opticks* related to light and color, they could be *employed* by man in his rationalization of natural phenomena, his role being that of informed observer or spectator. No such privileged position fell to him, however, under the laws of the *Principia*. True, he could now look about his cosmos with a deeper understanding of its order and system. But in that order he was simply another natural object, as subject to the Newtonian laws as the lowliest rock or pebble. Consider Newton's First Law of Motion: 'Every body continues in a state of rest, or of motion in a right line, unless it is compelled to change that state by forces impressed upon it'. This law (as well as the two succeeding) applies equally to apples, stones, projectiles, and planets. Animals, including man, enjoy a certain autonomy in respect to those laws, in the sense that they may *will* when, where, and what to move. But however or whatever they will, their resultant movements obey the Newtonian laws. Their capacity as thinking and willing *agents* is, in other words, abstracted from, and it is merely as (collections of) *bodies* that they figure in the Newtonian universe. So that for all practical purposes, in the context of Newton's laws the distinction between organic and inorganic objects—between vital and inert substances—is neutralized.

If Newton occasionally entertains questions involving organic objects, his interest is in the forces affecting the constituent bodies (the particles or corpuscles) of those objects. Thus at the close of the *General Scholium* he writes:

---

6. Keats' use of 'philosophy' in the lines cited from *Lamia* is to be understood in the sense of 'natural philosophy', or science. See the editorial footnote to these lines in Abrams et al., in *The Norton Anthology of English Literature*, 4th ed., vol. II, p. 845.

And now we might add something concerning a certain most subtle spirit which pervades and lies hid in all gross bodies; by the force and action of which spirit the particles of bodies attract one another at near distances, and cohere, if contiguous; and electric bodies operate to greater distances, as well repelling as attracting the neighboring corpuscles; and light is emitted, reflected, refracted, inflected, and heats bodies; and all sensation is excited, and the members of animal bodies move at the command of the will, namely, by the vibrations of this spirit, mutually propagated along the solid filaments of the nerves, from the outward organs of sense to the brain, and from the brain into the muscles. But these are things that cannot be explained in few words, nor are we furnished with that sufficiency of experiments which is required to an accurate determination and demonstration of the laws by which this electric and elastic spirit operates.

As we see, animals are treated by Newton simply as a species of gross bodies. As to the intrinsic nature of those bodies, Newton does not commit himself. To be sure, gross bodies are collections of particles, and these particles have properties—extension, hardness, impenetrability, mobility, inertia (*Principia*, book III, rule III); what the bodies consisted in, however, what their inner, or *substantive*, nature might be, was for Newton a question closed to human understanding. As he put it elsewhere in the *General Scholium*:

. . . what the real substance of anything is we know not. In bodies, we see only their figures and colours, we hear only the sounds, we touch only their outward surfaces, we smell only the smells, and taste the savors; but their inward substances are not to be known either by our senses, or by any reflex act of our minds.

In the same way the 'spirit' alluded to by Newton in the passage cited above and held to be responsible for the attraction of particles is given no characterization, mechanical or otherwise.[7]

7. The 'spirit' here in question, it is to be noticed, operates at near distances and is thus to be distinguished from universal attraction or gravitation; see Koyré (1968, 52n.) for discussion of this point.

The same inaccessibility to human understanding pertained to Newton's law of universal attraction, or gravitation. Since the possibility of action at a distance was rejected by just about everyone, including himself, Newton several times tried to fill this theoretical gap by positing an 'aethereal' medium along which such action would be propagated by successive impacts upon the fluid particles of which the medium was held to consist. Ultimately, however, in the absence of any empirical or experimental evidence for the existence of such a medium, Newton had to abandon this 'hypothesis'. The fact was that though the action of bodies was accurately predicted mathematically by Newton's inverse-square law, no observable or experimentally secured cause could be adduced which would explain why the law held.[8]

This recoil from specifying (physical) causes is typical of Newton's procedure. At the beginning of the *Principia* he sets out eight definitions. Number V defines centripetal force: 'A centripetal force is that by which bodies are drawn or impelled, or any way tend, towards a point as to a centre'. Definitions VI to VIII define, respectively, the absolute, accelerative, and motive quantities of that force. The absolute is that quantity which is exerted radially by a center on the spaces around it, and which varies in proportion to the size and intensity of the force that propagates it; the accelerative is a translation of the absolute quantity into its effect on the velocity of bodies in the orbit, the velocity varying inversely with the distance from the center; the motive is the quantity manifested in the motion (momentum) produced on the bodies in the orbit, this quantity being always proportional to the quantity of accelerative force. Having set out these relations in proportional terms, Newton concludes the explanation of definition VIII with the following statement:

> I . . . use the words attraction, impulse, or propensity of any sort towards a centre, promiscuously, and indifferently, one for another; considering those forces not physically, but mathematically; wherefore the reader is not to imagine that by those words I anywhere take upon me to decide the kind, or the

8. See Koyré (1968, 16); the inverse-square law states that the force of a body's attraction varies inversely with the square of the distance.

manner of any action, the causes or the physical reasons thereof, or that I attribute forces, in a true and physical sense, to certain centres (which are only mathematical points); when at any time I happen to speak of centres as attracting, or as endued with attractive powers.

A bit earlier, in the same explanation, he writes, 'I design here only to give a mathematical notion of those forces, without considering their physical causes and seats'.

Newton in fact was chary of adducing causes for just about any of the actions which his mathematical laws described with such precision. Since experiments on the phenomena did not disclose such causes, which could not therefore be induced from an examination of individual cases, to adduce them would be to feign hypotheses, a practice that Newton repeatedly declared himself against. If his laws accurately predicted the motions of bodies, Newton was satisfied; it was not necessary to know further what forces were responsible for that motion. Newton in fact took a narrow, one might say a positivistic, view of what constituted proper scientific method. In the *General Scholium* he writes,

> Hitherto we have explained the phenomena of the heavens and of our sea by the power of gravity, but we have not yet assigned the cause of this power. . . . I have not been able to discover the cause of those properties of gravity from phenomena, and I frame [feign] no hypotheses; for whatever is not deduced from the phenomena is to be called an hypothesis; and hypotheses, whether metaphysical or physical, whether of occult qualities or mechanical, have no place in experimental philosophy. In this philosophy particular propositions are inferred from the phenomena, and afterwards rendered general by induction.[9]

9. The same position is enunciated in query 31 of the *Opticks*:
As in mathematics, so in natural philosophy, the investigation of difficult things by the method of analysis, ought ever to precede the method of composition. This analysis consists in making experiments and observations, and in drawing general conclusions from them by induction, and admitting of no objections against the conclusions but such as are taken from

Newton's *Principia* was of course a great scientific achievement. Not the least of its merits was the comprehension of both terrestrial and celestial phenomena by the same set of laws.[10] It accomplished this generalization, however, by reducing apples, stones, planets, and animal life to mere collections of particles. In this way Newton was able to provide a uniform theory of the universe, one in which everything was subject to the same mathematical laws. But for these laws to operate, those particles, and the objects which they constituted, had to be regarded as passive and inert—any independent or autonomous motion would render those laws nonpredictive, and hence had to be regarded as beyond their scope. Under the Newtonian laws, therefore, no provision was made for nor any countenance given to the possibility that activity could reside or originate in natural objects. The contrast could hardly be greater between the insensible and subjugate form that nature takes in the frame of Newton's laws and the vitality felt by the Romantics to inhere in its most impassive features. The worldview of the *Principia* had to be completely overmastered before Shelley could express himself thus:

> The moveless pillar of a mountain's weight
> Is active, living spirit. Every grain
> Is sentient both in unity and part,
> And the minutest atom comprehends
> A world of loves and hatreds.
>
> [*Queen Mab*, IV, 139–46]

---

experiments, or other certain truths. For hypotheses are not to be regarded in experimental philosophy.

10. Aristotle, in a view that had prevailed through the Middle Ages, had postulated motions of different sorts for earthly and heavenly bodies. As Dijksterhuis (1957, 168) puts it,

The Aristotelian theory of the elements . . . , in connection with the distinction between natural and enforced motion, led to the conviction that the sublunary world, in which heavy and light bodies, composed of earth, water, air, and fire, by their nature perform limited, non-uniform rectilinear motions, was bound to differ *toto genere* from the superlunary world, in which celestial bodies, consisting of ether, by their nature carry out unlimited uniform circular motions. On this account, the idea of applying theories framed in connection with terrestrial phenomena to celestial phenomena was excluded *a limine*.

Newton's Relation to the
Romantic Temperament

If the Newtonian laws made no allowance for the possibility that activity could reside or originate in natural objects, neither did they envisage the possibility that such activity could ensue from the sympathetic reach of a human observer. We have seen that in the Newtonian universe matter was inert. What then was the status of mind? This question hardly arises for Newton. But it would assume major proportions once the mechanistic principles and mathematical solutions of Newton's work were overcome by a conception of the universe in which the human spirit counted for as much in the ontological scheme as did inanimate nature. And for the holders of this conception Newton's conclusions failed to satisfy. Thus Coleridge objected that it was not only physical objects that Newton's system reduced to passivity; the mind of man suffered the same fate. As he wrote in one of his letters (Griggs, II, 709), 'Newton was a mere materialist. *Mind* in his system is always passive—a lazy Looker-on on an external World. If the mind be not *passive*, if it be indeed made in God's image, and that too in the sublimest sense—the image of the *Creator*—there is ground for suspicion that any system built on the passiveness of the mind must be false as a system'.

This reaction, as the letter makes clear, was prompted by Coleridge's reading of the *Opticks*.[11] Although Coleridge does not indicate what in that work provoked him to react as he did, we may conjecture as a likely, or at any rate an adequate, source the passage in query 31 where Newton, in the course of presenting his idea of the Divine Nature, writes,

> . . . we are not to consider the world as the body of God, or the
> several parts as the parts of God. He is a uniform Being, void of
> organs, members or parts, and they are his creatures subordi-

---

11. It is not likely, however, that anything in the *Principia* would have caused Coleridge to alter his opinion, since nowhere in that work except in the *General Scholium* is the mind even mentioned; nor is man, who in the *Scholium* is introduced primarily by way of asserting the dominion of God, men being His servants.

nate to him, and subservient to His will; And He is not more
the soul of them than the soul of man is the soul of the species of
things carried through the organs of sense into the place of its
sensation, where it perceives them by means of its immediate
presence, without the intervention of any third thing. The
organs of sense are not for enabling the soul to perceive the
species of things in its sensorium, but only for conveying them
thither; and God has no need of such organs, He being everywhere present to the things themselves.

In this passage Newton is concerned primarily to dispel any
intimations of pantheism that might be located in his general
theological conception. What would have struck Coleridge,
however, was the status accorded in it to the human soul or
mind. When Newton says that the soul of man is merely the place
of sensation, that is, the terminal to which the senses convey their
impressions, when he says that it perceives things by its immediate presence, without the intervention of any third thing, he
makes of the soul a mere receptacle, a place that *receives* the
impressions made on the senses by the species of things in the
world. The soul, on this account, has no initiating or contribu-
tory function. It does not perceive the species of things *through* the
senses; perception, rather, is brought to it *by* them. Whether this
passage was in fact the one that provoked Coleridge's reaction is
of no great moment; what is pertinent is that it amply justifies the
claim that for Newton the mind was passive, a mere recorder of
sensations. No other function of the mind is here suggested. In
particular, the passage provides no basis for supposing that Newton even assigned ideation to the mind, objects being perceived
'without the intervention of any third thing'. It thus seems fully
to warrant the charge of materialism that Coleridge laid to Newton. In any case it is clear that between the Newton who accorded
such a niggardly function to the mind and the Coleridge who
counted among its capacities the esemplastic power of the imagination a gulf existed that was truly tremendous.

For Wordsworth too the limited character and meager function
assigned by Newton to the mind would have been insupportable.
The mind, for Wordsworth, had active, energizing powers. To

regard it as a mere recorder of sensations would have been un-thinkable. For him the external World is fitted 'exquisitely' to the Mind; between the world of nature and the mind of man there exists an interanimating tension. Willey (1961, 278–79) writes of this reciprocating tendency,

> In the ceaseless interplay of Mind and Nature sometimes the one and sometimes the other is predominant. [Wordsworth] speaks of two main states of his own soul, one the uncreative, in which he is under the 'despotism of the eye', and the mind is 'prostrate, overborne', a mere passive 'pensioner on outward forms', the other the creative, in which 'the mind is lord and master', and through its own 'plastic power' can transfigure without distorting all it contemplates, adding the 'visionary' quality to natural objects, darkening the 'midnight storm', or adding 'new splendour' to the setting sun.

It is of course the creative, the endowing power of the mind which, for Wordsworth, is salient in this interplay. This is made clear in *The Prelude* where, after describing the 'renovating vir-tue' vouchsafed by the 'spots of time', he writes,

> This efficaceous spirit chiefly lurks
> Among those passages of life that give
> Profoundest knowledge to what point, and how,
> The mind is lord and master—outward sense
> The obedient servant of her will.

> [XII, 219–23]

The Role of Providence in Newton's Scheme

Two characteristics of Newton's work stand out for us in this study: the virtual confinement of his results to the motion of material, insentient bodies, and his indisposition to specify physical causes. Fundamentally, these two characteristics of his work are correlative: since causes are essentially *active* (or activat-ing) principles, to specify them would necessarily project his results beyond the realm of passive objects; this, in turn, would necessitate a thoroughgoing revision of his fundamental laws.

The *Principia* describes motion but does not explain it. Or, to put this another way, it presents a mechanics but not a physics of motion. By restricting his account to material nature, by drawing back whenever there arose the question of physical cause, Newton made of the world a cosmic machine, an elegant but lifeless assembly, whose parts were subject to and involuntarily obeyed a set of abstract mathematical laws. Any spiritual interaction that might be thought to occur between man and nature was foreclosed by his scheme, in which spirit was absorbed and nullified by the purely mechanical action of objects in motion. Man was left to rationalize his relation to nature within the limits set by this scheme. For many in the eighteenth century that rationalization took the form of seeing nature as a domain detached from the spirit, accessible only to the intellect of man, the 'distancing' that this attitude implied being accepted as a necessary concomitant of the newly acquired understanding.[12]

This attitude did not everywhere prevail. It was called into question, however, not to rehabilitate the human spirit in its transaction with nature but to restore man's humility in the face of God. A temper had to be applied to the arrogance that the Newtonian scheme had engendered; man needed to be reminded that for all his vaunted knowledge and the sense of mastery it induced, the disposition of the world and all that lay within it—including man—belonged finally to God. Contrary to what many in their vanity and pride assumed, the scheme that Newton had devised did not really set man apart from and above the

---

12. Compare Burtt (1954, 301):

. . . the claim of absolute and irrefutable demonstration in Newton's name had swept over Europe, and almost everybody had succumbed to its authoritative sway. Wherever was taught as truth the universal formula of gravitation, there was also insinuated as a nimbus of surrounding belief that man is but the puny and local spectator, nay irrelevant product of an infinite and self-moving engine, which existed eternally before him and will be eternally after him, enshrining the rigour of mathematical relationships while banishing into impotence all ideal imaginations; an engine which consists of raw masses wandering to no purpose in an undiscoverable time and space, and is in general wholly devoid of any qualities that might spell satisfaction for the major interests of human nature, save solely the central aim of the mathematical physicist.

universe; it had only disclosed a portion of the power that was God's—the greater mystery yet lay beyond the ken of man. So Pope in 1732 would write,

> Superior beings, when of late they saw
> A mortal man unfold all Nature's laws,
> Admired such wisdom in an earthly shape,
> And show'd a NEWTON as we show an ape.
> Could he, whose rules the rapid comet bind,
> Describe or fix one movement of his mind?
> Who saw its fires here rise, and there descend,
> Explain his own beginning or his end?
>
> [*An Essay on Man*, 31–40]

It should be noted that the eighteenth century reaction of Pope and others was not so much a reaction against Newton as against his idolators, who, in their half knowledge, fancied that the *Principia* had settled once and for all the order of the universe, and who so congratulated themselves on this having been accomplished by a fellow mortal that they looked upon themselves as emancipated, by his proxy, from the larger metaphysical problems attendant on the human condition. Nicolson (p. 134), commenting on the burden of the lines of Pope cited above, writes, 'Pope's attitude . . . indicated a specific irritation at the extremes of adulation to which the Newtonians were going in the years immediately following the death of their idol, when they had so adored him that Newton bade fair to ascend to the throne of Deity, displacing God himself'. So that in those lines, 'It was not Newton, but the Newtonians, whom Pope castigated'.

The metaphysical problems raised by Newton's great work persisted, however. And their root was to be found in Newton's personal response to the conflicting demands made on his temperament by the claims of science and theology. For Newton the scientist was also a deeply religious man. Throughout his life, therefore, he struggled to reconcile his scientific conclusions with his religious principles. This reconciliation was not easy to effect. Despite the fact that he saw in all his scientific endeavors a witness to the power and efficacy of God, those endeavors, in their consequences, posed fundamental questions of a doctrinal nature. As to his personal religious attitude, there is evidence enough in the *Opticks* and *Principia* that Newton held firmly theistic convictions. To begin with, God for Newton was the First Cause, the Creator of the universe:

> . . . all material things seem to have been composed of . . . hard and solid particles. . . , variously associated in the first creation by the counsel of an intelligent agent. For it became Him who created them to set them in order. And if He did so, it's unphilosophical to seek for any other origin of the world, or to pretend that it might arise out of a chaos by the mere laws of Nature; though, being once formed, it may continue by those laws for many ages [*Opticks*, query 31].

In thus asserting the creative agency of God no theological difficulties were started, compatible as the attribution was with a wide range of religious views. Difficulties arose, however, when the question at issue was that of divine providence. To this question Newton in his two primary works gave a limited and—it may be said—a dispiriting answer. In considering this question we must keep in mind that those pronouncements of Newton on the providential role of God that were readily available during and after his lifetime were embedded in (two) works whose primary purpose was to give a *scientific* account of such purely physical phenomena as light and motion. Whatever thoughts Newton might have had about the role of providence in the affairs of *men*, the *Opticks* and the *Principia* were not the logical place to express them. In fact, it is only in the *General Scholium* of the latter and the late *Queries* of the former—thus in sections added after the first editions of those works—that God is invoked at all.[13]

As far as it is a question of the *Principia* and the *Opticks*, the single statement that may be adduced on the role played by

13. The *General Scholium* was added to the second edition of the *Principia* (1713); the 'metaphysical' queries, 28 and 31, first appeared in the Latin edition of the *Opticks*, translated by Samuel Clarke (1706). For these facts see Davis (1970, 63–65).

providence after the world's creation is the one occurring in query 31 of the *Opticks*, in which Newton, after specifying God as the First Cause (in the passage cited above), continues,

> For while comets move in very eccentric orbs in all manner of positions, blind fate could never make all the planets move one and the same way in orbs concentric, some inconsiderable irregularities excepted, which may have arisen from the mutual actions of comets and planets upon one another, and which will be apt to increase, till this system wants a reformation.

This function God is able to perform, Newton continues, since He is 'a powerful, ever-living agent, who being in all places, is more able by His will to move the bodies within His boundless uniform sensorium, and thereby to form and reform the parts of the Universe, than we are by our will to move the parts of our own bodies'. The agency to reform the universe is to be sure an important providential function; it is at the same time, however, the bare minimum that Newton could render, forced on him as it was by the necessities of his mathematical calculations. It was a function, in fact, dictated not so much by religious impulse as by the demands of scientific rigor. Commenting on this providential assignment, Burtt (1954, 297–98) writes,

> Historically, the Newtonian attempt thus to keep God on duty was of the very deepest import. It proved a veritable boomerang to his cherished philosophy of religion, that as the result of all his pious ransackings the main providential function he could attribute to the Deity was this cosmic plumbery, this meticulous defense of his arbitrarily imposed mechanical laws against the threatening encroachments of irregularity.

As we see, the providential role of God after the creation is limited to the periodic reformation of the celestial orbits, whose courses may have been perturbed 'by the mutual actions of comets and planets upon one another'. The assignment of this function to God was of course enough to distinguish Newton from the deists; considering, however, the wide and profound role that providence has been made to play in other theological doctrines, Newton's allotment can only be seen as exiguous. Here again it must be borne in mind that we are assuming that Newton's influence on his nonscientific contemporaries and successors was founded critically on the *Principia* and the *Opticks*, and that Newton's general views on God's providence, which were certainly more complex than what the scientific purpose of his two major works predisposed him to express, were not accessible to the general public.[14]

It is not part of my purpose to address in comprehensive fashion the religious views that Newton espoused, views which in fact diverged from strict orthodoxy in a number of respects. Newton lived in an age when the efforts of many devout and thoughtful men were directed toward establishing a natural religion, when it was sincerely believed that the exercise of reason ought to be sufficient for the realization of religious convictions. Newton's own work of course provided a powerful support and rationalization for this endeavor. When the cosmic plan was shown to be such a precise arrangement of physical bodies, all obeying a limited set of mathematical laws, and when it was this arrangement alone that was attributed to the power and wisdom of God (saving some minor periodic adjustments), it was a short step to the picturing of Him as a divine architect or mechanic— the perfect and supreme watchmaker in a widely shared concep-

14. Detailed discussion of Newton's position on providence is contained in Jacob (1976), who argues that for Newton God's providence acted in the 'world politick' as well as the 'world natural'. Jacob supplies a certain amount of evidence to show that Newton's personal views were such as to support such a conclusion and that he communicated such views to the churchmen of the period, who then preached a doctrine in which God's providence was as active in the affairs of men as in the natural order. Even granting that Newton's personal testimony may have been available to the churchmen, there were many at the time—particularly those who were to make poetic use of his results—for whom Newton's views would be derived exclusively from his published writings, and for those his position on the providential role of God would be construed, as I have tried to show, in a narrow and restricted sense. As opposed to Jacob, Westfall (1970) argues that for Newton the providential function was limited just to the reformation of the planets and thus that Newton's position on divine providence separates him only narrowly and precariously from that of the deists.

tion of the eighteenth century.[15] Newton, as we have said, was
no deist. At the same time, however, by his anti-Trinitarianism
(Newton was suspected of Arianism), by his attempts to rationalize miracles and his implicit discountenancing of particular providence, by his emphasis on reason rather than revelation, the
witness that he bore for the power of the Divine Being, with its
stress on His dominion rather than His care, was not such as to
satisfy those who looked to God for spiritual comfort and guid-
ance.[16]

Newton and the 'Active' Universe

Quite apart from the meagerness of religious comfort
that Newton's work afforded, and more important for purposes
of this study, was the dampening effect that it exercised on man's
sense of his relation to the natural world around him (although
these two results were not unrelated). In the eighteenth century,
as I remarked earlier, the effect was not seen as dampening; the

15. Compare Koyré (1968, 21):

Once more the book of nature seemed to reveal God, an engineering God
this time, who not only had made the world clock, but who continuously
had to supervise and tend it in order to mend its mechanism when needed (a
rather bad clockmaker this Newtonian God, objected Leibniz), thus man-
ifesting his active presence and interest in his creation. Alas, the very development of the Newtonian science which gradually disclosed the consum-
mate skill of the Divine Artifex and the infinite perfections of his work left
less and less place for divine intervention. The world clock more and more
appeared as needing neither rewinding nor repair. Once put in motion it ran
forever. The work of creation once executed, the God of Newton . . . could
rest.

16. Thus Coleridge writes,

' . . . all that a Teacher can do is . . . to demonstrate the hollowness and
falsehood of the Corpuscular Theory and of every other scheme of Philosophy which commences with matter as a jam datum, or under any disguise
substitutes the Lockian, and Newtonian—from God *we had* our Being—for
the Pauline—*In* whom we move and live and *have* our Being. The moderns
take the ὁ θεός as an hypothetical Watch-maker, and degrade the τὸ θεῖον
into a piece of Clock-Work—they live without God in the world' [Griggs,
IV, 768].

Compare also Griggs, IV, 760.

implicit cleavage that Newton's scientific work introduced between man and nature was subjected to a process of rationalization and ultimately embraced. The affective loss entailed by the embrace was discounted in light of the intellectual gain. Poets like Thomson and Akenside, as we have seen, exulted in their newly won understanding. It was enough to see Nature and to know her. Affinities with her might be felt, but any such stirrings would be private, individual matters; they were not comprehended or sanctioned by the prevailing metaphysic.

All this was consistent, of course, with the Newtonian dictum that matter was inert, lifeless, acted upon by 'aethereal' forces whose own nature was mysterious. The change in response to this metaphysical outlook came with the Romantics, with their notion of an 'active', a living universe. Dissatisfaction with the passive, spiritless conception of the universe that the Newtonian physics presented is expressed not only implicitly in their poetry but also explicitly in various of the Romantics' writings. Thus Coleridge in a letter of 1819 to the editor of *Blackwood's Magazine* would write,

> I cherish, I must confess, a *pet* system, a bye blow of my own Philosophizing; But it is so unlike to all the opinions and modes of reasoning grounded on the atomic, Corpuscular and mechanic Philosophy, which is alone tolerated in the present day, and which since the time of Newton has been universally taken as synonimous with Philosophy itself—that I must content myself with caressing the heretical Brat in private—under the name of the Zoödynamic Method—or the Doctrine of *Life* [Griggs, IV, 956].

By his emphasis on Life, on a philosophy in which natural objects are seen zoologically, not physically, Coleridge is responding to that aspect of Newton's work which bears on the relation between man and the phenomena of nature, a relation which, as I have tried to make clear, his work had the effect of attenuating—to the point almost of rupture—and which the poets of the Romantic age would have had to rethink and refashion if they were to express many of their deepest feelings.

Thus in another letter (to his brother George, 1798) Coleridge specifies the character of the poetry to which such a refashioning has led him. In this letter, after speaking of his disaffection with the affairs of every day, particularly as they involve political activities, Coleridge continues,

> I have for some time past withdrawn myself almost entirely from the consideration of *immediate* causes, which are infinitely complex and uncertain, to muse on fundamental and general causes—the 'causae causarum'—I devote myself to such works as encroach not on the antisocial passions—in poetry, to elevate the imagination and set the affections in right tune by the beauty of the inanimate impregnated, as with a living soul, by the presence of Life [Griggs, I, 397]

Apart from evincing clearly Coleridge's sharp divergence from the metaphysical scheme projected by Newton's physics, the passage has important bearings on the thesis being expounded in this book. In poetry, Coleridge says, the affections are set 'in right tune by the beauty of the inanimate impregnated . . . by the presence of Life', this to be accomplished by elevating the imagination. If inanimate objects are to be impregnated, poetically, by Life, it would seem to follow that poetic expressions attributing human or animate properties to such objects—rivers, trees, mountains—should be taken at their face values, as meaning what they literally say. That to form in the mind images of inanimate objects in such a guise should require an elevated effort of the imagination is understandable; equally understandable, it seems to me, is that the reader of poetry encountering such poetic expression should be required to make a comparable mental effort. It is this effort that I have called the act of conceiving of.

8

The Mind According
to Locke

What Newton tried to accomplish for the physical world Locke attempted for the human mind—to provide an account of its systematic operations. In the main, it is only correspondences of such broad generality that one can affirm in comparing the work of the two men. One would be indicating a correspondence of the same general nature in suggesting that each approached his task in a spirit of empiricism. Correspondences of this sort being granted, we are of course not led to expect that the results arrived at by Locke and Newton should coincide in any particulars or even that there should emerge any significant analogies. An awareness of the disparity between the fields that each explored would suffice to dispel any such expectation. At the same time, however, it may be suggested that the procedures which each assumed as methodologically necessary led, in their respective endeavors, to one parallel consequence that was of considerable theoretical significance. With Newton the empiricist constraints led to the repudiation of hypotheses; the same constraints on Locke led him to reject the notion of innate principles.[1]

---

1. To call Newton an empiricist *tout court* would of course be greatly to oversimplify. There are, however, grounds enough in his writings, for example in the four 'Rules of Reasoning' which stand at the head of book III of the *Principia*, to justify attributing to him an empiricist 'spirit'. These rules are discussed by Koyré (1968, 261–72), who cites a fifth rule in Newton's manuscripts that was never published, in which Newton rejects innate ideas and which is in other respects as well completely Lockian in substance. (In this essay Koyré discusses also the complicated and rather tortuous role that the notion of hypoth-

Locke and Innate Principles

Locke devotes book I of his *Essay Concerning Human Understanding* to denying that human beings on their entry into the world are possessed of any innate principles, either speculative or practical, that is, such as would govern their reasoning or dictate their conduct. Of the speculative it is denied that principles such as '*Whatever is, is*' and '*'Tis impossible for the same thing to be, and not to be*' are innate; of the practical, '*That one should do as he would be done unto*' and '*Parents preserve and cherish your Children*'. Locke's tactic to demonstrate that neither speculative nor practical principles are innate is to show for the former that they are not universally assented to, for the latter that they are not universally observed. Since, moreover, principles (truths, propositions, maxims) presuppose the ideas out of which they are formed, the denial of innateness for the one entails also the denial of the other. So that neither principles nor ideas are innate. Among the ideas thus denied as innate is the idea of God; among the principles, that we should worship God. This is of course not to say that we have no idea of God, or that we do not have and obey the principle that we should worship God; it is only to deny that the idea and the principle are innate in us. On the contrary, argues Locke, if we are to have them they must be acquired. And it is through experience that they are acquired.

Those who adhered to the notion of innate principles affirmed it in one of two versions: naive or modified (for some discussion see Yolton, 1956, 29ff.). According to the naive version, the human soul was 'engraven' with innate principles at birth, rational and moral precepts being thus determined in advance of any experience; according to the modified version, the soul was born with a *disposition* to respond to the occasion of experience in

---

esis played in Newton's developing thought.) The same hedging is indicated for Locke. Various commentators have pointed out that Locke's definition of knowledge, in book IV of the *Essay*, is 'rationalistic' in spirit, at the same time that his program for the acquisition of ideas (book II) is 'empiricist'; see, e.g., Yolton (1970, ix). In the context of Newton's attitude toward hypotheses and Locke's toward innate principles, however, it is the empiricist strain that is noteworthy.

accordance with 'innate' principles—thus to give unreflected assent, as though congenitally primed, to the proposition, for example, that the whole is the sum of its parts or the precept that children should honor their parents. Locke rejected both these positions, arguing against the naive version that if it were true children and idiots should be expected to know the innate principles (which they clearly did not) and against the dispositional version that, once granted the necessity of experience for the demonstration that these principles were known, the claim of innateness was not only tendentious but superfluous as well: all the truths that a man can come to know are on the same footing—acquired solely by the exercise of his reasoning powers upon the circumstances provided by experience. As he puts it (*Essay*, 2.1.2):

> Let us then suppose the Mind to be, as we say, white Paper, void of all Characters, without any *Ideas*; How comes it to be furnished? Whence comes it by that vast store, which the busy and boundless Fancy of Man has painted on it, with an almost endless variety? Whence has it all the materials of Reason and Knowledge? To this I answer, in one word, from *Experience*: in that, all our Knowledge is founded; and from that it ultimately derives it self.

The influence that Locke's epistemological views exerted on the intellectual temper of the eighteenth century was deep and pervasive. To a considerable extent their impact proceeded from their timeliness. The grounding of knowledge on experience and its restriction to what the mind can derive from that grounding, which Locke so unequivocally maintained, was a doctrine that comported well with the liberalizing currents—political, mercantile, and religious—that were gathering force in that period. The rejection of innate ideas and the reliance on experience to furnish the guiding principles of mind and conduct freed man, as it were, unto himself. He became in his own person the agent of his intellectual and moral development. (That this same freedom in a sense reduced him, diminished his significance in the divine order, was a consequence that wittingly or otherwise he was prepared to accept.) Coleridge, for whom Locke's rejection of innate ideas was the mere dismantling of a straw man and who thus could not bring himself to understand the 'prodigious impression' that Locke made on his countrymen, offered the following rationalization for his popularity:

> I verily believe myself that the case stood thus: we were becoming a commercial people; we were becoming a free people, in enjoyment, as we had always been in right. Mr. Locke's name, and his services, which of themselves would be sufficient to immortalize him, had connected his name with that of freedom, and that of the revolution from the natural attachment of old and established learned bodies to old and established political bodies which had been their protectors. It was not to be wondered at that those who were supposed to teach the philosophy of past times were found mainly amongst those who supported the old forms of government; it was [*also to be expected*] and ⟨*stated*⟩ that the same great revolution was to go on in mind that had been going on in state affairs, and that as King William had completely done away with all the despotism of the Stuarts, so Mr. Locke had done away altogether with the nonsense of the Schoolmen and the universalists. In consequence of which, people read ⟨*him*⟩ who had never once examined the subject or thought about it, and found monstrous absurdities [that is, innate ideas] that they themselves had never heard of before, and they found them most ably confuted [Coburn, 1949, 376].

Of course, the influence of Locke's thought extended considerably beyond that exerted by his position on innate ideas. Locke's writings included (among others) works on education, on government, on Christian doctrine. Moreover, the argument against innate ideas took up only the first book of the *Essay*. At the same time, however, because of the profound implications that it held for questions of religious faith, it was that argument that chiefly exercised the minds of his near contemporaries. It is occasion for some surprise, therefore, that the issue of innate ideas seems not to have arisen in that major 'philosophical' poem of the age, Pope's *Essay on Man*. That Pope was familiar with the writings of Locke there is no question. Johnson tells us that Pope read Locke (*Life of Pope*), and Pope himself attests to his familiarity:

> As drives the storm, at any door I knock,
> And house with Montaigne now, or now with Locke.
>
> [*Imitations of Horace*, Satire, II, i, 51f.]

The *Essay on Man*, however, is not an obvious beneficiary of this familiarity. To be sure, Pope's preoccupation with and treatment of the 'ruling passions' may owe something, if only tangentially, to Locke's reflections on the association of ideas (*Essay*, 2.33). Unlike Locke, however, for whom men's 'antipathies' usually result from an originally unnoticed juxtaposition of experiences, the (irrational) association of the derivative ideas then assuming an arbitrary government over human conduct, the ruling passions for Pope seem to be primary attributes implanted by God at birth:

> As Man, perhaps, the moment of his breath,
> Receives the lurking principle of death; . . .
> So, cast and mingled with his very frame,
> The Mind's disease, its ruling Passion came;
>
> [II, 133–38]

In view of the attitude that Pope adopts in the above passage, it is not likely that the *Essay on Man* should provide much support for Locke's position on innate ideas.[2] And in fact there is none.

But if the *Essay on Man* would seem to have been unaffected by Locke's position on innate ideas, there is evidence elsewhere that Pope did not entirely escape its influence. Thus an attitude very much in accord with Locke's insistence on experience as the necessary condition for knowledge may be inferred from the *Dunciad*, in a passage where the goddess Dulness, after decrying

2. Thus in the comprehensive edition of Pope's poem by Mack (1964), of the several analogues to Locke that are cited none pertains to his treatment of innate ideas.

the employment of the mind on 'metaphysical' problems, declares,

> O! would the Sons of Men once think their Eyes
> And Reason giv'n but to study *Flies!*
> See Nature in some partial narrow shape,
> And let the Author of the Whole escape:
> Learn but to trifle: or, who most observe,
> To wonder at their Maker, not to serve

and elicits from one of her minions the response:

> Be that my task (replies a gloomy Clerk,
> Sworn foe to Myst'ry, yet divinely dark;
> Whose pious hope aspires to see the day
> When Moral Evidence shall quite decay,
> And damns implicit faith, and holy lies,
> Prompt to impose, and fond to dogmatize:)
> Let others creep by timid steps, and slow,
> On plain Experience lay foundations low,
> By common sense to common knowledge bred,
> And last, to Nature's Cause thro' Nature led,
> All-seeing in thy mists, we want no guide,
> Mother of Arrogance, and source of Pride!

> [IV, 453–70]

Whereas the votaries of the true faith 'nobly take the high *priori* road' (line 471), it is the fate of those pitiable creatures who do not worship at the sacred shrine to attain to knowledge slowly and laboriously on the lowly foundations of experience.

From the acceptance of knowledge as grounded exclusively on experience it is a short and logical step to a focus on the importance of education. If born vacant of ideas, the mind was nevertheless susceptible of impression; it had only to be filled and formed. And this was the function of education—which is but formalized experience. Thus in the well-known couplet of Pope,

> 'Tis education forms the common mind,
> Just as the twig is bent the tree's inclined.

> [*Moral Essays*, I, 149–50]

Knowledge, if not innate, must be inculcated. The *fruits* of experience, in other words, must be transmitted from one generation to another. In this vein Lord Chesterfield writes to his son:

> I am apt to flatter myself, that my experience, at the latter end of my life, may be of use to you, at the beginning of yours; and I do not grudge the greatest trouble, if it can procure you the least advantage. I even repeat frequently the same things, the better to impress them on your young, and, I suppose, yet giddy mind; and I shall think that part of my time the best employed, that contributes to make you employ yours well.[3]

The same concern in the formation of young minds, with the implication of original vacancy, is expressed by Thomson in *The Seasons*:

> By degrees
> The human blossom blows; and every day
> Soft as it rolls along, shows some new charm,
> The father's lustre and the mother's bloom.
> Then infant reason grows apace, and calls
> For the kind hand of an assiduous care.
> Delightful task! to rear the tender thought,
> To teach the young idea how to shoot,
> To pour the fresh instruction o'er the mind,
> To breathe the enlivening spirit, and to fix
> The generous purpose in the glowing breast.
>
> ['Spring', 1146–56]

To this we may add the lines from Gray's *Elegy* beginning

> Perhaps in this neglected spot is laid
> Some heart once pregnant with celestial fire;
> Hands that the rod of empire might have swayed,
> Or waked to ecstasy the living lyre.
> But Knowledge to their eyes her ample page
> Rich with the spoils of time did ne'er unroll;

---

3. *Letters to his Son*, II, 174. Letter 151; cited in Maclean (1962, 39).

> Chill Penury repressed their noble rage,
> And froze the genial current of the soul.

[45–52]

These lines, taken together with those that follow, express the sentiment, 'There but for the lack of education lies a Hampden, a Milton, a Cromwell'.

Finally, we may instance a passage in which Locke's position on innate ideas is stated in unmistakable terms. The passage, from Blackmore's *Creation*, is cited by MacLean (1962, 34):

> When Man with Reason dignify'd is born,
> No Images his naked Mind adorn:
> No Sciences or Arts enrich his Brain,
> Nor Fancy yet displays her pictur'd Train.
> He no Innate Ideas can discern,
> Of Knowledge destitute, tho' apt to learn.

[VII, 228–33][4]

Coleridge's Reaction to Locke's *Essay*

The correspondences indicated in the preceding section are not adduced with a view toward demonstrating that the poets cited had the *Essay* of Locke before them as they composed their poems or even that its contents were actively in their minds. As generally in such cases, the influence was more likely of an indirect kind. A poet's mind, like that of any man's, is filled with and formed by ideas deriving from many quarters. Some of those ideas, however, from the authority of those who espoused them or from the force of a long tradition, would be predominant,

---

4. Blackmore is today not ordinarily regarded as a significant figure in the ranks of early eighteenth-century poets. Yet his testimony is not to be taken lightly. Compare the remarks of Lovejoy (1978, 135):

> his *Creation* [1712], which seems to most readers now one of the most tedious of the didactic poems of an age of tedious didactic poetry, was much admired by many of his contemporaries and eighteenth-century successors. Addison said of it (*Spectator*, 339): 'It was undertaken with so good an intention, and is executed with so great a mastery, it deserves to be looked upon as one of the most useful and noble productions in our English verse'.

making up in large part the intellectual equipment of the age. Frequently, in the development of those ideas a number of sources and currents can be distinguished. Thus the question of innate ideas, as already mentioned, was one that exercised the minds of many—churchmen and others—throughout the seventeenth century. Given the popularity of Locke's *Essay*, however (by 1706 it had appeared in five editions), the clear and uncompromising rejection that the notion of innate ideas received in book I must be counted among the more potent factors influencing those who adopted and proceeded from that position. As put by MacLean (1962, 20–21), 'The literature immediately following [the *Essay* of] Locke . . . abounds with notions of the mind as a *tabula rasa*, with democratic conceptions of mental equality, and with the idea of ruling passions, each of which owes its rise in part to Locke's denial of innate ideas'.

What Coleridge thought about Locke's position on innate ideas is expressed in many place, perhaps most forcefully at the beginning of chapter 9 of the *Biographia Literaria* where, after introducing for consideration the Aristotelian dictum *nihil in intellectu quod non prius in sensu*, he proceeds,

> How can we make bricks without straw? Or build without cement? We learn all things indeed by *occasion* of experience; but the very facts so learnt force us inward on the antecedents, that must be presupposed in order to render experience itself possible. The first book of Locke's Essays (if the supposed error, which it labours to subvert, be not a mere thing of straw, an absurdity which, no man ever did, or indeed ever could believe) is formed on a σόφισμα ἑτεροζητήσεως, and involves the old mistake of *cum hoc: ergo, propter hoc.*

The 'old mistake' referred to here is articulated by Coleridge in chapter 7 of the *Biographia* by way of criticizing Hartley's mechanical theory of mental operations; there he writes,

> The attention will be more profitably employed in attempting to discover and expose the paralogisms, by the magic of which such a faith could find admission into minds framed for a nobler creed. These, it appears to me, may all be reduced to one

sophism as their common genus; the mistaking the *conditions* of a thing for its *causes* and *essence*; and the process by which we arrive at the knowledge of a faculty, for the faculty itself. The air I breathe is the *condition* of my life, not its cause. We could never have learnt that we had eyes but by the process of seeing; yet having seen we know that the eyes must have pre-existed in order to render the process of sight possible.

The same fallacy—concluding that because it is under certain conditions that a thing is brought to light therefore that thing did not exist in the absence of or prior to those conditions—is expressed again by Coleridge in lecture 13 of his *Philosophical Lectures* when he says,

> Mr. Locke's phrases seem to say that the sun, the rain, the manure, and so on, had made the wheat, had made the barley and so forth; but we cannot believe that a man who was certainly a very wise man in his generation could have meant this and that he was only misled in the expressions from his not being made apprehensive of the consequences to be deduced from them. If for this you substitute the assertion that a grain of wheat might remain forever and be perfectly useless and to all purposes non-apparent, had it not been that the congenial sunshine and proper soil called it forth—everything in Locke would be perfectly rational. I am only standing in amazement to know what is added to it, for never have I been able to learn from repeatedly questioning these Lockians what was done. The only answer has been, 'Did he not overthrow innate ideas?' [Coburn, 1949, 379]

Coleridge's position seems to be that the question really to be addressed is simply whether we are born with the capacity to think, that the issue of innate principles—the claim that specific truths are implanted from birth—is a red herring, 'an absurdity which no man ever did or indeed ever could believe'. Thus in the same lecture he contends that Locke's rationale for the attainment of knowledge parallels in all respects the program of Descartes, with the one exception that Locke arbitrarily and gratuitously foisted onto it the notion of innate ideas in a form that Descartes never held, that in fact what Descartes understood by innate ideas was nothing other than Locke's ideas of reflection, an inborn power or capacity of humans which no one denied. Certainly for Coleridge the mind's 'reflective' capacity comprised among its modes the power to form and entertain conceptions that exceeded the lessons of experience. But this is a matter apart from the present considerations. Here we may simply say that whereas Coleridge (with some exasperation) agreed with Locke in rejecting (the strong form of) innate ideas, his notions of the mind's capacities went far beyond the straitened limits prescribed for it in Locke's *Essay*.

The Influence of Locke's *Essay* on Christian Theology

The status accorded the notion of innate principles (and ideas) had serious implications for fundamental doctrines of Christian theology. As Yolton (1956) makes clear, Locke's address of the question appeared at a time when it had already been the subject of intense discussion and debate. The threat to religion posed by Locke's contention lay primarily in his denying the innateness of moral principles. For the churchmen of the period it had been a ready and cogent argument for the validity and authority of such principles that they were imprinted *ab origine* by 'the Finger of God' and therefore, as divinely sanctioned, commanded obedience of all men.[5] The argument that knowledge of those principles was not innate but had to be individually acquired thus introduced a free space between the dictates claimed

---

5. Yolton (1956, 52) cites from a letter written to Locke in 1690 by his friend Tyrrell that the theologians were 'much scandalized that so sweet and easy a part of their sermons: as that of the Laws written in the heart, is rendered false and useless'. The same point is made by Ashcraft (1969, 200):

> The fact is, the doctrine of innate ideas did not want for defenders, and those who defended it most vigorously were theologians. The reasons for this are not difficult to understand. The belief in innate impressions sheltered ideas for which no other source or justification could be found. Whenever a doctrinal explanation was met with a challenge, the clergy retreated to the fortress of innate knowledge.

for God's will and the disposition of men to perform them. In consequence of this opening between dictate and performance the power and authority of the Church were diminished. Religious leaders saw in this weakening of their authority an invitation to skepticism and free thinking, an attitude in which religious orthodoxy would be replaced by a theology founded on the light of natural reason. The charge for the doing of good and the shunning of evil which the moral precepts enjoined would pass from the authority of the Church to the will of the individual.

Apart from its effect on organized religion, the interruption of man's affinity with God that was occasioned by the rejection of innate knowledge affected the attitude taken generally toward man's station in the universal scheme. In a subtle but substantive way the effect was to reduce man from the status of a being specially appointed for noble ends to a creature situated at the middle of an architectural design. Although this demotion—or devaluation—cannot be attributed directly or exclusively to Locke's denial of innate knowledge, it is clearly compatible or consistent with it. In fact, the position that Locke assigned to man in the chain of being is rather below the midpoint. In 3.6.12 of the *Essay*, in the course of discussing the notion that we have of spiritual beings, he argues that since we observe a scale of corporeal creatures descending below us, graded without 'Chasm, or Gap', and since we are 'in degrees of Perfection much more remote from the infinite Being of GOD, than we are from the lowest state of Being, and that which approaches nearest to nothing', 'we have reason then to be persuaded, that there are far more *Species* of [spiritual] Creatures above us, than there are [corporeal] beneath'. From our point of view it could be argued that the denial to man of innate knowledge has deprived him of a 'spirituality' the possession of which might have qualified him to occupy a true midpoint in the chain—as partaking of both purely corporeal and purely spiritual being.[6] Locke, however, has precluded this possibility for himself.

Without claiming for it a relation of logical consequence, one

6. For an examination of the effect that 'the notion of the full and infinitesimally graduated Scale of Being' had 'definitely to lower man's estimate of his cosmic importance and uniqueness', see Lovejoy (1978, 186ff.).

may still suggest that the 'realistic' or 'naturalistic' attitude taken by eighteenth-century writers toward man's place in the total scheme of things developed in considerable part under Locke's influence. Epistle 1 of Pope's *Essay on Man*, for example, includes the following on the great chain of being:[7]

> See thro' this air, this ocean, and this earth
> All matter quick, and bursting into birth;
> Above, how high progressive life may go!
> Around, how wide! how deep extend below!
> Vast chain of being! which from God began;
> Natures ethereal, human, angel, man,
> Beast, bird, fish, insect, which no eye can see,
> No glass can reach; from infinite to thee;
> From thee to nothing.
>
> [233–40]

Pope's intention in the first epistle is to temper man's overweening pride and bring him to the realization that *Whatever is, is right.* And his arguments are selected to serve that purpose. Much of the same material can be found in Locke, where it is employed without the moral urging but for the same practical purpose—to show that the sensory and rational faculties with which man is outfitted are particularly designed for his needs, that any increase or excess of those faculties would be harmful, not beneficial, to man. Consider these lines from Pope:

> The bliss of man (could pride that blessing find)
> Is not to act or think beyond mankind;
> No powers of body or of soul to share,
> But what his nature and his state can bear.
> Why has not man a microscopic eye?
> For this plain reason, man is not a fly.

7. The notion of a great chain of being had of course a long and consistent history before Locke came on the scene; it appeared in the work of continental writers like Pascal and Leibniz, for example. Its genesis, moreover, can be traced to two leading ideas, that of plenitude, to Plato, and that of continuity, to Aristotle; see Lovejoy (1978, chap. II). In considering its popularity in the literature of eighteenth-century England, however, it seems reasonable to nominate Locke as a likely source of influence.

> Say, what the use, were finer optics giv'n,
> To inspect a mite, not comprehend the Heav'n?
> Or touch, if tremblingly alive all o'er,
> To smart and agonize at every pore?
> Or quick effluvia darting thro' the brain,
> Die of a rose in aromatic pain?
> If nature thunder'd in his opening ears,
> And stunn'd him with the music of the spheres,
> How would he wish that Heav'n had left him still
> The whisp'ring zephyr and the purling rill?
>
> [Epistle 1, 189–204]

Compare these with the passage from Locke's *Essay* where he writes (2.23.12),

> The infinite wise Contriver of us, and all things about us, hath fitted our Senses, Faculties, and Organs, to the conveniences of Life, and the Business we have to do here. . . . If our Sense of Hearing were but 1000 times quicker than it is, how would a perpetual noise distract us. And we should in the quietest Retirement, be less able to sleep or meditate, than in the middle of a Sea-fight. Nay, if that most instructive of our Senses, Seeing, were in any Man 1000, or 100000 times more acute than it is now by the best Microscope, things several millions of times less than the smallest Object of his sight now, would then be visible to his naked Eyes, and so he would come nearer the Discovery of the Texture and Motion of the minute parts of corporeal things. . . . And if by the help of such Microscopical Eyes, (if I may so call them,) a Man could penetrate farther than ordinary into the secret Composition, and radical Texture of Bodies, he would not make any great advantage by the change, if such an acute Sight would not serve to conduct him to the Market and Exchange; if he could not see things he was to avoid, at a convenient distance; nor distinguish things he had to do with, by those sensible Qualities others do.[8]

8. Compare Thomson in *The Seasons*: after a section describing the myriad forms of life inhabiting nature, he continues,

    These, concealed
By the kind of art of forming Heaven, escape

Compare further the couplet

> Shall he alone, whom rational we call,
> Be pleased with nothing if not blessed with all?
>
> [Epistle 1, 187–88]

with Locke's *Essay* (1.1.5):

> Men may find matter sufficient to busy their Heads, and em-
> ploy their Hands with Variety, Delight, and Satisfaction; if
> they will not boldly quarrel with their own Constitution, and
> throw away the Blessings their Hands are fill'd with, because
> they are not big enough to grasp every thing.

Locke on Mankind's Cognitive Capacities

The strain of apologetics that one discerns in the preceding selections was occasioned in part by the need to offer a
rationale for man's position in the world—a position in which,
while much was afforded to his advantage, other benefits which
conceivably might have been allotted, were yet withheld from
him. Pope, whose design in the *Essay on Man* was ultimately
ethical, justifies the limitations on man's sensory and rational
powers within the general framework of a theodicy—'the Universal Cause / Acts not by partial but by gen'ral laws'. In Locke's
Essay, of course, there is no attempt at a theodicy. Nor is there
any consistent effort to construct a system of ethics. Thus the
Essay is not the place in which to find Locke's mature reflections
on man's relation to the divine order or on what moral principles
should regulate his conduct. What we do find there, however, is
Locke's assessment of man's cognitive capacities. And in this
assessment Locke is by no means liberal; rather, those capacities
are hemmed in by severe and extensive limitations. These limita-

---

> The grosser eye of man: for, if the worlds
> In worlds inclosed should on his senses burst,
> From cates ambrosial and the nectared bowl
> He would abhorrent turn; and in dead night,
> When Silence sleeps o'er all, be stunned with noise.
>
> ['Summer', 311–17]

tions have been illustrated in compendious form by Ashcraft (1969, 195f.), from whom I quote the following:

> What is striking about the *Essay concerning Human Understanding* is not the claims it advances on behalf of human reason, but rather its assertion of the meagreness of human knowledge. 'Our knowledge being so narrow' and our ignorance 'being infinitely larger than our knowledge', the 'clearest and most enlarged understandings of thinking men find themselves puzzled and at a loss in every particle of matter' [4.3.22; 3.6.9, 11]. In fact, Locke insists, 'the intellectual and sensible world . . . we can reach with our eyes or our thoughts . . . is but a point, almost nothing in comparison of the rest' [4.3.23]. . . . Throughout the work, Locke's denials are much more frequent than his assertions of our knowledge. Thus, 'we have no knowledge of the internal constitution and true nature of things'. That is, we are ignorant of the 'real essences' of sensuous objects [2.23.32, etc.]. The 'certainty of universal propositions concerning substances is very narrow and scanty'. Indeed, 'these are so few, and of so little moment, that we may justly look on our certain general knowledge of substances as almost none at all' [4.6.13, 15]. . . . And, Locke continues, 'If we are at a loss in respect of the powers and operations of bodies, I think it is easy to conclude we are much more in the dark in reference to spirits, whereof we naturally have no ideas' [4.3.17]. Similarly, questions relating to the nature of man's soul lie 'out of the reach of our knowledge' [4.3.6].

In the face of these limitations it is not to be expected that what Locke *allows* to the intellectual capacities of man should evince much amplitude. Innate principles being rejected, the contents of the human mind originate from direct experience of natural phenomena.[9] Exposure to these phenomena produces sensations, which furnish the mind with ideas. These are simple ideas, consisting in the mere registration of various physical qualities by the

---

9. Locke was a physical realist, believing that the objects of nature have an existence independent of the human observer; see 4.2.14.

several senses. Of this simple sort some are ideas of *primary* qualities, that is, qualities deemed inseparable from bodies; such are ideas of solidity, extension, figure, mobility, and number. The other major class of simple sensory ideas comprises those produced not by the (primary) qualities inherent in bodies but by the *powers* those bodies have to stimulate another order of sensations. By this means are produced the simple ideas of *secondary* qualities such as color, taste, consistency, and so forth.

On the ideas provided by sensation the mind can then perform operations. *Reflection* upon the ideas derived from sensation may produce another class of simple ideas, attendant upon the former. Thus from the simple idea of softness there may be engendered the idea of pleasure, to the simple idea of a body's extension may be joined the ideas of unity and existence. The exercise of reflection is not limited, however, to the formation of simple ideas. It has the power also to compare, combine, and enlarge the simple ideas—of both sensation and reflection. In this way are formed compound, complex, and abstract ideas: the ideas, for example, of a dozen or a mile, the ideas of murder or gratitude, the general idea of whiteness, seen now as comprehending the whiteness of chalk and of snow. Subsuming the several modes of reflection are the two faculties of the human mind: the will and the understanding. Abstracting from the volitional faculty (it not being relevant here), we can say that for Locke sensation and thinking (the exercise of the understanding) account for all the intellectual productions that a man is capable of. As he writes (2.1.24):

> Thus the first Capacity of Humane Intellect is, That the mind is fitted to receive the Impressions made on it; either, through the *Senses*, by outward Objects; or by its own Operations, when it *reflects* on them. This is the first step a Man takes towards the Discovery of anything, and the Groundwork, whereon to build all those Notions, which ever he shall have naturally in this World. All those sublime Thoughts, which tower above the Clouds, and reach as high as Heaven it self, take their Rise and Footing here: in all that great Extent wherein the mind wanders, in those remote Speculations, it may seem to be

> elevated with, it stirs not one jot beyond those *Ideas* which
> *Sense* or *Reflection*, have offered for its Contemplation.

We are struck in reading this pronouncement by a crucial
omission. By what mental faculty, we are moved to ask, is the
distance closed between the start from these lowly footings and
the achievement of those sublime heights? It is well and good to
assert that the mind in its most strenuous and elevated exertions
has still to dispose of the ideas derived from sensation and reflection. But if one acknowledges that the mind is capable of such
exertions, some account should be given of the faculty which
enables them to be made. We might consider the capacity of
reflection to produce complex ideas as supplying this link. But
the high reaches of reflection are reserved by Locke for ideas of
Deity and the discoveries of science. He shows no interest, on the
other hand, in those sublime thoughts occasioned by a communication with nature and that find their expression in works of art.
In short, the imagination as a productive or creative power is
accorded no significance.[10] In this neglect we reach what for the
poets of the Romantic period was an obnoxious and insufferable
deficiency in Locke's theory of mind.

To be sure, Locke does make allowance elsewhere for a mental
faculty which might be supposed to figure in the production of
imaginative conceptions. It seems to be his feeling, however, that
one should not be too much taken with its exercise. His attitude
toward this faculty, which he calls wit, may be inferred from the
following passage, which continues his discussion of the mind's
ability to discriminate among its ideas (2.2):

> If in having our *Ideas* in the Memory ready at hand, consists
> quickness of parts; in this of having them unconfused, and
> being able nicely to distinguish one thing from another, where
> there is but the least difference, consists, in a great measure, the
> exactness of Judgment, and clearness of Reason, which is to be

10. Locke shows almost no interest in the imagination. It is mentioned in the
Essay only rarely and then only in passing as one of the modes of thinking; see e.g.
2.1.20, 2.2.3. In the index which Locke added to the 2d edition there is no entry
under 'imagination'.

observed in one Man above another. And hence, perhaps, may be given some Reason of that Observation, That Men who have a great deal of Wit, and prompt Memories, have not always the clearest Judgment, or deepest Reason. For *Wit* lying most in the assemblage of *Ideas*, and putting those together with quickness and variety, wherein can be found any resemblance or congruity, thereby to make up pleasant Pictures, and agreeable Visions in the Fancy: *Judgment*, on the contrary, lies quite on the other side, in separating carefully, one from another, *Ideas*, wherein can be found the least difference, thereby to avoid being misled by Similitude, and by affinity to take one thing for another. This is a way of proceeding quite contrary to Metaphor and Allusion, wherein, for the most part, lies that entertainment and pleasantry of Wit, which strikes so lively on the Fancy, and therefore so acceptable to all People; because its Beauty appears at first sight, and there is required no labor of thought, to examine what Truth or Reason there is in it. The Mind without looking any farther, rests satisfied with the agreeableness of the Picture, and the gayety of the Fancy: And it is a kind of an affront to go about to examine it, by the severe Rules of Truth, and good Reason; whereby it appears, that it consists in something, that is not perfectly comformable to them.

As between judgment and wit, it is not hard to see where Locke's preference lies. Judgment serves the interests of truth, wit conduces to fancy; judgment is serious, wit is playful; judgment discriminates and thus avoids error, wit assembles congruities and produces pleasant pictures. It is clear that for Locke the imagination as a serious productive power has no place among our mental faculties. His 'wit' may be productive, but it is not serious. It may provide entertainment and diversion, but this function is superficial and fleeting. That it could serve to animate the most profound thoughts and feelings of the poetic temperament was a notion foreign to Locke's conception.[11]

11. That such thoughts and feelings might be expressed metaphorically was a notion not merely foreign to him, it was actually repugnant. Metaphor, we see, is

The Imagination as Treated by Addison

The meager and misprized role that Locke assigned to the 'imagination' was reworked and considerably deepened in the *Spectator* essays (nos. 411–421) written by Addison in 1712. (It is significant that Addison entitled this group of essays 'The Pleasures of the Imagination'.) The philosophy of mind that underlies Addison's discussion is essentially that of Locke, Addison's major and significant extension consisting in his orientation of the Lockian psychology toward works of art. The Lockian substructure appears at once in essay no. 411, in which Addison elevates the sense of sight over all other senses, as being the major source of our simple ideas: 'We cannot have a single image in the fancy [Addison says that he will refer to the imagination and the fancy 'promiscuously'] that did not make its first entrance through the sight'. 'But', he continues, 'we have the power of retaining, altering, and compounding those images which we have once received into all the varieties of picture and vision that are most agreeable to the imagination' (this last is practically a paraphrase of Locke; see above). Locke's simple and complex ideas become, when taken up by the imagination, material for inducing primary and secondary pleasures. In yielding the former pleasure the imagination is essentially receptive and passive, to yield the latter it becomes spontaneous and active.

As it does for Locke, the imagination for Addison stands in a somewhat invidious relation to the faculty of reason or understanding. 'The pleasures of the imagination, taken in their full extent, are not . . . so refined as those founded on some new knowledge of improvement in the mind of men; yet it must be confessed that those of the imagination are as great and as transporting as the other'. The pleasures of the imagination are prefer-

---

(mere) entertainment and pleasantry. It appeals to us because its beauty, being superficial, is so obvious. A metaphor satisfies by the agreeableness of the picture it presents to us; it is an illusion, however, to think that it can express any measure of truth. When to the sentiments that Locke here expresses on metaphor we add the strictures he lays down on figurative language elsewhere in the *Essay* (3.34), we see that any attempt to link metaphor and the imagination will find scant encouragement in Locke.

able to those afforded by mere sensual delights and are less taxing than those that may be achieved by the exercise of our serious mental powers:

> A man should endeavour to make the sphere of his innocent pleasures as wide as possible. . . . Of this nature are those of the imagination, which do not require such a bent of thought as is necessary to our more serious employments, nor, at the same time, suffer the mind to sink into that negligence and remissness which are apt to accompany our more sensual delights, but, like a gentle exercise to the faculties, awaken them from sloth and idleness without putting them upon any labour or difficulty.

According to Addison, the imagination reacts with pleasure in either perceiving or contemplating what is great, novel, or beautiful (no. 412). In the course of his subsequent discussion he makes a number of exceedingly pregnant observations, particularly in adumbrating views on the sublime that were later described in more systematic fashion by Kant.[12] From our perspective, however—that of the Romantic imagination—the significant aspect of Addison's treatment is his consistent and well-nigh exclusive coupling of the imagination with pleasure. The principle of pleasure is of course treated by most commentators as a staple component in our response to the beautiful (and the novel). From the Romantic viewpoint, however, to assess the imagination simply as a handmaiden to pleasure (significant as that role may be) would seem to accord it but a partial, hence inadequate, measure of its importance. Left out in this assessment of the imagination is what we might call its 'metaphysical' dimension, a dimension which for Coleridge in (primarily) his criticism and for Wordsworth in his poetry counted as perhaps its most significant property.

12. Compare for example his remarks in no. 418 on how we may find pleasure in the terrible when we feel ourselves safe from its effects with what Kant says in *The Critique of Judgment*, §28; cf. also his quite stupendous description of relative magnitudes in no. 420 and the respective roles that imagination and understanding play in the comprehension of such magnitudes with Kant's treatment of the same question in §26.

The 'Creative' Imagination

I refer to the 'metaphysical' dimension of the imagination to stress what to me appears to be its most significant aspect. Engell in his discussion of the imagination (1981, 8) makes a number of powerful claims for its efficacy, particularly in its culminative, late Romantic phase:

> The creative imagination became the way to unify man's psyche and, by extension, to reunify man with nature, to return by the paths of self-consciousness to a state of higher nature, a state of the sublime where senses, mind, and spirit elevate the world around them even as they enlarge themselves. . . . As the 'high Romantics' receive and develop the concept of the imagination, it becomes the resolving and unifying force of all antitheses and contradictions. It reconciles and identifies man with nature, the subjective with the objective, the internal mind with the external world, time with eternity, matter with spirit, the finite with the infinite, the conscious with the unconscious, and self-consciousness with the absence of self-consciousness. It relates the static to the dynamic, passive to active, ideal to real, and universal to particular.

These claims, if spectacular, are nonetheless justified. Moreover, any faculty achieving such results may fairly be called 'creative'. From my standpoint, however, the creativity of the imagination consists not in its function of reconciling and resolving differences or of identifying polar opposites; for me the imagination is creative in a more fundamental sense, namely, as constituting reality. By its exercise there is established a view or conception of the universe, a conception which is cogent for its holder, and which neither experience by itself nor experience processed by the canons of understanding and reason would have the capacity to produce. Given these extraordinary properties, it may well be asked whether it is simply the imagination per se that is the faculty in question. We shall address this question in the chapter that follows. For now, however, we shall continue to discuss the problem on the assumption that it is by means of the imagination pure and simple that the mind performs its 'creative', or conceptualizing, functions.

The Unsatisfactoriness of
Locke's Theory of Mind

According to the mechanistic views of Newton the world is subject to certain laws which regulate ineluctably the course and progress of its bodies, including man. To be sure, in some local, interior sense a human being, by an exercise of will, can effect movement and change; in a larger, cosmic sense, however, man is just as subject to the physical laws as are inert, inanimate objects. To this Newtonian picture of man as a body Locke added his analysis of man as a mind. In line with his empiricist views, the mind for Locke is determined in its constructive capacities by the physical world into which it is born. For Locke there is no question of a cooperative enterprise between the mind and the physical world, an activity out of which might emerge a personal, spiritualized conception of the universe. For Locke (as for Newton) the universe is given; the role of the mind is to understand it *as given*. The strongest possible mental ingredient, that is, innate ideas, having been repudiated at the outset, the function of the mind becomes that of registering and classifying perceptions, producing in the first instance simple ideas and in the second ideas that are more general and complex. The entire operation is simply one of processing experience, arriving in the course of this processing at ideas of various types and degrees of complexity. In all these operations the mind is reactive to a reality that is antecedently there; its function is to understand and rationalize this *preexistent* reality. Nowhere in the Lockian epistemology is allowance made for the possibility that the mind, by the exercise of a power native to it, could contribute to the constitution of that reality. The Lockian analysis of mind envisaged no such power and hence no such possibility.

Let us now compare this Lockian, functionalist conception of the mind's capacities—a conception in which the faculty of imagination plays no demonstrable role—with the conception held by

Coleridge of Shakespeare's mind, a mind endowed preeminently with that very faculty. If it should appear invidious to compare the 'common' mind analyzed by Locke with that of England's greatest poet, we should remind ourselves that it is precisely the absence of the imagination as a faculty involved in the construction of one's worldview that one has been alleging as a shortcoming of Locke's analysis of mind, and that thus to invoke for comparison a conception of mind in which that very faculty and that very function are highlighted is merely to prosecute the comparison in the terms that are proper to it.

Of the many respects in which the imagination may be said to condition one's view of the world the respect which for Coleridge chiefly stands out in the practice of Shakespeare is its power to unify and integrate elements that appear in themselves to be disparate or opposed. Enumerating the excellences that Shakespeare displays in *Venus and Adonis*, Coleridge comments (Rhys, 1919, 39–40),

> he had . . . unequivocally proved the indwelling in his mind of imagination, or the power by which one image or feeling is made to modify many others, and by a sort of fusion to force many into one;—that which afterwards showed itself in such might and energy in Lear, where the deep anguish of a father spreads the feeling of ingratitude and cruelty over the very elements of heaven;—and which, combining many circumstances into one moment of consciousness, tends to produce that ultimate end of all human thought and human feeling, unity, and thereby the reduction of the spirit to its principle and fountain, who is alone truly one. Various are the workings of this the greatest faculty of the human mind, both passionate and tranquil. In its tranquil and purely pleasurable operation, it acts chiefly by creating out of many things, as they would have appeared in the description of an ordinary mind, detailed in unimpassioned succession, a oneness, even as nature, the greatest of poets, acts upon us, when we open our eyes upon an extended prospect. Thus the flight of Adonis in the dusk of the evening:—

> Look! how a bright star shooteth from the sky;
> So glides he in the night fron Venus' eye!

How many images and feelings are here brought together without effort and without discord, in the beauty of Adonis, the rapidity of his flight, the yearning, yet hopelessness of the enamoured gazer, while a shadowy ideal character is thrown over the whole! Or this power acts by impressing the stamp of humanity, and of human feelings, on inanimate or mere natural objects:—

> Lo! here the gentle lark, weary of rest,
> From his moist cabinet mounts up on high,
> And wakes the morning, from whose silver breast
> The sun ariseth in his majesty,
> Who doth the world so gloriously behold,
> The cedar-tops and hills seem burnish'd gold.

Two types of integrating or, as Coleridge might say, coadunating powers are here attributed to the imagination. In its 'tranquil' operation it brings together in a single concept (or conceit) a collection of images and feelings which in the bare nature of things (that is, as they stand unvisited by the imagination) are disparate and unassociated. Effected on this mode is a unity of comprehension. One generic notion, that of extreme rapidity, is broached by the imagination as subsuming the flight of Adonis and the movement of a shooting star. As corollaries of this unity a number of subsidiary, context-dependent responses are engendered. In its 'passionate' operation the imagination impresses human feelings and emotions on inanimate or mere natural objects. Effected on this mode is a unity by diffusion. Sentience is projected through the universe. In order to understand Coleridge's meaning here we must regard the predicates 'gentle' and 'wakes' from a particular point of view. We are not to suppose that the poet applied the epithet *gentle* to the lark because larks are like certain humans who *properly* may be said to exhibit such a temperament; we are to read the term as an independently motivated description of a lark, a being which by its own nature and in its own right is capable of gentleness. The point is not that larks may *derivatively* be called gentle; it is that larks, like other things in the universe, exhibit any of a number of general affective, emotional, and temperamental characteristics. In the same way, the lark *wakes* the morning—not by analogy with what humans do to one another, but by way of performing an act which in a universe thus conceived of is performed by (and upon) many and sundry types of being. We are light years away here from considerations of poetic diction or the pathetic fallacy.

Of the two functions of the imagination, the tranquil and the passionate, it is obviously the latter which for my thesis is the relevant one. The effects of the imagination as it operates in its tranquil mode are essentially of a local or ad hoc nature. A similarity is discerned between two or more previously unrelated phenomena. When this similarity is presented, recognition of its unobviousness occasions in the reader a sense of discovery and hence a feeling of pleasure. But while similarity is a constant factor in all instances of the imagination's tranquil operation, the phenomena between which the similarity is discerned, and consequently also the notions that comprehend them, differ from instance to instance. So that, inasmuch as there is no systematic relationship among the elements which are variously shown to resemble each other, no consistent worldview can possibly ensue from the exercise of the imagination in this mode. Things are quite otherwise, however, with the imagination in its passionate operation. One and the same principle, that of impressing on inanimate or merely natural objects the stamp of humanity, may recur numerous times in the course of a poem's development. Thus Coleridge cites again from *Venus and Adonis* the lines

> Even as the sun, with purple-colour'd face,
> Had ta'en his last leave of the weeping morn,
> Rose-cheek'd Adonis hied him to the chase:

and comments, 'Remark the humanizing imagery and circumstances of [these] lines'. The consistent employment of this single principle, projecting itself again and again upon the various and sundry entities inhabiting a poem has the effect of generating a characteristic view of the world, a view in which nature is not a mere other phenomenon that man must learn to understand but one in which it is his partner in a great spiritual communion. Now the English poet to whom, preeminently, this worldview might be attributed is Wordsworth, and in terms of the exposition by Coleridge offered above, we might reasonably conclude that it was Wordsworth's imagination in its conceptualizing or world-creating activity that enabled him to construct it.

9

Wordsworth and the
Kantian Sublime

We ended the preceding chapter with the claim that Wordsworth employed his imagination in a conceptualizing or world-creating activity. Even though our study has several times brought us in view of such a conclusion, the claim itself is a large one and could stand some further grounding. It may be said, to begin with, that it is a fairly common fate of the imagination to have attributed to it unusual and extravagant powers. The fact is that human beings are capable of experiences—both of affective reaction and conceptual formation—whose mental seat it is hard to specify, and more often than not it has been held that these experiences are situated in the imagination. In one of his many allusions to the topic, Wordsworth said that imagination is 'the Power so called / Through sad incompetence of human speech' (*Prelude*, 1850, VI, 592–93). It may be suggested that the incompetence is not so much one of speech, that is, language, but of understanding, of insight into our cognitive processes. The phenomenology of the experiences which are here in question is extremely complicated; such experiences seem not to be the function of any single mental faculty but to involve, rather, a tension or interaction between faculties. Typically, this tension occurs when an experience is such as to strain or overload the capacity of our cognitive apparatus. In such cases the process seems to unfold in the space between imagination and conception. It is in this space that the 'thoughts' which follow upon such exceptional experiences are disposed. In this chapter I shall look more closely into the nature and function of this space.

We in fact earlier raised a question about 'thinkability', in chapter 6, where it was shown to be bound up with the approach to metaphoric construal that I have termed phenomenological. On our assumption that in some poems deviant sentences are to be taken literally, hence construed phenomenologically, the question arises as to what sort of thought is thereby engendered—what, if any, cognition, impression, image, or representation is entrained when we take at face value an expression like 'The rose is happy'. For all the interest that philosophers, linguists, and literary critics have shown in the question of linguistic deviance, the phenomenological conditions that might correspond to such sentences have been left essentially in a state of indeterminateness. Husserl maintains that deviant sentences, although grammatically well formed, project meanings that are 'false, foolish, or ridiculous'; although not senseless, they are contrasensical (*unsinnig*). Further, although in his discussion of intentionality Husserl allows that we may have intentions of nonexistent objects (Jupiter, the Tower of Babel), he is unhelpful on the question of what we might call the *propositional* intentions that would correspond to deviant sentences. Presumably, because such sentences are for Husserl semantically contrasensical, they promote no well-defined intentions.

Linguistic approaches to the problem are similarly unhelpful. The semantics associated with transformational grammar is concerned simply to identify the class of deviant sentences. This it does on purely formal grounds. In deciding that such sentences permit of no interpretation, such a semantics can obviously throw no light on their cognitive or other phenomenological import. The linguistics of British analytic philosophers, furthermore, typified by Ryle's characterization (1949, 16f.) of deviant sentences as comprising 'category mistakes', similarly denies to such sentences any semantic and hence cognitive interest. Finally, the work of literary critics, by the strategy that they adopt for interpreting metaphor, in effect rejects at the outset any possibility that deviant sentences might have cognitive content.

My own attempts to determine the mental state or process engendered by such sentences have likewise left their cognitive properties ill defined. In chapter 3 I introduced a distinction between conceiving and conceiving of and suggested that, although the mental counterparts of deviant sentences could not be projected as concepts, they could be formulated as conceptions, that while we could not think them, we could in some sense think about them; I said that where such a notion as a sea laughing is concerned we could, in thinking about it, delimit a space in our minds where such a notion might fit but that we could not fill that space with a concept, that in this process we project 'a schema, an abstract model or framework which, given the purpose of the exercise, we take to be a representation of that "object' ". Subsequently in that chapter I invoked the testimony of Kant (via Coleridge), and Newton, and Descartes, each of whom, in discussing the problem posed by infinity, drew a distinction comparable to the one I was elaborating. Newton contrasted the imagination with the understanding, claiming that however great the infinity we can imagine, there is always beyond that an infinity comprehended by the understanding, to which comprehension the (successive) efforts of the imagination cannot attain. In this process the understanding (for Newton) acts as a kind of asymptotic limit for the imagination. The extract from Kant makes a similar point, a point, it turns out, which plays a significant role in the discussion of the sublime which Kant advances in *The Critique of Judgment*. It seems to me that the cognitive and epistemological problems posed by deviant sentences bear certain affinities to those posed for our mental faculties by infinity, and that a case analogous to that which Kant makes for the relation between infinity and the sublime can be made for deviant sentences. I shall try to show this by examining in some detail the arguments and results that Kant presents in his third critique.

Reflective Judgment and the Finality of Nature

Kant's treatment of the sublime is preceded by his treatment of the beautiful, and since a good deal of the phenomenological background is presented by Kant first as respects the beautiful, it is necessary before discussing the sublime to consider some of the conclusions that Kant arrives at in his examination of the beautiful.

For Kant the beautiful and the sublime are properties associated with the reflective judgment. Judgment is *determinative* when it subsumes particulars under universals. This process is accomplished when the representation of an object is made to fall under one of the pure concepts of understanding—the categories (substance, causality, and so on). The categories being transcendental universals, furnished a priori by the understanding, judgment has merely to follow the laws of their application and thereby 'subordinate the particular in nature to the universal' (IV).[1] If this process is viewed from the standpoint of classification, it implies a system of twelve classes, one for each of the (twelve) categories. Nature, however, is so multiform, rich, and complex in its manifestations that mere subsumption under the categories and the gross taxonomy thereby implied leaves out of account a host of relations and affiliations that subsist among the various objects that nature presents to us (rocks, cows, and dogs, for example, are all substantial, but only the latter are animals). There thus comes into play the need for a class of empirical universals (concepts), and it is one of the functions of reflective judgment to supply those universals. In the *First Introduction* (V) Kant says, 'To *reflect* (or to deliberate) is to compare and combine given representations either with other representations or with one's cognitive powers, with respect to a concept which is thereby made possible'. It is the first of these two functions—the comparing and combining of representations—which is relevant here (the comparing with one's cognitive powers will concern us later, in our discussion of the beautiful). Where determinative judgment operates merely to subsume particulars under the a priori categories, reflective judgment one might think of as subsuming intermediate or collateral classes of particulars. In other words, the concepts of reflective judgment impose a *hierarchiza-*

---

1. Citations to Kant are to the edition (and translation) of Meredith (1952). Roman numerals refer to sections in Kant's *Introduction*, arabic numerals to sections in the text. Kant wrote an earlier introduction to the Third Critique, which is referred to as the *First Introduction* (Haden, 1965).

tion on the phenomena of nature. Now if these processes are in their turn to be determined a priori, reflective judgment stands in need of its own transcendental principle. As such a principle Kant introduces the finality of nature (V). According to this principle there is in nature a connectedness, a pattern or design, such that judgment in reflecting on the multifarious forms that nature in its particularity assumes will find itself confirmed if it disposes those forms in an arrangement which is orderly and systematic. Although these judgments are contingent relative to our understanding (as not subsuming their objects under the categories), they must proceed as though some principle, whose function is not seated in the understanding, validates them a priori. This principle is that of the finality of nature, a principle to which reflective judgment implicitly conforms in its providing of universals for particulars. These universals are then, to be sure, not the a priori categories; they are, rather, intermediate empirical concepts or universals by whose means is formed the network of species and genera which confers an order on the objects of our experience.

The fact that the system of species and genera holds as it does provides an implicit sanction for the reflective judgment to proceed as though the finality of nature were a principle valid a priori. In effect, then, the principle assumes that nature is adapted to our cognitive faculties, though the faculty in question is not the determinative judgment, since its a priori principles (the categories) are not the ones operative in these judgments but is, rather, the faculty of reflective judgment, which legislates the principle to itself. Particular judgments, when they operate to impose a regularity on the empirical aspects of nature, are thus only contingent for the understanding, following from none of its a priori principles. But they are necessary for reflective judgment, determined as it is to accord in its procedures with the principle of finality in nature.

The notion of finality is bound up closely with that of an end (or purpose). Kant defines an *end* as 'the concept of an Object, so far as it contains at the same time the ground of the actuality of this Object'. Further, 'the agreement of a thing with that constitution of things which is only possible according to ends, is called the *finality* of its form' (IV). In the light of these definitions we have to assume the finality of nature as resulting from a concept which envisaged that finality and whose implementation or realization caused that finality to manifest itself in nature. Yet the finality of nature is not a pure concept of the understanding. At the same time, it is an a priori principle, one which it is necessary that judgment follow if the particular appearances of nature are to be experienced not as random and haphazard but as united under a system of empirical laws. And since, as a form of finality the principle must derive from some concept,[2] Kant says that 'particular empirical laws must be regarded, in respect of that which is left undetermined in them by these universal laws [that is, those associated with the categories], according to a unity such as they would have if an understanding (though it be not ours) had supplied them for the benefit of our cognitive faculties, so as to render possible a system of experience according to particular natural laws' (IV). The existence of the understanding in question need not necessarily be assumed (Kant leaves this possibility open); rather, the reflective judgment simply arrogates the principle of nature's finality to itself. In doing so, it proceeds implicitly as though nature's finality ensued from a concept (of the putative understanding) which envisaged that finality as an end.

Aesthetic Judgments of the Beautiful

In reflective judgments typically there is both a subjective and an objective side, subjective necessarily, in that all our sensations of external objects conduce to inner representations and, moreover, in that the space in which such objects are intuited is (along with time) a pure aesthetic form. At the same time, representations of such objects comprise also an objective side, space imposing on the object its form, sensation presenting it as matter (VI). When objects are represented for us in this double-sided manner we can provide for them a concept and thus gain

2. As we shall see, however, this entailment does not always hold.

knowledge of the object. With the knowledge afforded us by a reflective judgment there is, theoretically, associated a feeling of pleasure, particularly when we connect the knowledge so afforded with other bits of knowledge. To be sure, a particular piece of knowledge thus acquired may be so routine for us that it no longer induces the feeling of pleasure. In the past, however, it may have done so for someone, and for us at present another particular piece may induce it. The feeling of pleasure in these instances follows from our recognition that the particular piece of knowledge we become cognizant of fits into a systematic scheme of relationships with other pieces of knowledge and is thus confirmatory of nature's finality.

There is one type of representation, however, in which the feeling of pleasure is induced quite apart from any accession of knowledge, where, that is, the representation is not referred to any concept. In the representation of such an appearance, therefore, no object falls under our cognition and, consequently, the pleasure cannot ensue from any access of knowledge. It is a pleasure of this type, one which thus serves no cognitive purpose, that is produced in experiencing the beautiful. The pleasure attending such a representation is in abstraction from any material sensation and is produced by apprehension of finality in the mere form of the object. Moreover, as having correlated with it no concept, the finality of which it is here a question is *without an end*.

If this type of pleasure does not result from any access of knowledge, it does not ensue either from the satisfaction of any personal or practical desire. To explain the significance of this remark it is necessary to point out that Kant in his critique of taste deals not only with the beautiful but also with the agreeable and the good, the latter of which qualities may both be viewed as involving a finality issuing from some concept (3–5). The agreeable, then, is that which produces a pleasure as satisfying a merely sensuous desire, the good that whose pleasure ensues from the utilization of an object that is good for some purpose or from willing a conduct that is good in itself. From this it follows that the agreeable and the good have associated with them an interest for the conceiving subject. And in order that this interest be served, an object or activity must be produced which represents finality. If I desire the gratification of some sense, then the object or activity that satisfies that desire must realize the concept which I antecedently formed as conducing to that result. Similarly, if I wish to realize a good, then the useful object or ethical conduct which fulfills that wish must conform to a prior concept of the good which would be accomplished by the production or performance of that object or conduct. In other words, the finality in these cases may be said to correlate with a concept which had that finality in view as its end. The finality of nature, as we have seen, is also regarded as the end of some concept, the only difference being that the concept having that finality in view is not one that in fact is seated in our judgment, either cognitive or practical; judgment simply legislates the concept to itself. In any case, however, the important consideration to emerge from this discussion is that in each of the three types of judgment here surveyed, finality is correlated with a concept whose end is realized—leading to knowledge in the case of nature and to the satisfaction of a personal or ethical desire where the agreeable and the good are concerned.[3]

Unlike ethical judgments, which are practical, and empirical judgments, which are cognitive (and leaving out of account at this stage responses that are purely sensuous), the judgment evoked by the beautiful is aesthetic. This follows from the fact that in such a judgment the finality apprehended of an object serves no purpose, that is, is without an end. Given Kant's definition of finality, namely, 'The agreement of a thing with that constitution of things which is only possible according to ends, is called the *finality* of its form', it might appear that the notion of finality without an end is a contradiction in terms. The key word, though, is 'agreement'. Kant is therewith allowing for cases, such as the one here in question, where no concept is involved but

---

3. Strictly speaking, the response of agreeableness is only physiological and does not presuppose the intentional production, via a concept, of an object. However, from experiences of agreeableness associated with certain objects, the promise of such a response may become incorporated in one's empirical concept of that object and thus motivate its production; see Guyer (1979, 188) for some discussion of this point.

where finality is nonetheless registered. I shall try to make this clearer.

Presumably, we experience a feeling of pleasure or satisfaction whenever one of our concepts is realized. We have seen this to be the case with practical concepts—of ethics or sensuous gratification—and with those cognitive concepts figuring in the classification of natural phenomena. In all these cases the pleasure ensues from the actualization or realization of the concept in question. Such concepts may be regarded as final causes, which lead to the actualization of the objects that were envisaged in the practical concepts and, where the concept of nature's finality is concerned, which ensures that natural phenomena will satisfy the concept. In all these cases the objects that 'fall under' the concepts represent a finality that the concept envisaged as its end. When an object is apprehended as beautiful, however, we experience a pleasure in its finality even though no concept—practical or cognitive—lies behind the object's materialization (or assessment). In such cases, therefore, the finality cannot be said to ensue from any concept, nor, consequently, can it be represented in any object. The finality is a function of the mere form of the object as this form is apprehended and reflected upon by the mind's faculties, and the pleasure is a correlate of this activity. Of the process involved Kant says the following (VII):

> If pleasure is connected with the mere apprehension (*apprehensio*) of the form of an object of intuition, apart from any reference it may have to a concept for the purpose of a definite cognition, this does not make the representation referable to the Object, but solely to the Subject. In such a case the pleasure can express nothing but the conformity of the Object to the cognitive faculties brought into play in the reflective judgment, and so far as they are in play, and hence merely a subjective formal finality of the Object.

In the conformity which the object displays to the cognitive faculties we presumably have an 'agreement with that constitution of things which is only possible according to ends', and which, consequently, can be regarded as instancing a finality of form.[4] Moreover, it is this formal, purely subjective finality which underlies a judgment of the beautiful. Such a judgment is not cognitive, since it offers up no object for the understanding to subsume, nor is it practical, since the object being apprehended realizes no end; it is aesthetic, in that the finality it presents is purely formal and its determining ground entirely subjective.

The pleasure induced by the apprehension of the mere form of an object in a purely subjective representation arises from the play of the cognitive faculties which the judgment in its reflection excites. Even though the process is one of mere 'play', however, the function of the imagination in apprehending such forms cannot occur without the reflective judgment 'comparing them at least with the *faculty* [my italics] of referring intuitions to concepts' (VII). The process in these cases is one of comparing, not subsuming, that is, the customary falling of the intuition under a concept does not occur here. In the process of comparing, though, the imagination is 'undesignedly' brought into an *accord* with the understanding, and it is from an awareness of this accord that a feeling of pleasure ensues.

The accord achieved characterizes reflective judgment in its aesthetic function. In the empirical function of the reflective judgment an intuition of an object is presented by the imagination to the understanding which, as we have seen, provides a concept for that representation. The object being thus cognized, the process has closure. In its aesthetic function the reflective judgment achieves no such closure. Since the representation of the object comprises only its formal aspect, no cognition via a concept is possible. At the same time, however, imagination and understanding, as mental faculties that are requisite for cognition in general, are activated as to their functions and excited to a condition of free play. The focus here is on the process, not on its termination. This process, as envisaging no conclusion and as

4. Kant deals further with this question in §10 where, after acknowledging that finality presupposes a concept whose causality manifests itself in an object as finality, he concludes that we may at times waive this requirement and observe a finality of form 'without resting it on an end'.

accompanied by a feeling of pleasure, propagates a series of representations kindred to and associated with that of the object in view. Thus, unlike an empirical judgment, in which a definite process is carried to its completion by a particular mental function, we have in an aesthetic judgment an indefinite process which engages the mind's total powers in an active and sustained preoccupation.

From the preceding discussion we can draw the following conclusions: an object is beautiful for us (1) when it is not cognized, when the imagination, in presenting a one-sided, purely formal intuition, effects merely an accord with the understanding, and (2) when the pleasure induced by the representation does not (since it cannot) depend on the accession of any knowledge but ensues precisely from an awareness of the accord which reflection upon the representation has engendered.

Aesthetic Judgments of the Sublime

Judgments of the beautiful, as we have seen, are aesthetic judgments which discern in their objects a finality without an end. Judgments of the sublime are aesthetic judgments of the same type, the difference lying in the nature of the objects which evoke them. Correlating with this difference in their evocation is a difference in the affections induced by the two types of aesthetic judgment. Judgments of the beautiful induce a feeling of pleasure, judgments of the sublime a feeling of respect. The feeling of pleasure results from an interaction of the imagination and understanding, the feeling of respect from an interaction of imagination and reason. Let us proceed now to examine in more detail Kant's analysis of the sublime.

Kant distinguishes two types of sublimity—the mathematical and the dynamical. This partitioning is required in that the feeling of the sublime, unlike that of the beautiful, where the mind is in a state of 'restful contemplation' (*ruhiger Kontemplation*), involves a mental *movement*, and in this movement the imagination may be referred (*bezogen*) either to the faculty of cognition or that of desire. The mathematical sublime is conditioned on the first type of movement, the dynamical on the second (24). We begin with a discussion of the former type.

The Mathematical Sublime

Mathematically, the sublime is what is absolutely great (25). This is a greatness whose standard of comparison is not outside itself, in which case the greatness would be merely relative; it is a greatness comparable to itself alone. When we say of something simply (*schlechtweg*) that it is great, we do this on the basis of an actual or tacit comparison with other objects. Such a judgment may be either aesthetic or logical. If the unit of measurement employed in the comparison is merely the intuition of a certain magnitude, say of the average size of a man or tree, then the judgment is aesthetic; if the unit is a mathematical concept—a foot or a mile—it is logical. Since the same object can, by selection of a different unit as standard of comparison, become either great or little, any estimate of greatness by these types of measure can only be relative. So that neither by a subjective judgment based on sensory apprehension, nor by an objective judgment based on a numerical measure, can anything be estimated as absolutely great. It follows that nothing in nature that allows of comparison with anything else can be absolutely great.

That magnitude which is comparable to itself alone is infinity. Thus the absolutely great is the infinite. Now the imagination is able, in concert with concepts of number supplied by the understanding, to achieve intuitions of increasingly greater magnitudes. Moreover, this operation can proceed ad infinitum. In this process of logically estimating magnitudes, however, nothing compels the imagination to grasp in a *single* intuition the sum or totality of the increasing orders of magnitude. Where the infinite is concerned this is in fact impossible, since it would imply using as measure a unit of which the infinite were a component. So that the estimation of anything as absolutely great cannot be a logical judgment, that is, one falling under a mathematical concept.

If anything is to be estimated as absolutely great it will have to be by an aesthetic judgment. We have already seen that aesthetic estimation of magnitude, if made comparatively, cannot lead to a judgment of absolute greatness. It is, however, on the basis of an aesthetic estimation that such a judgment can in fact be attained. In taking in a magnitude the imagination performs two operations: apprehension of the manifold and comprehension of that manifold in an intuition. If the object is small enough, the comprehension of what is apprehended takes place without difficulty. As the object becomes larger, however, this compatibility breaks down and there supervenes a trade-off between the two operations—the greater the scope of the apprehension the less becomes the possibility of comprehension in a single intuition. According to Kant it is for us a law of reason to bring every object of sense to wholeness in a single intuition. But in the presence of certain magnitudes, this demand cannot be satisfied; in particular, this failure occurs when the magnitude is absolutely great, or infinite. In the attempt to bring such phenomena to intuitive wholeness, we become aware of a tension or conflict between the striving of the imagination, 'that most unbounded of human faculties', and the requirement imposed by reason. For the attempt by the imagination to satisfy the idea of totality advanced by reason must necessarily fail, necessarily because an idea is a noumenon and as such cannot be supplied with an intuition. This very failure, however, is a boon, in that it makes us conscious of a supersensible faculty within us. For it is only through this faculty and its idea of totality that we are afforded a realization of absolute greatness, a realization that neither the sensible intuition of the imagination nor the mathematical concepts of the understanding enable us to achieve.

The Dynamical Sublime

Whereas a judgment of the mathematically sublime is evoked by a sense of nature's immeasureableness, a judgment of the dynamically sublime is evoked by a sense of its might. And just as by mathematical calculation we are unable to comprehend nature in its immensity, so are we unable by physical effort to resist its might. In the presence of the mighty in nature—erupting volcanoes, a storm at sea—our powers of resistance are nugatory. In their aspects, therefore, such phenomena may inspire us with fear. As Kant says (28), however, 'We may look upon an object as *fearful*, and yet not be afraid *of* it, if, that is, our estimate takes the form of our *simply picturing to ourselves* the case of our wishing to offer some resistance to it, and recognizing that all such resistance would be quite futile'. We are free, in other words, to remove ourselves in thought from the fearsome phenomenon and feel ourselves safe from its terror. Here again, therefore, in virtue of a supersensible faculty within us, taking the form now of practical ideas concerning our free agency (not the intellectual idea of totality), we feel ourselves elevated above mere phenomena, as independent of nature, and thus find a sublimity in our own powers of mind. For reflection on our physical frailty causes us to see how transitory are health, possessions, and physical survival, thus how vain our worldly concerns, and leads us by an exercise of our will to a consideration of moral precepts. In this process we see nature's might in a different perspective, one in which we are made aware of our own superiority.

Concerning the sublime we can state these conclusions: in the mathematically sublime the imagination's representation is inadequate to the idea of totality; in the dynamically sublime its representation is subordinated to the idea of freedom. Further, in raising us above what is infinite in nature reflection on the mathematically sublime discloses the mind's absolute greatness; in raising us above its fearsomeness reflection on the dynamical sublime discloses the mind's absolute dominion. Sublimity, therefore, is a human attribute, and not a manifestation of nature. As Kant says (23), 'We express ourselves on the whole inaccurately if we term any *Object of nature* sublime, although we may with perfect propriety call many such objects beautiful. For how can that which is apprehended as inherently contra-final be noted with an expression of approval? All that we can say is that the object lends itself to the presentation of a sublimity discoverable in the mind'.

A fundamental difference between the beautiful and the sublime lies therefore in the respective assignments that we make of the finality associated with each type of judgment. In a judgment of the beautiful the finality is represented in our perception of the object—in the sensory impression of its form. On this basis, even though the judgment issues from an interaction between the imagination and understanding, and as such is subjective, we are entitled to say of the *object* that it is beautiful. When we judge something sublime, on the other hand, we do this on the basis of a form which is perceived as contra-final. We therefore cannot say of the object that it is sublime. The finality, rather, is located in the mind, disclosed in that very interaction between the imagination and reason from which the judgment issues. So that Kant says (23), 'It [the sublime] gives on the whole no indication of anything final in nature itself, but only in the possible *employment* of our intuitions regarding it in inducing a feeling in our own selves of a finality quite independent of nature'. I will argue that a finality of this kind, one arising from the employment of our intuitions, is produced in certain minds when contemplating nature and that this finality, when expressed, betokens a state of mind that bears strong affinities to the state represented in Kant's analysis of the sublime. I shall refer to this state and the type of sublimity that I claim it represents as the conceptual sublime. As my chief exhibit for this type of sublimity I shall propose the work of William Wordsworth.

Before we move to this stage of the discussion, however, it is necessary to say a word about another facet of Kant's analysis, namely, that in which he introduces the notion of aesthetic ideas. Treatment of this topic is indicated because it is in this part of his discussion that Kant describes those properties which, according to him, define the poetic (artistic) sensibility. Since, according to my argument, the particular power informing the poetry of Wordsworth results from the temper and disposition of mind that I am calling the conceptual sublime, a part of that argument should show that that same power cannot also result from the generation and employment of aesthetic ideas.

Aesthetic Ideas

In §49 of *The Critique of Judgment* Kant discusses the faculty of mind that constitutes genius. In this connection he introduces the notion of aesthetic ideas, the ability to form which is the characteristic function of the genial mind. By an aesthetic idea, Kant says, he means 'that representation of the imagination which induces much thought, yet without the possibility of any thought whatever, i.e., *concept*, being adequate to it, and which language, consequently, can never get quite on level terms with or render completely intelligible'. This claim about the inadequacy of language to express aesthetic ideas resembles the claim I made earlier in my discussion of a sentence like 'The rose is happy', where I argued that the thought behind it is one which the sentence only imperfectly expresses. It might thus appear that 'The rose is happy' would be the characteristic expression of an aesthetic idea. But such is not the case. As will be made clear, the rationale that I provide for a sentence like 'The rose is happy' is not comprehended by Kant's notion of aesthetic idea.

At first glance it is not clear whether Kant intends as the concepts involved with aesthetic ideas those of the understanding or those of reason.[5] However, the question seems to be settled (in favor of rational ideas) in a passage where Kant introduces for discussion the subsidiary notion of *aesthetic attributes*. Here Kant writes,

> Those forms which do not constitute the presentation of a given concept itself, but which, as secondary representations of the imagination, express the derivations connected with it, and its kinship with other concepts, are called (aesthetic) attributes

5. Kant embroils his discussion by introducing the fact that poems realize intentions. Thus he observes of genius that, 'being a talent in the line of art, it presupposes a definite concept of the product—as its end. Hence it presupposes understanding, but, in addition, a representation, indefinite though it be, of the material, i.e. of the intuition, required for the presentation of that concept, and so a relation of the imagination to the understanding'. He observes further, 'it [genius] displays itself, not so much in the working out of the projected end in the presentation of a definite *concept*, as rather in the portrayal, or expression of aesthetic ideas containing a wealth of material for effecting that intention'. These two passages reflect an ambivalence present throughout the discussion in §49, as Kant shifts between considering the poetic process and its product. In the first passage above the focus is on the product, in the second on the process. It is in relation to the product that concepts of the understanding are involved; in relation to the process aesthetic ideas are involved. And those concepts whose attempted expression engenders such ideas are concepts of reason.

of an object, the concept of which, *as an idea of reason* [my italics], cannot be adequately presented.

He then adds, by way of illustration,

> In this way Jupiter's eagle, with the lightning in its claws, is an attribute of the mighty king of heaven, and the peacock of the stately queen. They do not, like *logical attributes*, represent what lies in our concepts of the sublimity and majesty of creation, but rather something else—something that gives the imagination an incentive to spread its flight over a whole host of kindred representations that provoke more thought than admits of expression in a concept determined by words. They furnish an *aesthetic* idea, which serves the above rational idea as a substitute for logical presentation, but with the proper function, however, of animating the mind by opening out for it a prospect into a field of kindred representation stretching beyond its ken.

In the above passage aesthetic ideas are conjoined with rational ideas as their counterparts. Such ideas (of reason) can be represented discursively, in terms of their predicates, or 'logical attributes', but they cannot be fitted with intuitions. It is to fill the cognitive space left open that the imagination propounds aesthetic ideas. For this purpose it recruits aesthetic attributes, which constitute an intuitive base upon which the imagination can exercise its elaborating powers. To present all this another way: a rational idea is one whose 'object' cannot be given in intuition. Such ideas can be described discursively, in terms of their predicates, but no object can be presented which corresponds to them. The poetic task, epitomized in the work of a genius, is to express these notions so as somehow to body them forth. This is accomplished by involving in their exposition (aesthetic) attributes drawn from objects of which our experience has provided actual intuitions. The intermingling of these secondary, derived attributes with the idea of the rational notion constitutes an aesthetic idea, an idea in which components of something sensuous and something abstract are held in a labile suspension and in response to which the imagination is activated to produce a widening scope of kindred representations.

In the production of these aesthetic ideas intuitions play a significant part. Whatever of past experience the mind can muster which it deems germane to the rational idea it brings into play. The imagination, controlled and guided by the rational idea, works upon these intuitions to the effect that a field of associated representations is produced. This field constitutes the body of the aesthetic idea. Its termini are the rational idea and an intuition figuring as aesthetic attribute. Between these termini there moves a shifting mass of impressions, associations, relations, and insights which the imagination has engendered in its effort to provide substantial form for the rational idea.

Let us now apply these notions to a passage from Wordsworth's *Prelude* (I, 269–85). Although the passage I have selected represents a high point in the poem, I have selected it not for that reason but because it contains a characteristic use of language and lends itself to an analysis in terms of aesthetic ideas. In the section preceding the passage Wordsworth is lamenting his inability to apply himself to the production of the poetic work of which he feels himself capable. Then comes the well-known turn of his thought (my italics):

> Was it for this
> That one, the fairest of all rivers *loved*
> To blend his murmurs with my nurse's song,
> And from his alder shades and rocky falls,
> And from his fords and shallows, *sent a voice*
> That flowed along my dreams? For this didst thou,
> O Derwent, travelling over the green plains
> Near my 'sweet birthplace', didst thou, beauteous stream,
> Make ceaseless music through the night and day,
> Which with its steady cadence tempering
> Our human waywardness, composed my thoughts
> To more than infant softness, giving me
> Among the fretful dwellings of mankind,
> A knowledge, a dim earnest, of the calm
> Which Nature *breathes* among the hills and groves?

We pass over the interrogatory form of the passage, which pertains to the narrative development of the poem, and fix our attention on Wordsworth's evocation of the river Derwent and the sentiments he associates with it. The river '*loved* to blend his murmurs with my nurse's song', it '*sent a voice* that flowed along my dreams', it gave 'a knowledge, a dim earnest, of the calm which Nature *breathes* among the hills and groves'. How are we to take these formulations?

Suppose we follow Kant and read the passage as expressing an aesthetic idea. To begin with, then, the rational idea that impels the passage is the refuge and comfort ('the calm') that nature offers from the disappointments and frustrations ('Was it for this') of human affairs. The aesthetic attribute by which the rational idea is presented is the river. Upon this attribute is elaborated a series of images in which the forms of nature are described as penetrating the consciousness of the young Wordsworth. We are then to suppose that over and between these images there lingers a kind of ideational mist, a dispersion of affective and cognitive particles that registers in some general way upon the reader's consciousness—in short, we are to discern in the passage an aesthetic idea.

Against this background let us consider the language of the lines cited, in particular the passages containing the words I have italicized, where nature is represented as loving, speaking, and breathing. For all the latitude implicit in Kant's account of aesthetic ideas, it contains nothing to suggest that these representations are to be taken otherwise than as ordinary metaphors, that is, simply as conveying the impressions that the forms of nature have made on Wordsworth's *poetic* sensibility. Nature, on this view, is seen as something insentient which Wordsworth has chosen to describe with these predicates simply to reflect the play of his artistic fancy. On this reading Nature is a collection of physical objects, a lifeless mechanism, with Wordsworth, drawing on his human responses, employing words pertaining properly to his own affections and merely transferring them to nature. Read in this way the metaphors amount to little more than poetic diction or pathetic fallacies.[6] A reading of this sort not only fails

6. Compare Wordsworth in the Preface to the *Lyrical Ballads*: 'The reader will find that personifications of abstract ideas rarely occur in these volumes; and, I

to do justice to the strong poetic feeling of these lines, it also degrades and trivializes the rational idea.

In my opinion, even if we grant that the lines from Wordsworth present an aesthetic idea, the quality of his poetry that makes Wordsworth unique among English poets remains unaddressed. In support of this claim it would almost be enough to adduce the lines from a poem of Frederick the Great which Kant instances as incorporating an aesthetic idea.[7] The main reason for the reservation, however, lies in the fact that Kant's notion of aesthetic idea is a general notion—any combination of rational idea and aesthetic attribute, if properly combined, can serve to generate an aesthetic idea. It would thus be possible in going through Wordsworth's *Prelude* to find in it a variety of different and unrelated aesthetic ideas. If we use aesthetic ideas as a basis, therefore, it is not likely that we should reach any understanding of the quality in Wordsworth's poetry that impresses us with its peculiar power. In what follows I shall propose a different reason for that impression, a reason deriving not from Wordsworth's ability to propound aesthetic ideas but from his characteristic cast of mind, a cast of mind that I have referred to as conceptually sublime.

---

hope, are utterly rejected as an ordinary device to elevate the style, and raise it above prose'. Although this statement applies to the personification of abstract ideas, we would not be mistaken, I believe, in attributing to him the same attitude toward indulgences in the pathetic fallacy.

7.   Oui, finissons sans trouble, et mourons sans regrets,
      En laissant l'Univers comblé de nos bienfaits.
      Ainsi l'Astre du jour, au bout de sa carrière,
      Répand sur l'horizon une douce lumière,
      Et les derniers rayons qu'il darde dans les airs
      Sont les derniers soupirs qu'il donne à l'Univers.

Commenting on these lines Kant says that in them the king

kindles . . . his rational idea of a cosmopolitan sentiment even at the close of life, with the help of an [aesthetic] attribute which the imagination (in remembering all the pleasures of a fair summer's day that is over and gone—a memory of which pleasures is suggested by a serene evening) annexes to that representation, and which stirs up a crowd of sensations and secondary representations [an aesthetic idea] for which no expression can be found'.

Despite Kant's respectful analysis of these lines, however, the fact remains that as poetry they are little more than commonplace.

From my attribution to Wordsworth of this conceptual sub-limity it follows (as I shall show) that his metaphors are to be taken literally. Returning then to the words italicized in the passage, let us take them at their face value, that is, literally. As soon as we do this, nature and the river are transfigured: the river does speak, nature does breathe. No longer are their concepts lifeless, of objects existing outside and apart from us; they be-come vitalized with the same forces that animate human nature. This reading is not one of a crass and stereotyped hylozoism, the establishing of a 'living' realm of objects separate from and un-connected with ourselves. It is a reading, instead, which implies a universal interanimation, a sense of something 'deeply inter-fused', the sense expressed with utmost seriousness in these lines (88–102) from *Tintern Abbey*:

> For I have learned
> To look on nature, not as in the hour
> Of thoughtless youth; but hearing oftentimes
> The still, sad music of humanity,
> Not harsh nor grating, though of ample power
> To chasten and subdue. And I have felt
> A presence that disturbs me with the joy
> Of elevated thoughts; a sense sublime
> Of something far more deeply interfused,
> Whose dwelling is the light of setting suns,
> And the round ocean and the living air,
> And the blue sky, and in the mind of man:
> A motion and a spirit, that impels
> All thinking things, all objects of thought
> And rolls through all things.

In these lines we have the testimony of the mature Words-worth ('not as in the hours of thoughtless youth'), where Words-worth is speaking in his most serious strain. Whenever he speaks in this strain, and such is surely the case in the lines cited from *The Prelude*, we are justified, even obligated, to take what he says seriously, however contrasensical may appear to be his pairing of subjects and predicates. Indeed, it is my contention that Wordsworth's metaphors, taken literally, are not contrasensical if read against a context in which Wordsworth's thoughts are understood to be conceptually sublime.

Kant has defined the mathematical sublime as a feeling induced by a sense of nature's immeasureableness, and the dynamical sublime as a feeling induced by a sense of its might. Both these feelings arise in the presence of certain natural phenomena of which, because of their immensity or fearsomeness, we can gain no coherent intuitions, with the consequence that neither the faculty of understanding nor that of desire can provide a concept under which to subsume the experience.[8] As Kant says, such phenomena are inherently contra-final, that is, their forms cannot be apprehended in an intuition. In the effort to rationalize this contra-finality we are made aware of an idea or principle of reason and in the process become conscious of a supersensible faculty within us. Sublimity is therefore estimated of ourselves, of that power of the mind which transcends and governs those mental faculties that dispose of the sensible in experience.

The Conceptual Sublime

What I am arguing is that a place must be made for a third type of sublime—the conceptual—and that it is this type of sublime that the passages from Wordsworth reflect. It will be recalled that the rational ideas which the contemplation of the sublime in nature elicited were those ot totality for the mathematical and of freedom for the dynamical sublime. These ideas are for Kant a priori principles which operate in the conceptual

8. Reference to the faculty of desire where the dynamically sublime is concerned is apparently based on the passage from §28 already cited in which Kant says that in the presence of a fearsome object our estimate may take the form of 'simply picturing to ourselves the case of our wishing [my italics] to offer some resistance to it, and recognizing that all such resistance would be quite futile'. In §24, cited earlier, Kant says that the feeling of the sublime involves a mental movement, and that in this movement the imagination may be referred either to the faculty of cognition or to that of desire. Thus the imagination merely 'refers' to the faculty of desire. This 'reference', however, is not brought to completion in that faculty but finds its resolution in an idea of reason—that of freedom.

and practical behavior of all men. I suggest that an idea which for Wordsworth was a cornerstone of his mature beliefs had a status and played a role which for him individually was as fundamental as the ideas of totality and freedom were for Kant in general. I refer to his idea of the oneness, the integrity of the created world, the idea of man and nature as participating in a unity of sovereign disposition.

> In progress through this verse my mind hath looked
> Upon the speaking face of earth and heaven
> As her prime teacher, intercourse with man
> Established by the Sovereign Intellect,
> Who through that bodily image hath diffused
> A soul divine which we participate,
> A deathless spirit.
>
> [*Prelude*, V, 13–18]

The idea for Wordsworth was not to bring intuitions to totality or completeness, a striving which for Kant was a universal principle of reason; it was intead that the world as created *is* a completeness and totality, a conviction which for Wordsworth was an article of personal faith: 'in all things I saw one life' (*Prelude*, II, 410–11). Moreover, where Kant's rational principles are a priori and hold for all men, Wordsworth's idea was a posteriori and vouchsafed to but few. Thus, alluding to his master idea, he writes,

> I mean to speak
> Of that interminable building reared
> By observation of affinities
> In objects where no brotherhood exists
> To common minds.
>
> [*Prelude*, II, 382–86]

The formation of this idea entails a conceptual effort, an effort which bears all the marks of the sublime. From early childhood Wordsworth responded to the forms of nature. The feelings evoked in him by these forms were besetting and profound. They posed a challenge to the common notion that nature and man represented different orders of being. To rationalize this challenge Wordsworth conceived of the idea of oneness. This idea was neither a concept available a priori nor someone's doctrine of pantheism that Wordsworth simply adopted as his own; it was a product of Wordsworth's thought working on persistent intuitions which found no resting place among his ordinary concepts. For Kant the sublime is evoked by objects, phenomena of nature. The contra-finality which sets in train the mental operations that culminate in a sense of the sublime inheres in the *forms* of nature. For Wordsworth, on the contrary, the sublime is evoked by *thoughts* upon nature. This fact changes the mental dynamic that grounds the sense of sublimity. When this sense is evoked by a form of nature, the operative mental components are imagination and a principle of reason. The inability of the imagination to form of the object a whole of intuition brings to consciousness a principle of reason, and this consciousness, in making us aware of a supersensible faculty within us, warrants for us the superiority of our minds over nature. Wordsworth's actuating interest in nature, however, was not in the physical magnitude or power of its individual forms. His interest was in the intimations he received from nature of some universal kinship, in a feeling it engendered of a 'primal sympathy', a feeling he expressed by saying,

> To me the meanest flower that blows can give
> Thoughts that do often lie too deep for tears.
>
> ['Ode: Intimations of Immortality', 203–04]

The problem for Wordsworth was to sustain and rationalize this feeling in a general atmosphere in which nature was thought of as a merely physical background for the worldly pursuits of men, as a collection of objects between which and the human spirit 'no brotherhood exists to common minds'.

In Kant's two types of sublimity the rational principle serves as a kind of limit toward which the imagination, in its effort to supply an intuition, strains but cannot reach. The sense of the sublime in these cases results from the tension set up between these two mental components. Wordsworth's epistemological situation was different. His intuitions of nature as sentient were in direct conflict with the concept of nature as a merely physical organism, a concept fostered only too easily by the affairs of everyday life. That it required an effort to sustain those intuitions is indicated by Wordsworth in the following lines, where he speaks of the need to 'shrink back'

> From every combination that might aid
> The tendency, too potent in itself,
> Of habit to enslave the mind—I mean
> Oppress it by the laws of vulgar sense,
> And substitute a universe of death,
> The falsest of all worlds, in place of that
> Which is divine and true.

[*Prelude*, XIII, 136–43]

In a footnote to this passage the editors remark, 'Wordsworth's "universe of death" . . . is one in which the individual is enslaved by the unimaginative reliance on the senses and on purely habitual perception'. In any universe fashioned solely out of perceptual apprehension, one in the construction of which the mind was quiescent and the senses dominant, the concomitant impression of nature would be that of a physical organism, a mechanical arrangement of objects. Unlike the standard Kantian challenge, therefore, in which the imagination must be spurred to approach a rational idea as a limit, the intellectual task for Wordsworth was, rather, to overcome an impression of nature that disaccorded with deep and strongly held intuitions. The fact that these intuitions were felt by Wordsworth already as a boy need not in any way have relieved or mitigated the severity of the conflict. In any case, what overcame this conflict for Wordsworth and produced for him a condition of finality was the conception of an 'active' universe, a universe in which man and nature were parts of a single, unified whole, and through which there coursed a common vivifying spirit ('a soul divine'). The effort to attain to this conception, involving deep and protracted thought, discloses a supersensible faculty within us and in the process makes us aware of a greatness of soul that transcends man and nature, intimating the presence of divinity. The sense of the sublime in this case arises from the consciousness that by our own mental efforts to rationalize the impressions made upon us by nature we bring ourselves, by a conceptual effort, to an awareness of something greater than nature, greater than ourselves, something of which nature and man are but corporeal manifestations.

The Egotistical Sublime

Since the time that Keats made the attribution, most commentators have agreed that a certain individualistic tone or attitude in Wordsworth's poetry is felicitously characterized by the phrase 'Wordsworthian or egotistical sublime'. In his commentary on this attribution, Weiskel writes (1976, 49), 'The egotistical sublime is not "negative" or dialectical. In Kantian terms, the sudden "movement" of the mind is greatly slowed and the phenomenal or sensible ego is aggrandized in place of the self-recognition of the noumenal reason. But Kantian terms are not quite adequate, for this is a "positive" sublime that in the end would subsume all otherness, all possibility of negation'. Weiskel goes on to say (p. 50), 'In the egotistical sublime the two Kantian poles of sensible nature and eschatological destination collapse inward and become "habitual" attributes of what was to be called Imagination—a totalizing consciousness whose medium is sense but whose power is transcendent. Apocalypse becomes immanent; the sublime a daily habit'. These remarks are part of a profound and penetrating analysis that Weiskel offers of Wordsworth's poetic temperament.

The Kantian sublime is negative in that it materializes from the imagination's defeat in its effort to achieve intuitional fullness, an effort enjoined upon it by an idea (totality, freedom) of reason. As attempting to negotiate closure between sense and idea the effort of the imagination is also dialectical. The egotistical sublime, on the other hand, is positive. To be emphasized in its analysis is not the imagination's failure to bridge the mental space lying between the Kantian poles of sense and idea; to be emphasized instead is its success in 'comprehending' the sublime experience. Rather than being defeated by the experience, it is enhanced by it. In the process of compassing the experience, the imagination becomes conscious not of its limitations but of its power. As I have tried to show, however, there are grounds for reconsidering the assignment of all this 'power' to the imagination. In the artistic designs and productions that one commonly refers to the ('creative') imagination, there is undeniably a conceptual component. Therefore, if the egotistical sublime is rationalized as an aggrandizement of the imagination, to the essential exclusion of any role that other mental faculties might play in its expression, then the egotistical sublime would seem to be an inadequate vehicle for the power assigned to it. At the same time, Keats's observation must be presumed to have some point. In what follows, I shall try to adjudicate between the claims of the conceptual and the egotistical sublime in Wordsworth's poetry.

By way of illustrating the 'positive' nature of the egotistical sublime, Weiskel cites some lines from the Mount Snowdon passage of *The Prelude*, where Wordsworth describes the capacities of those who, like himself, are possessed of 'higher' minds:

> Them the enduring and the transient both
> Serve to exalt; they build up greatest things
> From least suggestions; ever on the watch,
> Willing to work and to be wrought upon,
> They need not extraordinary calls
> To rouse them; in a world of life they live,
> By sensible impressions not enthralled,
> But by their quickening impulse made more prompt
> To hold fit converse with the spiritual world,
> And with the generations of mankind
> Spread over time, past, present, and to come,
> Age after age, till Time shall be no more.
> Such minds are truly from the Deity,
> For they are Powers; and hence the highest bliss
> That flesh can know is theirs—the consciousness
> Of whom they are, habitually infused

Through every image and through every thought,
And all affections by communion raised
From earth to heaven, from human to divine.

[XIV, 100-18]

Weiskel comments that, despite their grandeur, these lines appear to be 'alloyed with a kind of massive complacency'. Indeed, it would not be going far afield to find in them an excessive self-satisfaction. In any case, Keats's attribution would appear to be just. Our task, therefore, is to see whether there is any inconsistency in maintaining for Wordsworth both an egotistical and a conceptual sublime.

That the conceptual and the egotistical sublime are compatible with one another follows from the fact that each is used to characterize a different aspect of Wordsworth's poetic production. The conceptual sublime refers to Wordsworth's metaphysical outlook, an outlook that saw nature as 'alive', an outlook that, in consequence, saw a communion of deep, almost mystical proportions as obtaining between man and nature. The egotistical sublime, by contrast, refers not to any metaphysical outlook but to a mental or psychological attitude, that of a somewhat overweening self-regard, an attitude that grew for Wordsworth out of a sense of his intellectual (spiritual) distinctiveness. For Wordsworth there are 'common minds' and 'higher minds' (Prelude, II, 386; XIII, 90). The higher minds are divinely favored ('such minds are truly from the Deity'): to them it is given to perceive 'affinities / In objects where no brotherhood exists / To common minds' (the insight underlying the metaphysical outlook). It is from the recognition in oneself of this 'gift', this specially dispensed endowment, that the sense of intellectual distinctiveness derives. This sense then manifests itself in a characteristic attitude, that of regarding oneself to have been providentially elected, and I would argue that it is the manifestation of this attitude in Wordsworth's poetry that the phrase *egotistical sublime* is appropriately used to describe.

The sense of communion is definitively expressed at an earlier point in the Mount Snowdon passage. Speaking of the 'huge sea of mist' which there enveloped him and his companions, Wordsworth writes,

> . . . we stood, the mist
> Touching our very feet; and from the shore
> At distance not the third part of a mile
> Was a blue chasm, a fracture in the vapour,
> A deep and gloomy breathing-place, through which
> Mounted the roar of waters, torrents, streams
> Innumerable, roaring with one voice.
> The universal spectacle throughout
> Was shaped for admiration and delight,
> Grand in itself alone, but in that breach
> Through which the homeless voice of waters rose,
> That dark deep thoroughfare, had Nature lodged
> The soul, the imagination of the whole.
>
> [*Prelude*, XIII, 53–65]

In meditating that night on his experience, the scene he had witnessed appeared to him to be 'The perfect image of a mighty mind'; continuing, Wordsworth writes,

> One function of such mind had Nature there
> Exhibited by putting forth, and that
> With circumstance most awful and sublime:
> That domination which she oftentimes
> Exerts upon the outward face of things,
> So moulds them, and endues, abstracts, combines,
> Or by abrupt and unhabitual influence
> Doth make one object so impress itself
> Upon all others, and pervades them so,
> That even the grossest minds must see and hear,
> And cannot chuse but feel. The power which these
> Acknowledge when thus moved, which Nature thus
> Thrusts forth upon the senses, is the express
> Resemblance—in the fullness of its strength
> Made visible—a genuine counterpart

And brother of the glorious faculty
Which higher minds bear with them as their own.
This is the very spirit in which they deal
With all objects of the universe:
They from their native selves can send abroad
Like transformation, for themselves create
A like existence, and, when'er it is
Created for them, catch it by an instinct.

[*Prelude*, XIII, 74–96]

Constituents of the scene on Mount Snowdon are the moon, hills, the sea, and mist (XIII, 41–48). Dominant among these elements are the waters (torrents, streams) 'roaring with one voice'. The mist produced by these waters, by spreading through the constituent elements of the scene, effects upon them a synthesis and unification. All this, however—the mist and the effected synthesis—has its origin in the 'blue chasm', which is represented as 'the soul, the imagination of the whole'. This unifying power or function of nature, projected from the chasm and expressed in the mist, is then, in the second passage, called the 'express resemblance . . . of the glorious faculty which higher minds bear with them as their own' (ll. 86ff.). The same 'spirit' that is manifested by nature when she 'transforms' the objects of the universe animates those (higher) minds which, like nature, are able to transform (by combining or synthesizing) those same objects. Both nature and the imagination of the elected few are in this sense 'creative'. In Wordsworth's case the form taken fundamentally by this 'creativity' consisted in the welding of man and nature into an idea of organic and mutually inspiriting relatedness; it is this idea that I have referred to as the conceptual sublime. Various occasions might move Wordsworth's imagination to implement this idea or to find it instantiated (actually two aspects of the same process; cf. XIII, 93–96), but the underlying idea is a conceptual construction which, by the nature of its phenomenological genesis, I have characterized as sublime.

The note of egotism obtrudes here (as elsewhere) in the invidious comparison that Wordsworth makes between 'grossest minds', for whom it is only when nature produces objects or scenes that are prodigiously 'creative' that they 'cannot chuse but feel' her power, and minds of nobler constitution, who deal in that transforming spirit habitually—who respond to the slightest variations effected upon the objects of nature and who are also able out of their own minds to produce forms comparable to those produced by nature.

Metaphoric Worlds

If the thoughts expressed by Wordsworth in the lines cited from *The Prelude* are in fact conceptually sublime, then we as readers have imposed on ourselves a corresponding conceptual task—in some way to approximate to the thoughts that animated Wordsworth in the writing of such lines. I believe that the only way this is possible is to take his metaphors literally. Doing so *forces* us to conceive of a world in which nature is 'alive', in which a community of spirit exists between ourselves and the objects of nature. To conceive of a river as loving, of nature as breathing, opens up for us a world different from the ordinary world of our senses and cognitions. This is a metaphoric world, a world of our own making, a world, it is my contention, that Wordsworth realized in his own thought and on the basis of which he wrote such lines as those cited from *The Prelude*.

The judgment has often been made that Wordsworth's poetry is in its profounder moments sublime. Such a judgment is not really justified if its basis is simply that Wordsworth took high themes as his subject and treated them with high seriousness. Many poets have done this without their poetry eliciting a similar judgment. The sense of the sublime in Wordsworth's poetry is occasioned by his transforming conception of the world, by the feeling he consequently transmits of a profound and interenlivening relationship as obtaining between man and nature. It is this conception lying behind and informing his poetry that projects into it a sense of the sublime. Thus, if we are to participate in its sublimity, we must read his poetry in a temper and disposition of mind such as animated Wordsworth in the writing of it. That state of mind, I contend, may be induced by a literal reading of his metaphors. Such a reading forces us to conceive of a world or state of affairs whose nature, in its abrogation of the canons that govern existential relations in our world, is estranged from common notions of reality and may rightly be termed metaphoric.

References

Abrams, M. H., gen. ed (1979). *The Norton Anthology of English Literature*, 4th ed., 2 vols., New York and London, W. W. Norton and Co.

Addison J. (1975). *Joseph Addison: Essays in Criticism and Literary Theory*, Northbrook, Ill. AHM Publishing Corp.

Akenside, M. (1863). *The Poetical Works of Mark Akenside*, ed. C. C. Clerk, Edinburgh, James Nichol..

Aristotle (1907). *The Poetics of Aristotle*, 4th ed., ed. and tr. S. H. Butcher, London, MacMillan and Co. Ltd.

Aristotle (1968). *Metaphysics*, tr. R. Hope, Ann Arbor, Mich., University of Michigan Press (Ann Arbor Paperbacks).

Aristotle (1973). *The Categories, On Interpretation*, ed. and tr. H. P. Cooke, Cambridge, Mass., Harvard University Press (Loeb Classical Library).

Ashcraft, R. (1969). 'Faith and Knowledge in Locke's Philosophy', in J. W. Yolton, ed., *John Locke: Problems and Perspectives*, Cambridge, England, Cambridge University Press, pp. 194–223.

Augustine, St. (1961). *Confessions*, tr. R. S. Pine-Coffin, Baltimore, Md., Penguin Books.

Averroes (1969). *Averroes Middle Commentary on Porphyry's 'Isagoge' and on Aristotle's 'Categoriae'*, ed. H. A. Davidson, Berkeley and Los Angeles, University of California Press, and Cambridge, Mass., The Mediaeval Academy of America.

Beardsley, M. (1962). 'The Metaphoric Twist', *Philosophy and Phenomenological Research* 22:293–307.

Black, M. (1962). 'Metaphor', in *Models and Metaphors*, Ithaca, N.Y., Cornell University Press.

Black, M. (1964). *A Companion to Wittgenstein's 'Tractatus'*, Ithaca, N.Y., Cornell University Press.

Blake, W. (1968). *The Poetry and Prose of William Blake*, ed. D. V. Erdman, Garden City, N.Y., Doubleday and Co., Inc.

Burke, K. (1970). *The Rhetoric of Religion*, Berkeley and Los Angeles, University of California Press.

Burrell, D. C. (1973). *Analogy and Philosophical Language*, New Haven and London, Yale University Press.

Burtt, E. A. (1954). *The Metaphysical Foundations of Modern Physical Science*, Garden City, N.Y., Doubleday and Co., Inc. (Doubleday Anchor Books).

Casey, E. S. (1976). *Imagining: A Phenomenological Study*, Bloomington, Ind., and London, Indiana University Press.

Chomsky, N. (1965). *Aspects of the Theory of Syntax*, Cambridge, Mass., The MIT Press.

Coleridge, S. T. (1919). *Coleridge's Essays and Lectures on Shakespeare and Some Other Old Poets and Dramatists*, ed. E. Rhys, London and Toronto, J. M. Dent and Sons, and New York, E. P. Dutton and Co. (cited as Rhys).

Coleridge, S. T. (1949). *The Philosophical Lectures of Samuel Taylor Coleridge: Hitherto Unpublished*, ed. K. Coburn, New York, The Philosophical Library (cited as Coburn).

Coleridge, S. T. (1956–71). *Collected Letters of Samuel Taylor Coleridge*, vols. I–VI, ed. E. L. Griggs, Oxford, The Clarendon Press (cited as Griggs).

Coleridge, S. T. (1983). *Biographia Literaria*, 2 vols., ed. J. Engell and W. J. Bate, London and Princeton, N.J., Routledge and Kegan Paul and Princeton University Press (Bollingen Series LXXV).

Copleston, F. C. (1955). *Aquinas*, Harmondsworth, Middlesex, England, Penguin Books.

Cragg, G. R. (1964). *Reason and Authority in the Eighteenth Century*, Cambridge, England, at the University Press.

Davidson, D. (1978). 'What Metaphors Mean', *Critical Inquiry* 5:31–47.

Davies, M. (1982–83). 'Idiom and Metaphor', *Proceedings of the Aristotelian Society*, New Series, 83:67–85.

Davis, J. W. (1970). 'Berkeley, Newton, and Space', in R. E. Butts and J. W. Davis eds., *The Methodological Heritage of Newton*, Toronto, University of Toronto Press, pp. 57–73.

Denbigh, K. (1968). *The Principles of Chemical Equilibrium*, Cambridge, England, Cambridge University Press.

Derrida, J. (1974). 'White Mythology: Metaphor in the Text of Philosophy', *New Literary History* 6:5–74.

Descartes, R. (1931). *The Philosophical Works of Descartes*, tr. E. S. Haldane, and G. R. T. Ross, 2 vols., Cambridge, England, Cambridge University Press.

Dijksterhuis, E. J. (1969). 'The Origins of Classical Mechanics from Aristotle to Newton', in M. Clagett, ed., *Critical Problems in the History of Science*, Madison, Wis., University of Wisconsin Press, pp. 163–84.

Doležel, L. (1988). 'Possible Worlds and Literary Fictions', in S. Allén, ed., *Possible Worlds in Humanities, Arts and Sciences*, Berlin and New York, Walter de Gruyter, Inc.

Eckermann, J. P. (1930). *Conversations with Goethe*, tr. J. Oxenford, London, J. M. Dent and Sons Ltd.

Engell, J. (1981). *The Creative Imagination: Enlightenment to Romanticism*, Cambridge, Mass., and London, England, Harvard University Press.

Fontanier, P. (1977). *Les figures du discours*, Paris, Flammarion.

Gray, T. (1969). *The Poems of Thomas Gray, William Collins, Oliver Goldsmith*, ed. R. Lonsdale, London and Harlow, Longmans, Green and Co., Ltd.

Gumpel, L. (1984). *Metaphor Reexamined*, Bloomington, Ind., Indiana University Press.

Guyer, P. (1979). *Kant and the Claims of Taste*, Cambridge, Mass., and London, Harvard University Press.

Haden, J., tr. (1965). *First Introduction to the Critique of Judgment*, Indianapolis, Ind., The Bobbs-Merrill Co., Inc.

Hanson, N. R. (1971). *What I Do Not Believe, and Other Essays*, ed. S. Toulmin and H. Woolf, Dordrecht, Holland, D. Reidel Publishing Co.

Hintikka, J. (1969). *Models for Modalities*, Dordrecht, Holland, D. Reidel Publishing Co.

Hughes, G. E. and Cresswell, M. J. (1972). *An Introduction to Modal Logic*, London, Methuen and Co., Ltd.

Hume, D. (1966). *An Enquiry Concerning Human Understanding*, La Salle, Ill., Open Court.

Husserl, E. (1967). *Ideas*, tr. W. R. Boyce Gibson, New York, The Humanities Press.

Husserl, E. (1970). *Logical Investigations*, tr. J. N. Findlay, 2 vols., New York, The Humanities Press.

Jacob, M. C. (1976). *The Newtonians and the English Revolution, 1689–1720*, Ithaca, N.Y., Cornell University Press.

Jakobson, R. and Halle, M. (1956). *Fundamentals of Language*, The Hague, Mouton.

Jakobson, R. (1960). 'Closing Statement: Linguistics and Poetics', in T. A. Sebeok, ed., *Style in Language*, New York and London, The Technology Press of MIT and John Wiley and Sons, Inc., pp. 350–77.

Jesperson, O. (1964). *Language*, New York, W. W. Norton and Co., Inc.

Kant, I. (1952). *The Critique of Judgement*, tr. J. C. Meredith, Oxford, The Clarendon Press.

Kant, I. (1965). *Critique of Pure Reason*, tr. N. K. Smith, New York, St. Martin's Press.

Katz, J. J. (1972). *Semantic Theory*, New York, Harper and Row.

Keats, J. (1958). *The Poetical Works of John Keats*, 2d ed., ed. H. W. Garrod, Oxford, The Clarendon Press.

Klubertanz, G. P. (1960). *St. Thomas Aquinas on Analogy*, Chicago, Loyola University Press.

Koyré, A. (1968). *Newtonian Studies*, Chicago, University of Chicago Press (Phoenix Books).

Kripke, S. A. (1972). 'Naming and Necessity', in D. Davidson and G. Harmon, eds., *Semantics of Natural Language*, New York, Humanities Press, pp. 253–355.

Lakoff, G. and Johnson, M. (1980). *Metaphors We Live by*, Chicago and London, University of Chicago Press.

Levin, S. R. (1976). 'Concerning What Kind of Speech Act a Poem Is', in T. A. van Dijk, ed., *Pragmatics of Language and Literature*, Amsterdam, North Holland Publishing Co., pp. 141–60.

Levin, S. R. (1977). *The Semantics of Metaphor*, Baltimore and London, The Johns Hopkins University Press.

Levin, S. R. (1979). 'Standard Approaches to Metaphor and a Proposal for Literary Metaphor', in A. Ortony, ed., *Metaphor and Thought*, Cambridge, England, Cambridge University Press, pp. 124–35.

Levin, S. R. (1981). 'Allegorical Language', in M. W. Bloomfield, ed., *Allegory, Myth, and Symbol*, Cambridge, Mass., Harvard University Press, pp. 23–38.

Levin, S. R. (1982a). 'Are Figures of Thought Figures of Speech?', in H. Byrnes, ed., *Contemporary Perceptions of Language: Interdisciplinary Dimensions = Georgetown University Round Table on Languages and Linguistics 1982*, Washington, D.C., Georgetown University Press, pp. 112–23.

Levin, S. R. (1982b). 'Aristotle's Theory of Metaphor', *Philosophy and Rhetoric* 15:24–46.

Locke, J. (1979). *An Essay Concerning Human Understanding*, ed. P. H. Nidditch, Oxford, The Clarendon Press.

Lovejoy, A. O. (1964). *The Great Chain of Being*, Cambridge, Mass., and London, Harvard University Press.

Mac Cormac, E. R. (1985). *A Cognitive Theory of Metaphor*, Cambridge, Mass., MIT Press.

MacLean, K. (1962). *John Locke and English Literature of the Eighteenth Century*, New York, Russell and Russell.

McFarland, T. (1985). *Originality and Imagination*, Baltimore and London, The Johns Hopkins University Press.

Milton, J. (1952–55). *The Poetical Works of John Milton*, 2 vols., ed. H. Darbyshire, Oxford, The Clarendon Press.

Mulligan, R. W. (1952). *Truth*, translated from the definitive Leonine text (translation of *Quaestiones disputatae de veritate*), 3 vols. (1952–54), Chicago, Henry Regnery.

Newton, I. (1952). *Optics*, New York, Dover Publications, Inc.

Newton, I. (1962). *Unpublished Scientific Papers of Isaac Newton*, ed. and tr. A. R. Hall and M. B. Hall, Cambridge, England, Cambridge University Press (cited as Hall and Hall).

Newton, I. (1974). *Mathematical Principles of Natural Philosophy*, tr. A. Motte (1729), rev. F. Cajori, Berkeley and Los Angeles, University of California Press.

Nicolson, M. H. (1966). *Newton Demands the Muse*, Princeton, N.J., Princeton University Press.

Pavel, T. G. (1986). *Fictional Worlds*, Cambridge, Mass., and London, Harvard University Press.

Pegis, A. C., ed. (1948). *Introduction to Saint Thomas Aquinas*, New York, The Modern Library.

Phelan, G. B. (1948). *Saint Thomas and Analogy*, Milwaukee, Wis., Marquette University Press.

Piper, H. W. (1962). *The Active Universe*, London, The Athlone Press.

Pippard, A. B. (1966). *Elements of Classical Thermodynamics*, Cambridge, England, Cambridge University Press.

Plato (1945). *The Republic of Plato*, tr. F. MacD. Cornford, London, Oxford, New York, Oxford University Press.

Pope, A. (1931). *The Complete Poetical Works of Pope*, ed. H. W. Boynton, Boston, Houghton Mifflin Co. (Cambridge edition, The Riverside Press).

Pope, A. (1950). *Alexander Pope: An Essay on Man*, ed. M. Mack, New Haven, Yale University Press.

Prickett, S. (1970). *Coleridge and Wordsworth: The Poetry of Growth*, Cambridge, England, Cambridge University Press.

Quine, W. van O. (1963). *From a Logical Point of View*, New York, Harper and Row (Harper Torch Books).

Quintilian (1953). *The Institutio Oratoria of Quintilian*, 4 vols., tr. H. E. Butler, Cambridge, Mass., Harvard University Press (Loeb Classical Library).

Richards, I. A. (1936). *The Philosophy of Rhetoric*, Oxford, England, Oxford University Press.

Ricoeur, P. (1977). *The Rule of Metaphor*, tr. R. Czerny et al., Toronto, University of Toronto Press.

Ricoeur, P. (1978). 'The Metaphorical Process as Cognition, Imagination, and Feeling', *Critical Inquiry* 5:143–59.

Ross, J. F. (1976). 'Analogy as a Rule of Meaning for Religious Language', in A. Kenny, ed., *Aquinas: A Collection of Critical Essays*, Notre Dame, Ind., University of Notre Dame Press, pp. 93–138.

Rousseau, J.-J. (1966). *On the Origin of Language*, tr. J. H. Moran and A. Gode, New York, Frederick Ungar Publishing Co.

Russell, B. (1976). *Human Knowledge: Its Scope and Limits*, New York, Simon and Schuster.

Ryle, G. (1949). *The Concept of Mind*, New York, Barnes and Noble Books.

Sartre, J.-P. (1965). *What is Literature?* tr. B. Frechtman, New York, Harper and Row.

Searle, J. (1969). *Speech Acts*, Cambridge, England, Cambridge University Press.

Searle, J. (1979). 'Metaphor', in A. Ortony, ed., *Metaphor and Thought*, Cambridge, England, Cambridge University Press, pp. 92–123.

Shelley, P. B. (1948). *The Complete Poetical Works of Percy Bysshe Shelley*, ed. T. Hutchinson, London, Oxford University Press.

Smith, D. W. and McIntyre, R. (1984). *Husserl and Intentionality*, Dordrecht, Boston, Lancaster, D. Reidel Publishing Co.

Thomson, J. (1965). *James Thomson: Poetical Works*, ed. J. L. Robertson, London, Oxford University Press.

Toulmin, S. (1960). *The Philosophy of Science*, New York, Harper and Row (Harper Torch Books).

Vico, G. (1968). *The New Science of Giambattista Vico*, tr. T. G. Bergin and M. H. Fisch, Ithaca and London, Cornell University Press.

Weiskel, T. (1976). *The Romantic Sublime*, Baltimore and London, The Johns Hopkins University Press.

Westfall, R. S. (1970). *Science and Religion in Seventeenth-Century England*, n. p., Archon Books.

Willey, B. (1961). *The Eighteenth Century Background*, Boston, Beacon Press.

Wittgenstein, L. (1968). *Philosophical Investigations*, Oxford, Basil Blackwell.

Wittgenstein, L. (1961). *Tractatus Logico-Philosophicus*, London, Routledge and Kegan Paul.

Wordsworth, W. (1940–49). *The Poetical Works of William Wordsworth*, 5 vols., ed. E. de Selincourt and H. Darbyshire, Oxford, The Clarendon Press.

Wordsworth, W. (1979). *The Prelude, 1799, 1805, 1850*, ed. J. Wordsworth, M. H. Abrams and S. Gill, New York, W. W. Norton and Co.

Yolton, J. W. (1956). *John Locke and the Way of Ideas*, London, Oxford University Press.

Yolton, J. W. (1970). *Locke and the Compass of Human Understanding*, Cambridge, England, Cambridge University Press.

Index